K

Unraveling French Cinema

For Ethan, Chloë, and Phoebe
who have been my beacons these past forty years.

UNRAVELING FRENCH CINEMA

FROM *L'ATALANTE* TO *CACHÉ*

T. JEFFERSON KLINE

WILEY-BLACKWELL

A John Wiley & Sons, Ltd., Publication

This edition first published 2010
© 2010 T. Jefferson Kline

Blackwell Publishing was acquired by John Wiley & Sons in February 2007. Blackwell's publishing program has been merged with Wiley's global Scientific, Technical, and Medical business to form Wiley-Blackwell.

Registered Office
John Wiley & Sons Ltd, The Atrium, Southern Gate, Chichester, West Sussex, PO19 8SQ, United Kingdom

Editorial Offices
350 Main Street, Malden, MA 02148-5020, USA
9600 Garsington Road, Oxford, OX4 2DQ, UK
The Atrium, Southern Gate, Chichester, West Sussex, PO19 8SQ, UK

For details of our global editorial offices, for customer services, and for information about how to apply for permission to reuse the copyright material in this book please see our website at www.wiley.com/wiley-blackwell.

The right of T. Jefferson Kline to be identified as the author of this work has been asserted in accordance with the Copyright, Designs and Patents Act 1988.

Library of Congress Cataloging-in-Publication Data

Kline, T. Jefferson (Thomas Jefferson), 1942–
 Unraveling French cinema : from *L'Atalante* to *Caché* / T. Jefferson Kline.
  p. cm.
 Includes bibliographical references and index.
 ISBN 978-1-4051-8452-6 (hardcover : alk. paper) – ISBN 978-1-4051-8451-9 (pbk. : alk. paper) 1. Motion pictures–France. I. Title.
 PN1993.5.F7K58 2010
 791.430944–dc22

2009020176

A catalogue record for this book is available from the British Library.

Set in 10/12.5pt Galliard by SPi Publisher Services, Pondicherry, India
Printed in Singapore by Ho Printing Singapore Pte Ltd

1 2010

Contents

Acknowledgments

The present volume evolved out of classes I taught at Boston University and at the Teachers As Scholars seminars founded by my friend Henry Bolter. I thus have Boston University and Henry to thank for their encouragement and support. I could not, however, have constructed these ideas without the generations of wonderful students who so actively participated in discussions of these films over the years. My gratitude extends as well to my friends, the late Charlie Bernheimer and the very present Jean Oudart, Tom Conley and Roy Grundman, who read and critiqued various parts of this book. Without Jayne Fargnoli, however, these pages would have remained in scattered notes and essays and never been brought together as they have been here. Jayne came to see me one day, demanded that I write this book, and helped give it shape as it evolved. Her constant enthusiasm, creativity, and encouragement have been my companions for the past two years and I cannot thank her enough for all that she has done to bring this project to fruition. Her colleagues, Margot Morse and Gail Ferguson, also gave of their considerable expertise to bring these pages to press. Nowadays, no one can properly do film studies without having a "genie" as a "techie." Shawn Provencal has been that genius for me, helping with quiet amusement at every technical and electronic stage of this process.

Introduction

What is French Cinema?

One of the first responses my students offer to the question, "What's your feeling about French film?" is to groan, and say, "I like French films, but I just don't get them, they're no fun!" Which is another way of saying, without having to admit it, "I don't like French films!" Why not? "There's not enough plot, not enough action! And when there *is* a plot, it doesn't seem to lead to a clear ending. And besides, there are too many other things going on that seem to interfere with my enjoyment of the story." In other words, for them, French films are too unlike the Hollywood films we all grew up watching to allow for a degree of pleasure comparable to what they're used to. So … why bother? Why indeed?

It will be our purpose here, to re-present French film in ways which dare to ask this question head on and which hold the promise of proposing answers that I hope will convince you that French film "matters." It is my belief that a deeper understanding of what makes the French think and act the way they do – considerations that explain why they make movies the way they do – will lead to a greater appreciation of their art and, yes, even to the *enjoyment* of the questions they put *to* and *on* the screen before us.

You are embarking, then, on a voyage of initiation into the complexities of French cinema and in the ways in which French filmmakers have, practically from the invention of film itself, focused as much on the question,

"What is cinema?" as they have on the storyline of their films. In order to reach a deeper understanding of this essential difference between French cinema and Hollywood or other national cinemas, we will need to look carefully at a series of examples of the ways French directors shape their films around two potentially divergent goals: one being the narration of a story and the other being an elaboration of some theory about film itself. Despite the many differences we shall discover among the set of films to be discussed in these pages, we shall also discover some fundamental connections and it will be from the set of these common concerns that we may deduce and define what is so "French" about French film.

Hollywood is not just a financially successful American industry; it exports to the entire world a very particularly American way of looking at that world. Unless we step outside the Hollywood model we fail to grasp the extent to which that model replicates instinctively for a worldwide audience the very American motto "Just do it!" that Nike had the genius to lay claim to. American directors have historically refused to get theoretical about their work, preferring to think about storyboards, available actors, budgets, and markets. The gulf that separates Hollywood from East Coast intellectualism may have something to do with the freeing up of Hollywood to develop a cinema that relies on the star system, on simplicity of genre and plot and a style, entirely based on the notion of continuity, which makes the movies easy to follow and understand. For Hollywood, the entire cinematic enterprise, technologically and stylistically, is in service of telling a good story. In addition, the world market targeted by Hollywood made for films that would be globally pleasing, mainstream, and visually comprehensible to a wide variety of audiences. On the other hand, French cinema (despite some of the great French studios' geographic distance from the Metropolis) never broke away from the highly intellectual, avant-garde and artistically experimental ferment of Paris. The names of two major studios tell us much about their industries: Hollywood's global and even extraterrestrial ambitions are expressed by the name Universal Studios whereas the very problematic history of the French industry is captured by the self-defeating name, Studios de l'Albatross.

After the elections of 2007, the new Minister of Finance, Christine Lagarde, stepped forward to announce that it was time for the French to stop being so ... *French*! In evident frustration at her compatriots' inability to "just do it," she complained: "France is a country that thinks. There is hardly an ideology that we haven't turned into a theory. We have in our libraries enough to talk about for centuries to come. This is why I would like to tell you: enough thinking, already! Roll up your sleeves!"[1] Her words should come as no surprise to any non-Frenchman who has struggled with that country's cinema. It is, after all, more than geography, language or even cuisine that makes the French French (and their cinema so indelibly "foreign" to Anglo-Saxon audiences). Indeed, what finally separates French cinema from Hollywood and other national cinemas and defines it can be discerned not only by the totality of films produced and shot on French soil, nor by the history of the various movements and genres that have occupied French filmmakers (such as le Film d'Art, Impressionism, or Poetic Realism), but rather this very Gallic tendency to "think … to turn ideology into theory" Lagarde (2007) and to write (inject) theory into every cultural artifact they produce. In the following pages, then, we will be examining the many ways in which the "shadow of theory" guides, problematizes, and ultimately defines the very charged and intricate existence of the seventh art in France.

The report near the end of 1894 that Louis Lumière had, "in one night, invented the Cinematographe," won France the title of the cradle of the cinema,[2] and, following the first public demonstration of Lumière's apparatus in Paris on March 22, 1895 there followed the production and promotion of hundreds of short films that were to establish France as the world's leader in film exports. Sadly, however, the French domination of world production was short-lived, for the French had thoroughly underestimated the competition from America, and, in general, failed to appreciate the rapid evolution of the technology they believed belonged solely to them. Their failure to capitalize on their early advantage was predicated on three quite symptomatic elements that would haunt the French industry throughout its first three decades: the rapid dissemination of theoretical assumptions about the medium that caused many disagreements about the way forward; a series of misguided assumptions about the cultural sophistication of film audiences; and finally the enormous difference between the size of the audiences that could be attracted by Hollywood and by French films.

The Lumières' invention of the Cinematograph came at the end of a century whose major thinkers were Geoffroy Saint-Hilaire, Darwin and Marx, that is to say, the framers of the theories of evolution and revolution. Consequently, throughout the nineteenth century, scientists of all different stripes found themselves taking up the search for an *unmediated representation of nature in movement.*[3] As Alan Williams has pointed out, the French behaved throughout the 1800s as though they were rehearsing for the invention of cinema by pursuing simultaneously the development of photography, the science of the optical synthesis of motion, and the analysis of movement.[4] When it finally did occur at the end of the century, the invention of the cinema was thus not undertaken in order to provide mass entertainment, but rather to perfect a tool for scientific analysis. Louis Lumière would insist that his "endeavors were the endeavors of technological research, never what they call 'mise-en-scène.'" The Lumière brothers saw themselves as *scientists* whose subjects filmed by the camera could best be compared to "the behavior of a micro-organism under the biologist's microscope, or the movement of stars at the end of the astronomer's telescope."[5] French cinema in fact, would never lose this spirit of theoretical inquiry (a trait it shared with all the other arts and human sciences in France throughout the twentieth century). It is entirely in this spirit that the Lumières baptized their invention as the *Cinématograph (writing* in movement), while Edison, across the Atlantic, decided to baptize his machine the *Vitascope* (a vision of *life*). These two terms perfectly capture the entire set of differences that will come to define and oppose classical Hollywood cinema to its French counterpart. Whereas the early success of the French cinema was due to the fascination exerted by documentary films on all kinds of subjects, it was soon overtaken and overrun by an American medium that focused on the art of vivid storytelling.

Another reason for the early failure of the French film industry lay in the assumptions that circulated about the cultural sophistication of this new art. Because of its early successes at fairs, then in vaudeville halls and peepshows, the cinema was assumed by the French intelligentsia to appeal to lower-class audiences whereas members of the upper-middle class refused to "buy into" this kind of lowbrow entertainment. In America, the medium was quickly aimed at a more affluent, urban, and upwardly mobile social stratum.[6] Because they remained blissfully unaware of the dangers of foreign competition, the French producers did not immediately seek to broaden the cultural and financial appeal of their product. At the end of the First World War with France in economic ruins, the French found themselves trying to choose between two financially untenable options. The more disastrous solution grew out of the misperception that Hollywood's "epic" approach could be replicated in France. However, because Hollywood could, by the mid-1920s, count on audiences of upwards of 100 million viewers for its most popular films, the Americans could afford to lay out ten times the sums available to French producers. What worse way could there have been to react to the competition from Hollywood than to imitate "a financial adventure with unusually high financial risks"?[7] The result could only have been further economic ruin. The big studios, Pathé and Gaumont, went bankrupt trying to make super-productions that might compete. Their films attempted to replicate the very factors that made what David Bordwell has termed the "classical

Hollywood style" so dominant: (1) "rules that set stringent limits on individual innovation; (2) the production of a realistic, comprehensible, and unambiguous story; (3) the use of artifice through techniques of continuity and 'invisible' storytelling; and (4) a fundamental emotional appeal that transcends class and nation."[8] However much their productions had the "look" of Hollywood, they could not complete with American distribution and ultimately brought the industry to its knees.

The dissolution of the big studios left the French cinema in the "happy" position of being able to become itself. The plethora of independent companies that were spawned by the failure of the big studios brought with them the sensible realization that France could never compete with Hollywood on its own terms and the certainty that another route had to be pursued: quality films that stressed film's poetic possibilities. And so it was that many smaller French producers and directors focused their efforts on reaching an urban, educated audience by creating various versions of *Le Film d'Art*, a cinema consecrated to reproducing intellectually acceptable literature and theater, borrowing the techniques and actors of the Parisian stage.

Much of the inspiration for the new alternate cinema had already come from a flurry of journals that were founded to contest the mainstream industrial practice. Henri Diamant-Berger's *Le Film* from its inception (1916) encouraged an independent strain of film criticism that rapidly morphed into a nascent film theory articulated not just by journalists but by the "new wave" of young film directors that invaded the studios after the First World War. This first joining of theory and practice would allow French cinema proper to be (re)born and would, in one form or another, endow the French cinema with a set of indelibly "Gallic" tendencies that would characterize its most important productions from that era to the present. The journal *Ciné pour tous* followed in 1919, *Cinéa* in 1920 and *Mon Ciné* in February 1922. In the March 1921 issue of *Cinéa*, Louis Delluc fired the first critical broadside against the Hollywood colonizers: "Let the French cinema be French! Let the French cinema be cinematic!"[9] In this call to arms, Delluc rallied his colleagues to reject the idea that French cinema must become Americanized or disappear, and, furthermore, to reject a cinema that was, as he put it, merely instinctive and where the director was "secondary to the author's intentions."[10] René Clair would note disdainfully, "American technique is completely in service of the progress of the story. In America, films are immediately accessible, whereas in France they require an effort of the intelligence alone."[11] For his part, Pierre Porte saw Hollywood film as merely "an instrument to convey actions, a machine to recite stories and incapable of anything resembling speculations."[12] Elie Faure would go so far as to call the American film industry "primitive and at the same time barbarous."[13]

To resist this invasion of the American barbaric and instinctual pleasure palace, a band of young French directors began asking the question that was later to animate André Bazin and the entire post-WWII generation of cineastes, "What is cinema?"[14] Although this question never arises in Hollywood directors' published musings on their medium,[15] the French almost immediately began an attempt to define film as "a work of art," a kind of "painting and sculpture developing in time,"[16] which "translates, develops, explicates or intensifies reality."[17] Jean Epstein predicts that "within five years we will compose cinematographic poems."[18]

From this position it was but a short step to see the cinema as a language, "a form of ideographic writing"[19] and Jean Epstein set out "to establish the premises for a cinematic grammar or rhetoric ... a grammar peculiar to itself."[20] This new "cinégraphie" would become, in Abel Gance's words, "a new language, a mode of expression of rhythms and truth."[21] All of this talk about cinema as poetry with its own language represented a concerted effort to raise the seventh art from the gutter of lower class entertainment to the salons of Paris's intellectual elite, a concern frequently betrayed by such proclamations as: "Our cinema requires an effort of the intelligence alone,"[22] with its "unique specificity."[23] Film was conceived of as "a veritable art infused with artistic and intellectual elements;"[24] "a vision we have *intellectually conceived* to transmit to film;"[25] and representing "an evolution on the intellectual plane."[26] The cinema director, then, must be "a poet, scholar, scientist",[27] working with the "hope of raising the intellectual level of the cinema," to "a science that one writes with living words."[28]

We are so far indeed from the Hollywood pleasure palace that in this writing in the 1920s we even encounter the idea that cinema "must never be a place where the viewer finds pleasure. It must be something that disturbs ... [and is] completely intolerable for the viewer."[29] The same theorist who cried "Let French cinema be French" would go on to assert that the role of the French cinema is to cause *alarm*.[30] In describing the efficaciousness of the close-up, Jean Epstein will rejoice that "pain is within reach."[31] We cannot help but consider how much Antonin Artaud's vision of a "theater of cruelty" resonates with this ambition for French film. All of which leads one critic to wonder whether "the Latin genius might be badly suited to the art of the screen? It's a genius especially well suited to eloquence and conclusive reasoning, but perhaps hostile to the elliptical and silent power of film.... The French mind," he bemoans, "may be too rational to possess those qualities of frankness and impulsiveness" requisite to good film.[32]

This arrangement of a series of independents awash in film theory and battling the "imbeciles" (the word is Louis Delluc's[33]) who peopled the major studios in both France and America will henceforth become an intermittent yet ultimately dominant model for the French film industry. In the 1930s the particular slant of the theoretical debates and the persons mobilizing them would shift, but the overall pattern persisted of "a large number of small and undercapitalized production companies working in competition and combination with each other,"[34] the result of a weak industry and extremely healthy "subclass" of "*auteurs.*"

Of course, since it was centered in Paris, cinematic debate entered the political arena as well during the twenties and thirties. No matter what the subject, however, theoretical debate and film production continue unabated today.

Part of the French tendency to theorize can be said to derive from larger cultural issues. The "difficulty" of French film derives in part from several factors endemic to the French and which, if properly delineated, should enable non-French readers better to appreciate their culture. The first might be said to derive from the presence in the French educational system of a dialectical or confrontational method of discourse which guarantees that, for the most part, their cultural expressions begin with questions about the nature of any activity undertaken, and an immediate supposition that the "accepted" course of action needs always be defended against an expected critique, and that any pragmatic or concrete action requires elaborate theoretical justification. This in turn might explain the abiding existence of large numbers of carefully delineated political factions in their culture: a spectrum of national political parties and perspectives that must constantly be defined, redefined, debated and tested.

When we attempt to measure the impact of this mentality on the arts, we can immediately understand the very intellectual turn things take in the Parisian art scene. The French critic, Georges Altman, writing in 1931 suggested that 'The French preference for reasoning and demonstrating at all costs, of explaining and classifying may vitiate French film at its foundations."[35] Twenty-five years later, François Truffaut will claim that "By American standards, French film directors are all intellectuals."[36] A well-known critic of the thirties, Emile Vuillermoz, remarks, "Each of us knows that, in [France] there are well-established customs of candor. We take great stock in our independence in thinking and speaking and we flatter ourselves that this gives proof of our impartiality, our clear-sightedness and our independence of judgment."[37] (In other cultures, such aggressive debate may be considered "impolite" or simply a distraction from the need to act – to "just do it". In France, then, active debate and the need for definitions are considered not just a requisite step in any process but a socially necessary and even pleasurable activity!) And while we would not agree with Mr Altman that French film has been *vitiated* by these tendencies, they would explain why their cinema requires some special introduction for a non-French viewer.

It shall be the purpose of this book to explain the impact of such debates in the realm of cinema on our enjoyment (or bewilderment in the face) of French film. I intend to present these questions in clear enough language to enable the non-French public to enter *pleasurably* into them. Understanding this cultural particularity will, I believe, help the reader appreciate and even *enjoy* discovering its role in film. My approach in these pages is not intended to replace the excellent histories of French film such as Alan Williams's *The Republic of Images,* Susan Hayward's *French National Cinema,* or Phil Powrie's and Keith Reader's *French Cinema,* each of which provides a more comprehensive historical perspective on French film than I intend here.[38] Instead, I have chosen to focus more specifically on what makes French film so particularly bewildering for so many of its would-be admirers.

The cultural mindset I have described, then, would explain why the notion of Auteur Politics (first codified in the "silent" era of the 1920s and "rediscovered" during the New Wave in the 1950s) must be so central to thinking about the French cinema. Understanding French film must inevitably come to terms with a set of film directors who chose to work *against* the easy accessibility of their products rather than *in obeisance to* the escapist expectations of the average filmgoer. The great directors in France more often than not saw themselves as renegades against whatever tradition world cinema was attempting to impose on them. (And such impositions were often devastating to the great studios of France that regularly went bankrupt when they attempted to outdo Hollywood spectaculars that regularly operated on budgets ten times greater than those available to French directors).

The history of French film from the 1920s on provides an excellent example of this imperative toward an alternative cinema. Unlike those producers of formulaic studio productions which, if immediately crowd pleasing, were nevertheless quickly forgotten, the "pantheon" of French directors includes primarily artists whose films so infuriated their opening night audiences that they were immediately censored (as in the case of Jean Vigo's first film), ignored (as in the case of many of Abel Gance's early films), or violently denounced by the public (as in the case of Renoir's *Rules of the Game,* when the audience reacted to the film by trying to burn down the theater!). The "rediscovery" of these films presents important milestones in the evolution of the medium, its language, and its possibilities.

The idea that film is a "language" goes hand in hand with the French idea of the director as "auteur/author." The great French film directors thus created their films in the spirit a writer might compose an essay. (In this regard we should note how often the French filmmakers refer to filming as writing: Marcel L'Herbier will refer to shooting as "the realization of French film poetics"; [39] Jean Epstein will call cinema "a calligraphy in which the image is a sign, complex and precise"; [40] Alexandre Astruc will coin the phrase "camera stylo" and Agnes Varda will invent the term "cinécriture.") The "thesis" of their films might be hidden beneath an entertaining storyline but the interpretation of the film will not yield up its entire meaning until the implicit thesis is factored into the story. Sometimes this will involve a very great degree of subtlety. More often the thesis will "disturb" the storyline and/or continuity of the film and cause the unwary viewer some discomfort. But discomfort is, in the French esthetic, only a goad to look further, to deepen our search for meaning. The pleasure of watching French films will come, then, from integrating thesis and story into a new and deeper meaning. To state this is to understand that Hollywood's "whodunit?" might be translated into French as a "why-dunit?" What we shall do, then, is gradually shift the emphasis in viewing a French film from the question, "what happens?" to the question, "how does the film communicate what happens?" as well as to the question, "why is film the perfect medium to express this particular idea/event?"

One of the first differences that emerges from the confrontation of Hollywood and French cinemas, and one that almost inevitably produces the "discomfort" associated with French film, centers on the opposition continuity/discontinuity. When the Hollywood directors plan a film they do so on a "storyboard" which enables them to establish a fluid sense of the continuity (in both space and time) between scenes. When French directors begin their work, they make a "découpage" – a "cutting board."

This deceptively simple difference of vocabulary reveals a huge dichotomy: for Hollywood, to make a film means to capture the seamless dramatic flow of events and the role of editing is to ensure that this motion is felt to be logical and uninterrupted; for the French, to make a film excites an immediate awareness that films are made up of lots of little pieces (24 different frames a second, bits of scenes taken from different perspectives, successive scenes pasted together through a process called "montage"). This difference in conception is itself symptomatic of the huge cultural divide that separates the Anglo-American cultural, psychological, and philosophical matrix from the French. In the course of this excursion, we will see quite graphically how these various differences will come to be played out in cinematic terms. It is my hope that, in the long run, you will come to grasp and, yes, *enjoy* the significant ideas that have animated French intellectual and cultural history from the early twentieth century to the present. And all of this will flow directly from a very careful analysis of a series of emblematic films. A discussion of film codes and how to "read" a film will allow the reader the tools to understand how a film "means." Throughout this adventure, we will repeatedly discover that French films offer their audiences "double the pleasure" of enjoying a storyline and searching for a new understanding of the medium itself.

Let us begin, then, by going back to the question that has so animated the last one hundred and ten years of French cinema: "What *is* cinema?" Each of these chapters delineates a particular theory of film that moves from the question that so animated French critics and filmmakers of the 1920s: is the cinema a form of poetry? Jean Vigo's film *L'Atalante* will provide an excellent subject on which to examine this question and to decide whether images are chosen purely for their *poetic* [evocative] value rather than for their *narrative* [story] value. Within ten years of Vigo's enterprise however, a countering assertion will be advanced that argues that film's photographic medium cannot but represent reality itself and that film must therefore adhere to the real. Jean Renoir's *Rules of the Game* will illustrate how such a theory can be put into practice.

The idea that the film apparatus recreates the conditions of dream was also proposed in the 1920s but the idea did not receive serious critical attention until Jean-Louis Baudry reintroduced it in a watershed essay in the late 1960s.[41] It wasn't long before this notion found its most complex representation in François Truffaut's *The Story of Adele H.* (1975). As convinced as we may be by Truffaut's "demonstration," the idea will be contested by Benoit Jacquot, who will propose instead an analogy between watching a film and undergoing hypnosis. A close analysis of Jacquot's *Seventh Heaven* will demonstrate the strengths of this assertion. But whether film is like dream or hypnosis, it tends, according to several French filmmakers, to recreate earlier experiences in our lives – either experiences of connection to loved ones or of a nostalgia that *lost* connection, suggesting the possibility that film is equivalent to the state of mourning. In Anne Fontaine's *How I Killed My Father* we will see an illustration of the potential connections between film and mourning as psychic structures.

Beginning with the Occupation, filmmakers will increasingly question the practices and traditions of film. Marcel Carné will use *The Children of Paradise* (1944) to have the cinema aggressively invade the spaces and traditions of the theater, and to suggest that the real artist must be a *criminal* to effect the necessary overthrow of these traditions. His character, the famous assassin, Lacenaire, will inspire Robert Bresson to offer a

Pickpocket as his hero in a continuing "criminal" rejection of everything theatrical in cinematic practice. Bresson's contemporary, Jean-Luc Godard, will add a third persona to this idea of the cinema as crime in *Breathless* (1959). And so, by the time Carné's poet-assassin, Bresson's artist-pickpocket and Godard's revolutionary-thief have "strutted and fretted their hour" upon the screen, French film has been wrenched from its "Tradition of Quality" and the French film industry has "lost its way."

If the "film as crime" is necessary to reroute an art form bogged down in tradition, then the film as map becomes necessary to chart a new way for the silver screen. Louis Malle and Krystof Kieslowski will offer films that propose new maps of the cinematic that will lift French film out of its rut and offer renewal. Malle's *Les Amants* and *Damage* will suggest two new forms of orientation for the cinema, while Kieslowski's *Red* turns all our ideas of maps upside down in his reordering of the way we make connections in the world.

Finally, because film represents the control *and manipulation* of our access to perceived "reality" by a single, all-powerful director, at least one filmmaker will suggest that film represents a form of terrorism. In reviewing Michael Haneke's *Caché*, we will discover some very uncomfortable connections between the cinema, our experience of the news media and state terrorism. Our transition to French film of the twenty-first century will not be a comforting one.

We shall, in this way, encounter the ways in which film's very ontology (being) may be connected to: the real, to poetry, dreams, hypnosis, mourning, crime, mapping, or even terrorism. In each case, a film will be analyzed in ways that will allow us to participate in and extend our meditation on this particular work of art to other films. And, inevitably, our itinerary will bring us into contact with the major intellectual trends of twentieth century French thought: existentialism, structuralism, psychoanalysis, and deconstruction.

So let us begin our investigation, looking for all the different ways (and they are legion!) that the French can construct a definition of the seventh art itself while, at the very same time, appearing merely to tell a good story. Keeping these two purposes in view will not be easy, but it will prove well worth the challenge.

Suggested Further Reading

Abel, R. (1984), *French Cinema: The First Wave, 1915–1929*. Princeton, NJ: Princeton University Press.

Abel's study provides the most complete view of the early years of French cinema, combining discussions of the economic, technological and intellectual trends of the first third of the twentieth century. His discussions of particular films are compelling and intelligent.

Andrew, J. D. (1976), *The Major Film Theories*. Oxford: Oxford University Press. Andrew gives a useful overview of the major European film theorists and allows us to place Bazin's work in a larger theoretical context.

Braudy, L. and Cohen, M. (2004), *Film Theory and Criticism*. Oxford: Oxford University Press. The indispensable anthology for anyone wishing to sample writing on the cinema from across a wide spectrum of perspectives and categories. Almost every theorist mentioned in this volume is represented in this anthology.

Williams, A. (1992), *Republic of Images*. Cambridge, MA: Harvard University Press.
The first several chapters of Williams's study in particular present a fascinating history of the invention of cinema as emanating from a "bricolage" of three different preoccupations dear to the nineteenth century: photography, the analysis of movement, and the optical synthesis of movement.

1
Cinema and/as Poetry
L'Atalante's Apples as Poems

"*It is the essence of poetry that liberates us from the reality of the accepted and firmly established world, in which we believe we are living, to open up to us the multiform relations of other worlds which are possible, however evanescent.*" (Leo Spitzer, 1963)

As the discussion of the development of the French film industry in the Introduction should make clear, the failure of the major French studios early on lay in their belief that "the classic Hollywood style" could be replicated in France.[1] The plethora of small independent producers that followed the big studios' demise also favored the rise of "auteurs" who were freed from the concerns of big-market popularization, and who, being French, immediately launched into a heated debate over the direction the seventh art was meant to take. From a fairground attraction, French film was transformed into "a work of art," a kind of "painting and sculpture developing in time."[2] Such was the euphoria surrounding this rebirth of cinema as "le film d'art," Jean Epstein would announce that "the cinema is poetry's most powerful medium," and predict that "within five years we will be writing film poems."[3]

From this position it was but a short step to see the "cinema as a language ... a form of ideographic writing,"[4] and Jean Epstein set out "to establish the premises for a cinematic grammar or rhetoric ... a grammar peculiar to itself."[5] This new "cinégraphie" would become, in Abel Gance's words, "a new language, a mode of expression of rhythms and truth."[6] Throughout the 1920s, French critics and filmmakers increasingly advanced this idea of cinema as poetry with its own language. In this hotbed of debate, the filmmakers became "poets … working in the hope of raising the intellectual level of the cinema"[7] struggling against a tradition they abhorred, more outlaws than participants in an industry. Indeed, the filmmaker as outlaw was to become a favorite signature of French cinema for the next eighty years.[8]

As students of French cinema, we cannot jump unthinkingly into this debate without asking, "What is poetry?" – just as we began our meditation on Gallic film with the question, "What is cinema?" The answer would have been relatively easy in earlier times, when poetry was recognized as much by its adherence to formal conventions as by the elevation of its discourse. Until the advent of Baudelaire's prose poems in the mid-nineteenth century, no French poet would dream of writing verse that was not set in a standard form (the sonnet, for example, must have 14 lines, each line twelve syllables and each line rhymed with others in recognizable patterns). Poetry, for the most part, eschewed the vulgar language of the street in favor of a style whose vocabulary aspired to higher standards of elocution. This classic tendency is nowhere better captured than in Keats's lines:

> Beauty is truth, truth beauty, – that is all
> Ye know on earth, and all ye need to know.

This attitude would persist until Victor Hugo famously debunked it in his *Préface de Cromwell* where he would argue that "the drama is the grotesque in conjunction with the sublime," that poetry must not limit itself to flattering its subject but must instead treat the entire range of human experience. To accomplish his aim, Hugo argues that the language of poetry can no longer be limited by esthetic rules, but must seek to break all rules. As a result of this evolution, through the realism of the nineteenth century and concluding in the relativism of the twentieth century, we no longer feel at ease in attempting to define poetry along formal lines.

How then should we go about it? By what means shall poetry be defined? Let's try an experiment that may help.

Suppose that on a given day in January, the 15th for example, we picked up the morning paper and read: "Yesterday, an automobile speeding down I 95 at a speed police estimated to be ninety-five miles per hour, hurtled into a sycamore tree. Its three occupants were pronounced dead on arrival at St Lazarus's Hospital in Dedham." We would normally adopt what we might call a "referential" (*not* a reverential) attitude toward this news item, culling from it the needed information on this accident.

Suppose, on the other hand, we were to rearrange these same words in the following manner:[9]

HARD FACTS

Yesterday
An auto
mobile
speed
        ing down
I
Ninety-five
at a
speed
    police
estimated
TO BE
Ninety-five
Miles   an   hour
Hurtled into a
Syc
amore   tree
Its   three
Occupants were
        pronounced
DEAD
on arrival at

St. Lazarus Hospital in

Ded
    ham.

    Milosh Afterman (translated from the French by Al Foreman-Smith)

Let's assume, for the moment that this second text is a poem – not because it strikes us as "poetic" but simply because the arrangement of the words on the page announces it as such. Take a few minutes, then, and jot down as many differences as you can find between these two sets of identical words differently arranged on the page.

You will have noticed that the "poet" has chosen to arrange his text vertically rather than horizontally, that he has created a bizarre arrangement of spacing, and that he has elected to capitalize some words and to break others into fragments. You would no doubt add that, were any journalist to present this form of the text to his editor, the former would either be summarily dismissed or sent home to sober up.

Now if I were to ask you to tell me the difference in the *function* of the word "yesterday" in each text, you might have more difficulty in answering. Certainly the function of "yesterday" in the news item is purely referential: it tells us that the accident happened on January 14. But in the poem? There being no dateline, we are forced to conclude that the text has a timelessness about it which is disconcerting. The word beckons to us, urges us to consider its various possibilities. Indeed, from this perspective, we can now see that each of the words in the poem is waving to us like so many circus clowns, each vying for our attention, each disguised behind a mask whose significance escapes yet fascinates us. The frustrating conclusion (which drives so many readers away from poetry) is that the meaning is no longer evident, unambiguous, easy to grasp. If these words no longer point to a real event, what *do* they point to? What are they *up* to? As Joyce's Molly Bloom would say, "Tell us in plain words!"

As we search for answers, our eye moves up and down the page trying to make some "sense" of this jumble. What begins to emerge is a pattern of repetitions (which formerly might be called rhymes): the word "speed" is isolated in such a way that its repetition becomes a kind of uncanny theme for the poem as a whole. The words "DEAD" and "Ded" are also paired suggesting a connection between the two sets of rhymes. And now the connection between the *capitalized* "TO BE" comes into play with the *capitalized* word "DEAD." "Speed TO BE DEAD" would seem to be one of the subliminal messages this poem is *trying simultaneously to hide and to express*. But then the capitalized "I" re-emerges to join itself to this set. "I speed TO BE DEAD" hauntingly whispers to us from among the words on the page, now drawing other fragments into its nexus. The word "syc" [sick] now adds its infectious connotations to this message. Does the repetition of "ninety-five" suggest a date or an age?

Other uncanny messages begin to appear. Certainly when we read the news item, we do not linger over the fact that the car was not driven into but, seemingly of its own volition, "hurtled into a tree." In the poem, however, the emphasis caused by the fracturing of the AUTO mobile makes a case for some HAL-like machine[10] which, having discovered its own robotic power, has elected to run amok. (In the process the poetic car and tree have been typographically shattered and its three allegorical passengers separated violently from each other and their lives).

Now we might wonder why the poet has chosen to begin his poem with "yesterday," a word unanchored from any specific historical moment and left afloat in our consciousness. If you say the word a few times, you might, as many of my students have done, find yourself humming the Beatles song, "Yesterday, all my troubles seemed so far away." Or you might, as still others of my students have done, find yourself remembering Macbeth's celebrated soliloquy:

> Tomorrow and tomorrow and tomorrow
> Creeps in this petty pace from day to day
> To the last syllable of recorded time;
> And all our *yesterdays* have lighted fools
> The way to dusty death. Out, out, brief candle!
> Life's but a walking shadow, a poor player
> That struts and frets his hour upon the stage
> And then is heard no more: it is a tale
> Told by an idiot, full of sound and fury,
> Signifying nothing.[11]

In other words, because it is a *poetic* text, it is likely to call up memories of other poetic texts we have encountered, and to gain new meanings by its association with them. In this case, the word "yesterday" evokes both the possibility of innocence and dreadful foreshadowing.

Happily, again because it is a poem, we do not necessarily have to choose between these two different possibilities. Like the contents of our own unconscious, both meanings may entertain an uneasy coexistence. The poem, in all its mystery, neither demands nor allows us to be sure of a single interpretation. When, over the years, I have asked my students to give me their interpretation of this "poem", many different and entirely plausible possibilities have emerged:

- The poem alludes to the increasing mechanization of our lives and warns us of impending disaster. But, given the allusion to Lazarus, perhaps it is not too late!
- The poem alludes to our sick tendencies toward self-destructive behavior.
- Because of the allusion to Lazarus, the poem is a modern retelling of Christ's miraculous power to save us from the jaws of death.
- Because it was translated from the French, the poem may allude to the death of Albert Camus and two companions who, in 1960, were killed

as they were driving along a French national road and crashed into a sycamore tree.

- And, perhaps stretching the limits of interpretation, the poem may allude to the discovery in 1895 of the cinema, in which movement was introduced, allowing the actions of the past to survive forever on celluloid.

You may have found other interpretations of your own! Whichever one(s) we choose, we shall nevertheless have noticed that a number of important characteristics of poetry have emerged from our experiment:

- Poetry asks us to adopt an attitude quite opposed to the one we employ when reading journalistic or informational material. We do not look for its words to refer to or narrate events in the real world but instead to imagine or interpret events.
- A poem presents us with a rebus, an enigma, a riddle to be solved and its pleasure derives, as in sudoku, crosswords or jigsaw puzzles, from making the pieces fit in a comprehensible way. Unlike the other puzzles we have mentioned, however, there may be more than one possible solution.
- The words in a poem (unlike those in the newspaper) demand to be read individually and then linked by association with other words in the poem and those in other poems.
- Whereas a news item is to be read once, from left to right, from beginning to end, to gather information, a poem is to be read repeatedly, forwards, backwards and intermittently to seize the multiple connections between words.
- Words in poems are assumed to be dense, to have the possibility of meaning several different things; that is, they are metaphorical and allow meanings to move (the original denotation of the Greek word μεταφορά) from one sign to another.
- The poem is timeless and is both complete unto itself and never entirely finite (because it can allude to other texts).
- Whereas journalism should be unequivocal and straightforward, poetry seeks to be multivalent and metaphorical.
- In almost every respect, poems and dreams are to be interpreted by like means.

Whether poetry takes a particular form, voice, stance or rhythmic arrangement is no longer a defining characteristic of the genre. What *does* seem to define it, in modern times, is rather the set of attitudes and approaches we bring to it.

But you must be asking, "Of course, this is all well and good for poetry written with words whose meanings and arrangements are accessible to the reader, but what is the corresponding message delivered in film? How can we possibly 'read' a film the way we read poetry?" Indeed, we must discover how a film makes meaning. For the most part, we tend to restrict our understanding of film's meaning to the events of the story and the lines spoken in the dialogue. In this respect, film operates much as literature does, through narrative codes (What happens? Who wins? Who loses?) and/or through sociological codes (What is the setting? What is the social class of the characters at the outset? Does their situation change or remain static? Does the film carry a social or political message that we should take away with us?). *On the Waterfront*, for example, presents a situation in which individual freedoms are being threatened by the strong-arm tactics of the corrupt dockworkers' unions in New York in the 1950s. The film tells the story of a heroic individual who dares to stand up to the union bosses and liberate his co-workers from these oppressive conditions. The director Kazan's message seems utterly American, pitting the heroic individual against the oppressive machine that would crush him. His revolt against the bosses – even against his own family – is undoubtedly inspirational, and is doubly so given the performance of the iconic Marlon Brando. And yet the film was produced at a time when unions were struggling on behalf of workers who had faced equally catastrophic conditions when they opposed corporations unfettered by union representation. The "classic Hollywood style" promotes a single interpretation (the heroic individual's defeat of the corrupt unions), itself unfettered by the very complicated political situation of the time.

Narrative and sociological codes, however, can themselves be complicated by cinematic ones – and this will be especially true of a cinema that seeks to maximize poetic style. To appreciate these other cinematic codes, then, we must ask what in film corresponds to the "poetic effects" of our illustration of poetry. Fiction film does, of course, work through narrative, costume, scenery, and dialogue to produce a story. But none of these elements are specific to the cinema. If, instead, we ask, as the French were doing throughout the 1920s, "what elements of film are, in fact, *specific* to the medium?" we arrive at another entirely different set of potential meanings.

Specific to the cinema is the *combination* of codes that are produced by the set of properties of the apparatus that has recorded and arranged the "events" we see: the camera, the composition of the shot, the lighting, the soundtrack and of course, the editing. Each of these elements is capable of producing a multitude of different effects: *the camera* can remain stationary or travel. While stationary, it can pan horizontally or vertically, or can zoom toward or away from its object. It can vary its focus to capture one or another aspect of the scene. In every one of these camera effects we can discover a different meaning. When it "travels," it can be moved horizontally on wheels or tracks, or vertically on a crane or a plane. It can also be carried, and the hand-held camera usually produces a very immediate sense of being in the action of the scene rather than experiencing it as an observer.

Because we see the film on a rectangular screen, any given shot is framed like a painting. Each of these *compositions* can communicate something about the scene, whether the space is ordered or not, whether the space feels open or restricted, whether the image feels symmetrical or not. All of these elements are carefully arranged to produce specific ideas in the spectator's mind.

Likewise, *the lighting* of the scene can produce different interpretations according to the source, power, and coloration of the lighting. Harsh frontal lighting would create an entirely different interpretation of events than would a soft bath of diffused light. Back lighting can produce a halo. Points of light can draw our attention to various elements in the scene before us.

The possibilities of *the soundtrack* are also infinite: sound can originate directly from the fictional world we are watching (called diegetic sound), or can have its source outside that world as, for example, the music that thrills us into the first images of *Star Wars*, or in the extra-diegetic voice that announces that Truffaut's *The Story of Adele H.* is taking place in Halifax during the American Civil War. Sounds "off," originating in the world of the film but not yet visible, can produce relief or terror.

The uses of *editing* are also so complex and varied that we can only suggest their range here. Rudolf Arnheim, who authored *Film as Art*, and Sergei Eisenstein, the great Russian director and theorist, both argued that editing is the primary source of poetry in cinema since, through rapid juxtapositions of elements, the cinema can replicate poetic metaphor. A crowd descending the stairs of the Paris Metro followed immediately by the image of a flock of sheep leaves little doubt as to the poetic possibilities of the seventh art. Beyond such juxtapositions, much meaning can be derived from the use of an overlap dissolve in which one image fades gradually into another, as opposed to the use of a fade to black which can either serve as mere punctuation, or, in the hands of Jim Jarmusch, be felt as an eerie loss of consciousness from which we awaken uneasily. Special editing effects such as the iris (where the image is erased by a shrinking circle, imitating the closing of the human eye) or a wipe (where one image "chases" the next across the screen) add to the stock of techniques available to the film's editor. When the French began to experiment with editing in the 1920s they produced films which included shots of merely two to three frames, accelerating the pace of the film so dramatically that the spectators experienced a degree of vertigo. The Japanese, on the other hand, especially Ozu, derive enormous power from extremely long takes of a scene with little action. The effects of editing, so minimized in the classical Hollywood style, with its emphasis on continuity, will become extremely important to the French as they maximize the poetic rather than the narrative aspects of their art.

Once aware of the multiplicity of possibilities that await us as we sit down in the darkened space of the theater, we should feel alarmed. If meaning is to derive from so great a number of different elements, how can we possibly keep track of all of them, much less integrate them into an interpretation of what we have seen?

In my classes, I ask my students to form seven different groups, each group responsible for one single "code" in the segment we are seeking to analyze: one group looks at the camera work, another the lighting, a third the composition, a fourth the soundtrack, a fifth the editing, and a sixth is asked to examine whether the segment contains any direct messages to the viewer (audience address).[12] From all of these various elements, we will patiently "construct" together a sense of the messages that are being projected before us. As a test of how much will be learned from paying attention to the *specifically cinematic* events before us, I also ask the seventh group to report on what happens in the scene, absent of any cinematic analysis. This will allow us to measure the difference between watching the film for its story and the appreciation that should come from seeing the many meanings that are "added" by the director in his choice of the specifically cinematic codes at his disposal.

(As readers of this book, you might want to gather a group of friends and rent a DVD, then, with each person responsible for a specific cinematic code, look at the opening segment of the film. I believe you will be amazed and delighted at the results of your collaborative effort! I will wager that the film in front of you will open up its "secrets" in a remarkably dramatic way.)

Such an approach should allow us to appreciate the specifically *cinematic* effects of a particular scene. When we then apply the other lessons of our literary poetic exercise, we can begin to appreciate such elements as repetition, rhyme, rhythm, and theme when we read the film (as we read the poem) backwards and forwards. Because the cinema was originally invented and intended by its inventors to provide a scientific document of the world around us, it always has some aspect of journalism to it – that is, it likely seems, by its very photography to begin, like the newspaper article, as a purely referential document. Just as we can rearrange the journal article poetically, so we can see that, in every fiction film, what initially appears to be merely referential has a multitude of poetic effects that, when analyzed, can become visible and can greatly enhance our reading of the words/ images before us. Let us, then, bolstered by this appetite for poetic analysis, turn from the poem to Jean Vigo's *L'Atalante* to discover in its *specifically cinematic poetics* the world of meanings that awaits us.

The Poetry of Jean Vigo's *L'Atalante*

"There is no way of completely understanding the films of Jean Vigo," wrote the celebrated French film critic, André Bazin, "unless we try to discover ... what particular kind of tenderness, of sensual or sentimental affection they reflect." Bazin invites us to pause for a moment to reflect on Vigo's life – and to do so is to become convinced of how absolutely miraculous it is not only that he managed to overcome extraordinary adversity to create his films, but that *L'Atalante* should have survived.

Jean Vigo was born on April 26, 1905, making him a contemporary of Jean-Paul Sartre. It didn't help his start in life that his father, Miguel, a poor but committed anarchist, lived in drafty, unheated rooms, ate rarely and badly, and dragged his son to one smoke-filled meeting room after another – nor that Jean celebrated his third Christmas in his father's jail cell. Luckily he was frequently exiled to his grandparents' home in Montpellier in the south of France. On August 6, 1917, the twelve-year-old Jean watched as gendarmes searched his house and dragged his father off to jail. One week later, Miguel was found assassinated in his cell. Left virtually orphaned, since Miguel's wife Emily had never professed motherhood to any observable degree, Jean spent his teenage years in various boarding schools where he suffered from a variety of arbitrary regimes that would be exposed in his film, *Zero for Conduct*.

By age 21, Jean had developed what was to be a lifelong passion for the cinema and hoped to sign on with Abel Gance for his production of *Napoleon*, but tuberculosis brought Vigo back to Montpellier and from there to a sanatorium in the nearby mountains. There he met Elizabeth Lozinska ("Lydou"). On their return to Nice in 1928, they married and used Lydou's father's wedding gift of 100,000 francs to buy a Debrie movie camera. After some preliminary shots of the Nice zoo, the two decided to make a "surrealist documentary" about Nice, which initially got good reviews at its premiere in Paris, but was a commercial failure and quickly slipped from view.

By July 1932, Vigo had met the financier, Jacques-Louis Nounez, who helped produce Jean's first fiction film, *Zero for Conduct*. Of this short film, shot under impossible conditions in the dead of winter, Vigo said, "I deliberately made *Zéro de conduite* a realistic film,"[13] but Vigo's sense of "realism" is clearly closer to surrealism than to the more commonly accepted meanings of the term realism.[14] When it was first shown, Vigo announced, "I wanted *Un Chien Andalou* to be projected here today because … the directing is meticulous, the lighting skillful, the images and visual associations perfectly coherent, the dreams impeccably logical. It is a marvellous confrontation between the rational world and the subconscious … These are rare qualities indeed in a film."[15] Vigo sounds remarkably like an orthodox surrealist in his praise of Buñuel's film and even more like the visionary father of Surrealism, André Breton.[16] Immediately after *Zéro*'s opening in Paris in April 1933, however, the Catholic Church called for it to be banned and the board of censors took action, deeming it "a threat to civil order." The film wouldn't be shown again until its rediscovery after the Second World War.

As if knowing he was running out of time, Vigo went to work immediately on his only full-length fiction film, *L'Atalante*. Sadly, once again, production was delayed until winter had set in, which meant that Vigo's health would be fatally compromised, and he took to his bed almost immediately after completing the editing. He rose only twice before his untimely death a few days after the film ended its short run at the Coliseum Theater in Paris. His first full-length fiction film was to be his last, and was then to be cut apart, "massacred," to appeal to more popular taste by his producers at Gaumont, and was only rediscovered and reassembled in its original form 25 years after its release.

Like the news item of our "experiment," *L'Atalante* could easily be reduced to its storyline and then dismissed as a slow-paced realistic chronicle of the marital difficulties of a bargeman (Jean Dasté) and his new bride (Dita Parlo). After the briefest of marriage ceremonies in Juliette's rural village, Jean whisks her off to a very restricted life on his barge, punctuated by episodes of drunkenness of Jules and the mate (Michel Simon), and furious outbursts of Jean's jealousy. Jean consents to one brief outing at the Café des Quatre Nations, where a young traveling salesman (Jules Margaritis) invites Juliette to dance with him and inflames her imagination with visions of Paris. As a result of this interloper's behavior, the interlude ends up serving as yet another excuse for her jealous husband to confine his new bride to her dreary quarters. Juliette escapes from the barge, however, and flees to Paris where she is fascinated by store windows full of magical scenes. Soon, however, she loses her purse to a pickpocket and wanders disconsolately around the city. After her disappearance, Jean grows despondent and old Jules must take over captaining the barge. Things grow so bad that Jules finally decides to head to Paris to look for Juliette. He discovers her in a record store, listening to sea shanties, brings her back to the barge and restores her to her husband. In the final shots of the film, Jean and Juliette appear to be happily reunited.

Not much of a plot, you are no doubt thinking – and you're right. Several viewings of this film make it abundantly clear that Vigo's talents did not lie in the art of clever plot construction. It should doubtless come as no surprise to learn that the story was based on a lamentably art-less novel by Jean Guinée, and this choice was imposed on Vigo by his producers at Gaumont. In fact, Vigo was to direct much of his creative energy to circumventing the banality of Guinée's story by any means he could. Despite those impositions, most film scholars agree that Vigo's film is among the dozen greatest French films, some would even argue that this "may be the greatest film ever made."[17] How can we understand this "greatness?" Clearly Vigo's talents lay more in *how* the story is told than in *what* happens and his art, as we shall appreciate, lies in his ability to transform a rather drab story into poetry and to translate graphic into cinematic writing.

If we take another look (or several looks) at *L'Atalante*, many of the characteristics that we discovered in our discussion of poetry begin to emerge. Already in the first scene of the film, for example, a series of very *enigmatic* elements bleed through the somber realism of the wedding pro-cession. You might take a few minutes to take another look at this scene which opens the film and runs until the couple boards the barge and the captain waves goodbye to the wedding party. Using the set of codes we introduced at the outset of this chapter, let's look at the way Vigo uses sound, camera angles, montage, and composition to create an unusual set of expectations for his viewers. Significantly there is almost no dialogue in this first sequence.

A quick establishing shot of the barge, prominently baptized as *L'Atalante*, greets the viewer at the opening of the film and is followed by a shot of the village church identifying the source of the bells we hear chiming – a natural association between the wedding that has just taken place and the barge on which the newlyweds will live. This would not be an unusual piece of montage except for the fact that two "problems" present themselves almost immediately. The first is the burst of smoke emanating from an unidentifiable source and whose purpose seems to be

Plate 1.1   The wedding procession goes haywire

to over-cloud an otherwise perfectly clear day. (Those familiar with Vigo's earlier film will remember that a similar mist arises in the opening minutes of *Zero for Conduct*). The second is that Vigo's montage suggests a close proximity (visually and auditorily) between river bank and church. This proximity is natural enough when we consider that one of the village's "industries" is logging, given the pile of logs adjacent to the barge later in the scene. Naturally one would assume that village and river are spatially connected for commercial and other reasons.

The procession we are to witness, however, continues not along a short roadway from village to river port, but out of the village left to right *away from the viewer*, then quite abruptly (the result of a jump cut) from right to left *moving now toward the viewer* without any explanation of the overall geography. Our "map" of events is further confused when the next shot has the couple (all alone now) weaving in and out among a set of three giant haystacks which dwarf and isolate them. The rest of the wedding party has been hopelessly lost from view, so accelerated is the married couple's pace. Apparently never discovering any thoroughfare, the young couple now struggles through a patch of very tall weeds, emerging at the top of a high hill which has the effect of lending them an otherworldly separateness. From there they descend onto a recently plowed and visibly muddy field, are next discovered in woodland, and finally emerge from yet another wooded area to pick their way through the scattered logs that obstruct their path. As they arrive, finally, at the barge, they are magically reunited with the rest of their party. As if this radically disjunctive voyage were not confusing enough, Vigo's editing moves back and forth between shots of the mournfully subdued married couple to another, very disturbing twosome. Through this use of what is called parallel montage (because the back-and-forth cutting emphasizes the connections between two different series of events assumed to be taking place at the same time), Vigo establishes the uncomfortable sense that these two couples are uncanny doubles of each other. This doubling, though not at first explicit, becomes unmistakable late in the sequence when the boy returns from his search for a bouquet looking like nothing so much as a bride crowned with an "aura" of weeds and wild flowers. What is most disturbing about this parallelism is that the couple Old Jules and the boy emerge from the church *before*, i.e. *in lieu of*, the newlyweds and proceed to perform a wild burlesque of marital relations, Jules constantly abusing his more feminine partner, pushing him, dragging him, shouting orders to him and sending him off to replace the flowers he has lost. Not only do these two violently pop up (through Vigo's montage) in the serenity of the wedding procession but, ironically, lend to it the only vitality we are to witness. In addition, through this editing technique we can surmise that Vigo has "rhymed" two different (and deeply opposed) elements, thereby (as we saw in the "poem" above) creating a fundamental ambiguity. Specifically, the suggestion that Jean and Jules are but versions of "the husband" allows us to perceive a pattern in the film that is not immediately evident and that tends to be overshadowed by the plot of the film.

If we pay closer attention to the soundtrack throughout this procession, we will hear the wedding bells give way to a solemn tolling and observe the celebrants, uniformly dressed in a most funereal black, as they follow reluctantly along, "witnessing" the delivery (dare we say "sacrifice") of one of their young women to an alien. "Don't cry!" is the first voice we hear, and, now sensing we are privy to a funeral rather than a wedding (there will be no festivities), we end up, like the "mourners," helplessly standing by as a daughter is torn from her mother's side, thrown like a chattel onto a swinging beam and "hoisted" onto the barge. Viewers should take a good long look at the "dead" face of this sacrificial victim just before she is "tossed" aboard, for there have been few more mournful portraits in the history of cinema than Dita Parlo's distraught visage.[18] In retrospect, we can appreciate just how directionless was their wedding

Plate 1.2 Juliette's solemn visage

procession, how little it followed any sort of forward progress, route, or map and how it ends in the place where "crossing over" must inevitably allude to the river Styx rather than the Seine and how the undue speed of their progress might uncannily recall the "I speed TO BE DEAD" of our poetic experiment.[19] In this regard, notice how, in Vigo's editing, Jean and Juliette start off moving toward the future (left to right) but immediately find themselves walking away from any sense of progression (abruptly shifting direction from right to left) and then on to a vaguely circuitous, unmarked course. One is reminded of Dante and indeed, just as the dark forest – *selva oscura* – in which Dante finds himself at the beginning of *The Inferno* (1.2) is described in vague terms, perhaps as an indication of the protagonist's own disorientation, Vigo's portrayal of Juliette's disorientation is paramount. The psychological and spiritual nature of this disorientation stresses two very important elements of both poem and film: first, we are encouraged to understand these journeys to be symbolic; and second, film and poem are carefully structured so that we must read "backwards" from later events to gain a fuller understanding of this first scene.

Again, to recall our investigation of poetry, the film opens with *an enigma* to be solved: Why does a wedding ceremony devolve into a funeral procession? What might it mean that Juliette's marriage joins her to some form of death? Would this be the death of her former self or some darker purpose? Part of our sense of that enigma derives from the possible *allusion* to Dante's *Inferno*. To solve this enigma we will have *to read the film forwards and then backwards* and to appreciate *through a process of association* the ways the film's different scenes can be connected into a highly *symbolic arrangement.*

One of the ways of understanding Juliette's "death" in the first scene, surely the most literal of the possibilities, is her absence from her native place, a meaning punctuated by her mother's tears as she leaves. An immediate second interpretation, perhaps no less obvious, is her entombment in the coffin-shaped barge. No doubt her expectations of escape from the confines of her native village are dashed not only by the reduced quarters that swallow her up in the bowels of the craft, but also by Jean's constrictions of her pleasures. He limits her activities to washing, sewing, and cooking, and angrily switches off the radio when she seeks news and music from Paris.

But Vigo is hardly content to limit his story to the limitations of her story. Instead, as director (and saboteur of Jean Guinée's very normative plot), he offers her a visit to another realm. Juliette arriving trance-like at the boat finds herself among a plethora of cats, one of whom is thrown abruptly into view. Thereafter, life on the barge takes on the elements of a dreamscape: scenes are shrouded in mist or mysterious light – in one scene she appears to be walking on water – and the multifarious and almost Halloween-like cats seem at times to rule this world, "seeking the silence and the horror of darkness … who seem to fall into a sleep of endless dreams" like some Baudelarian vision.[20] What seems to be at stake here is, I would suggest, a struggle pitting Jean against all of the others, indeed against *otherness itself.* What is truly carnivalesque[21] about this world is that, ironically, the straight-laced, rule-bound and severe Jean ends up symbolizing death whereas the decadent, grotesque Jules, almost daemonic in his eeriness, seems to represent life forces. Jean, who might have served Juliette's desire for freedom, seems to personify repression, whereas Jules, a man seemingly meant to follow the captain's rules, embodies the unleashing of the unconscious. In her descent into the forbidden Hades of Jules's cabin, she will encounter a world more separate in its exotic and erotic possibilities than any she might have imagined.[22]

Juliette seems to embody desire: desire for intimacy, desire for the forbidden, desire for the exotic. In her first moments on board, she lies longingly on the deck of the barge in her pure white dress as a personification of oxymoron: the collapsing of opposites, the erasure of contradiction that Freud hypothesizes when he says "What, in the conscious, is found split into a pair of opposites often occurs in the unconscious as a unity."[23] In her scenes with Père Jules, we gradually understand that she has more than names in common with him: indeed Vigo has effected a remarkable condensation of these two characters. Of course, at first, nothing could seem more removed from possibility than this juxtaposition: she is so young, so pure, so beautiful; he so old, so filthy, so grotesque. Truly a case of beauty and the beast in which beauty and beast uncannily double each other. On the morning after her arrival on the barge, for example, she emerges wearing a shirt like Jules. Later he sits at her sewing machine, tries on her dress and dances provocatively, as if attempting to rob her of her femininity.

When Juliette sneaks into Jules's cabin, she finds there a veritable *vitrine* (Jules's word, meaning a store window display) of objects whose fantastic juxtaposition has a distinctly surreal feel to it: a conch shell, a disquieting puppet of a musical conductor, a tusk, a broken record player, and even a pair of severed hands. "There is a story *behind* every object" says Jules, as if parroting the father of Surrealism, André Breton. The scene recalls Lautremont's text, used by Breton as *the* illustration of the surrealist image: "Beau comme la rencontre fortuite sur une table à dissection d'un parapluie et d'une machine à coudre [As beautiful as the chance encounter on a dissecting table of an umbrella and a sewing machine.]" Breton famously calls man "an inveterate dreamer, who has trouble assessing the objects he has been led to use, objects that his nonchalance has brought his way or that he has earned through his own efforts or what he calls his luck."[24]

And, as if sleepwalking through a surrealist milieu, Jules takes a knife and slices his finger while Juliette lasciviously licks her lips as she stares at the blood pulsing from his thumb.[25] As the personification of surrealism, Jules cannot fail to awaken Juliette's dreamy desires. She can virtually taste his exotic eroticism.

The uncanniest thing of all, in my view, is that Jules does not appear just once in *L'Atalante*, he reappears in the figure of the *camelot*, the traveling salesman-one-man-band. The actor, Gilles Margaritis, bears an uncanny physical resemblance to Jean Daste, who plays Jean, and to Jules's musical puppet. He seems to extend the dreamlike state of Jules's fantastic cabin off the barge and into the light of day. He first appears riding his bike in between the couple as they walk toward the *Café des Quatre Nations* (exactly as shots of Jules had interrupted the continuity of the wedding march!). Inside the café he opens a trunk that uncannily resembles Jules's cabin in its ability to spawn strange and wonderful objects. Like Jules, but

Plate 1.3   Jules slices his finger

now in a physically beautiful avatar, the *camelot* embodies a spirit of carnival and of the irruption of dream into the waking state. He performs magic tricks while singing hypnotic (almost Orphic) songs, and, like his bestial double, dances around wildly, pulling Juliette *through a latticed window*, a gesture that recalls Juliette's earlier descent into the "sacred space" of Jules's seductive cabin or Alice's headlong plunge into Wonderland. When, exasperated, the café owner tries to punch this sprite, Margaritis feigns a fainting spell that replicates exactly the collapse of the eerie marionette in Jules's cabin. After Jean wrenches Juliette from this enchanted place and returns her to the prison-like barge, this trickster will return (just as Freud predicted in his theory of the return of the repressed) to excite Juliette's desire for an exotic adventure.

We might pause here, to think again about the relationship between poetry and film. In retrospect, as we look at these two segments (Jules's cabin and the *camelot*'s café), we can appreciate how much they serve the function of poetic rhyme. Just as the repetition of the words "speed," "ninety-five," and "TO BE DEAD" in our poetic experiment function as rhymes to link up different moments of the "narrative" of the accident into more poetic meaning, Vigo's doubled scenes suggest versions of the story of a couple on a barge that move us well beyond the film's realism to a mythopoetic level. The two doubles of Jean – Jules (the beast) and the *camelot* (as his beautiful double) – not only awaken Juliette's appetites for the exotic and the erotic, they point the way for Jean's own oneiric transformation. Juliette can no longer be contained in the straitjacket of her new husband's failed imagination and her revolt causes Jean to need to break out of his own death-like captaincy of the barge. Beautiful and sinister alternatives must be explored.

No wonder then that, invited by both of the figures of dream in her life, Juliette succumbs to her desire for the exotic and escapes to Paris in search of this newfound *otherness*.

Once in Paris she pauses before a store window (*vitrine*) displaying dolls that recall Jules's puppet, yet are uncannily distorted by Juliette's own image mirrored in the store window. Vigo's poem works constantly with this overlay of interior/exterior mindscapes. But along with this dreamy recall of Jules's cabin, Paris is the site of trauma. A pickpocket violently grabs Juliette's purse and his aggression will lead her from ecstasy to bewildered despair.[26]

Jean, likewise, doubling Juliette, gives in to despair. Growing increasingly despondent, he loses control of the boat and ultimately rushes off directionless in a symbolic replay of the wedding procession. His wanderings culminate in a desperate and chaotic rush to the sea – a "retour à la mer" (sea and mother are homonyms in French) that signals his capitulation to a "sea" of unconscious forces greater than reason.[27] We should notice what happens to reason, linear thinking and authority in the face of this loss of control: poetry and the dreamwork begin to operate in parallel processes – intuition, free association, and ambiguity.

From this point on, Jean will have access to the absent Juliette only through means that are specifically *cinematic*: first in the remarkable parallel cutting of the two lovers in separate beds, each polka-dotted with an eerie lighting that signals the oneiric nature of their encounter. Next, Jean will dive beneath the barge to seek Juliette's image that is achieved by a superimposition (or dissolve) of two images, Juliette's "floating" body on the watery deep where Jean is swimming. This is a scene that can only be understood as a surreal union of dreaming and desire. We recall that in one of the first scenes on the barge, Juliette had told Jean, "Don't you know that you can always find your beloved by dousing your head in water? ... You'll see me when you want to." It is as if she were paraphrasing Breton who wrote: "Everything tends to make us believe that there exists a certain point of the mind at which life and death, the real and the imagined, past and future, the communicable and the incommunicable,

Plate 1.4   Juliette's floating body

high and low, cease to be perceived as contradictions."[28] That "point of the mind", Freud would argue, occurs every night of our lives.[29] "In the dreamwork," Freud noted, "representation by the opposite plays a … great … part…. Dreams are not merely fond of representing two contraries by one and the same composite structure, but they … often change something in the dream thoughts into its opposite."[30] For Jean, as Vigo, Freud and Breton seem to be telling us in concert, can only reach happiness when he abandons his need for control. "Surrealism" wrote Breton, "aims quite simply at the total recovery of our psychic force by a means which is nothing other than the dizzying descent into ourselves, the systematic illumination of hidden places and the progressive darkening of other places, the perpetual excursion into the midst of forbidden territory."[31] And so, just as Juliette's desire has been awakened by the "poetry" of the exotic figures of Jules and the *camelot*, Jean's only means of retrieving his lost love is through recourse to a similar "point of the mind, where life and death, the real and the imagined" come into play. He must invent a "poetry" of his own.

It is important to emphasize that, for Vigo, it is the cinema that is best able to render the conflation of such "contradictions." Vigo was undoubtedly drawn to the cinema precisely because it enabled him to "translate" such deeply poetic notions both through the use of montage as metaphor and by the superimposition of such powerful images as we encounter here in *L'Atalante.*

Ultimately the reunion of the estranged couple can only be effected by the "medium," Jules, who seems to know, as if he himself had already traced it, his feminized namesake's path into Paris. Uncannily, as if in a trance, he crosses the same bridge she had taken, and walks directly to the street, then to the store, then to the booth where she is playing "their song." Only when Jules and Juliette are themselves merged through this "medium of the unconscious" will she be able to return to her "legitimate" husband, who is himself now transformed through poetry.

What makes Vigo's cinema so remarkable is that he manages to tell his story without the overly disruptive style of Buñuel's *Andalusian Dog* or the too obvious recourse to mythic representation that we encounter in Cocteau's *Beauty and the Beast.* The genius of Vigo's poetic style lies, as we have seen, in his ability to transform realism (the news item or what the French would call "le fait divers") into a cinematic version of poetry in which we are forced to read backwards and forwards, to see deeper connections between people, various obscure objects of desire and several allusions to other poems and myths, all of which allows us to appreciate the ambiguity rather than the simplicity of experience. Moreover, by shifting the story of *Beauty and the Beast* to Ovid's tale, *Atalanta,*[32] Vigo allows us a (re)vision of the latter tale in which Ovid's *one* man bearing *three* apples (*trois pommes*) is cine-poetically transmogrified by Vigo into a vision of *three* men condensing into *one* poem (*un poème*) – a poem every bit as grotesque and sublime as *Beauty and the Beast,* but now stripped of its fantastic suspension of disbelief and disguised as a simple tale of everyday life. What appears to be a "fait divers" about barge life in 1934 is transformed through Vigo's ciné-poetic vision into a poem of despair, disintegration, and potential reintegration. Poetry is, at every turn, not only the *medium* but the *implicit subject* of this film. That duality of purpose is certainly the element that makes this film so *French.*

Ultimately we cannot know what the future holds for Jean and Juliette. Perhaps that is why the last shot of the film follows the *Atalante* moving enigmatically through a limitless expanse of water, onward into the night. The film offers no comfortable closure, only immense possibility. It also offers us a model for looking at other films, whether French or not, with a new appreciation of their many possibilities that seem, like the final bird's eye view of the barge, to sail along at some distance beneath our eyeline level. The entire film seems to whisper to us, as Juliette does to Jean, "You can see me if you really want to" – in a place submerged *beneath* and *between* the real images, a space that comes into view only when we rewind or unravel the reel of images, reading – poetically – backwards and forwards to allow the visual rhymes to be seen and heard. In this space, too, we hear the whispered questions that are so insistently posed and so insistently *French*, 'What is cinema?' and its 'double,' 'What is poetry?' But neither Juliette nor Vigo, nor French cinema itself, for that matter, ever seem to be entirely satisfied with the answers.

Suggested Further Reading

Andrew, J. D. (1984), *Film in the Aura of Art*. Princeton, NJ: Princeton University Press.
   Contains an excellent essay on Vigo's films.
Bordwell, D. and Thompson, K. (1990), *Film Art: An Introduction*. New York: McGraw Hill.
   The best introduction to film analysis, Bordwell and Thompson provide an overview of the technology of film production and technique. There is also a useful section on French Impressionism and Surrealism that provides an excellent context for the present chapter.

2

Cinema and the Real
Renoir's *Rules*

"*Cinema is a matter of style ... and style is a moral fact. An angle, a shot in film has its own moral. A tracking shot, for example may be moral or not moral. There is an ethic in the style of many directors.*" (Bernardo Bertolucci)[1]

There could perhaps be no greater contrast than that between the opening images of Jean Vigo's *L'Atalante* and those of Jean Renoir's *Rules of the Game*. Vigo's film uses what appears to offer an objective view of a marriage procession moving through a small French provincial town, yet begins almost immediately to undermine the camera's objectivity in all sorts of playful ways. Rapid cutting between the composed and solemn newlyweds and the hilariously frenetic couple of Jules and the cabin boy quickly subverts any sense of continuity or rational arrangement. The odd sightlines and weird itinerary of Jean and Juliette are captured from increasingly strange camera positions. The doubling of one couple by another eerily suggests some ulterior arrangement that we cannot quite fathom and leads us to move beyond the question of "what's happening?" to a bewildered state of fractured consciousness. All in all, what we discover quite rapidly is that we are in a *poetic* rather than a *realistic* mode.

Renoir's 1939 film, on the other hand, places the film's spectator immediately into a scarily familiar situation: we are immersed in an excited crowd of people, surging forward to greet the aviator, André Jurieux (Roland

Toutain) as he makes his record-setting landing at Le Bourget. The camera's position in the crowd allows us to experience directly this excitement, the jostling, the surge toward the plane, once it touches down, breaking through police lines and moving dangerously close to the spinning propellers of the small craft. Obstinately dogging the steps of the newswoman covering this scene for French radio, we claw our way to a position close enough to the hero to observe his first remarks to the world on his heroic achievement. There's nothing eerie or disjointed about this moment; Renoir uses few cuts to bring us to this proximity with our main character, and what few he uses are felt to be logical and continuous. Nor is the scene the least bit dreamlike despite the nocturnal darkness of the landing field. We are, quite simply, there!

Another remarkable difference between Vigo's "cinema*n*tics" and Renoir's cinematics lies in Renoir's refusal to allow his camera to entirely isolate the subjects of our interest. While André attempts to ask his friend Octave (Jean Renoir) whether Christine has come to the airport to meet him, the radio reporter can be seen behind them forcing her way between them, brutally interrupting their conversation and causing us to lose focus on their own connection. The soundtrack imitates this visual chaos by constantly threatening to drown out André's voice with the crowd's tumultuous uproar. Indeed, throughout this scene (and in most of the scenes of this film) we rarely seem to benefit from a properly framed or limited scene that would allow us to fix our attention on one particular character, grouping, or object (as we might on a theatrical stage for example); there is almost always *too much to see.*

We might say that what Renoir has done is to imitate the way we look at the world around us, not always certain of what requires our undivided attention, constantly distracted by things in our field of vision that don't necessarily conform to our particular expectations. Renoir's cinematics often give us the impression we are walking down a crowded street where there are many events happening all at once, any of which would be worthy of our attention, but whose sum total cannot quite be taken in by a single glance.

Is this merely a question of style? Well, it *might be* were it not that this is a French film – i.e. a "genre" where there are rarely if ever questions of style that are not the result of much deeper concerns. Indeed, one of the things we must attempt to understand is the way Renoir's style in this opening scene constitutes *one of the most important subjects of his film.* Although there are certainly literary aspects to his work, Renoir's basic approach to the techniques of filming here is much more *intentionally and programmatically* realistic than poetic. Why should this be? Could we not

Plate 2.1 The reporter barges in

simply see his realism as a fashionable conformity to the trends of late 1930s' French style? Or does the film (as I believe we shall discover) actually constitute a meditation on the *necessity* of realism in cinema?

Now, just as we could not have a discussion of cinema and poetry without first understanding the premises of poetry, we must now pause to attempt to understand how we might speak of realism in a creative work of fiction. Our best guide in this effort would be a critic by the name of André Bazin, who published his first essay on film in 1945 (that is to say six years *after* Renoir made *Rules*). In "The Ontology of the Photographic Image,"[2] Bazin set out to explain the conundrum of "realistic fiction," i.e. how something that is meant to be an illusion can aspire to be real. He immediately establishes a distinction between what he calls "pseudorealism" which would be content with "illusory appearances," the kind practiced by all of the arts up until the invention of photography, and the birth of "true" realism. "Photography and the cinema are discoveries," Bazin assures us, "that satisfy, once and for all and in its very essence, our obsession with realism."[3] And what is the essential difference, we might ask, between these two media and all the other arts? All the arts before photography necessitated the intervention of the eye and hand of the artist. As Bazin argues it, "The fact that a human hand intervened cast a shadow of doubt over the image." No matter that painting may have, in some cases, looked more realistic than photography, the fact that photography was the first "unmediated" rendering of the world made it forever different from its predecessors. Bazin trumpets:

> For the first time, between the originating object and its reproduction there intervenes only the instrumentality of a nonliving agent. For the first time an image of the world is formed automatically, without the creative invention of man…. All the arts are based on the presence of man, only photography derives an advantage from his absence…. Viewed in this perspective, cinema is objectivity in time."[4]

This particularity of cinema is more than just a characteristic; "objectivity in time," according to Bazin, constitutes the very ontology (*the* defining characteristic) of the seventh art.

When we recall that almost nothing happens in the world of French cinema without a theoretical rationale, we can understand the importance of Bazin's thinking for some of the filmmakers around him. If indeed, the very ontology of cinema is the real, then not only is true cinema realistic, but anything that takes away from this realism constitutes a betrayal of the nature of cinema. Knowing this kind of thinking to be central to Jean Renoir's conversations with André Bazin allows us to better understand the "rules" of *The Rules of the Game*.

Bazin's call for cinema to obey its ontology is not just idealism or an arbitrary requirement to be imposed on his friends who were practicing the seventh art. The critic had deeper reasons for making these demands. But we can best discover the nature and importance of Bazin's rationale by returning to Renoir's film.

We had left André Jurieux swearing childishly in front of a nationwide radio audience that Christine's refusal to come to his heroic landing is "disloyal." But we do not know, and will never really learn, on what he bases this accusation. Are he and Christine lovers or just friends? Has she made promises that she could not keep? But this is not *Citizen Kane* and there will be no "Rosebud" to provide the "aha!" answer to this question. No, Renoir is, in the end, too wise to believe that the "truth" of the matter has anything to do with the behavior of the people who surround Christine and André. He is much more of a realist than a police investigator about this. What interests Renoir, as we will see, is not what actually transpired between Christine and Jurieux but rather the skein of others' responses (and beliefs) and how these responses and beliefs are gradually woven into an almost inevitably tragic net that catches everyone up and leaves no one untouched.

When we finally see our "lovers" together for the first time, André has been invited to La Coliniere, the country home of Christine's husband, Robert, the Marquis de la Chesnaye (Dalio). As André steps out of the downpour outside into the atrium of this chateau, Christine (Nora Gregor) rushes to his side and, holding his hand, makes the following confession to all of the assembled guests:

> Dear friends, I must let you into a little secret about my relationship with André Jurieux. That's to say that I played a small part in the success of his exploit. And this is how: during his preparations, André often came to see me. We spent many hours together – very pleasant hours – hours passed under the sign of that rare thing, friendship. He told me about his plans and I listened to him. It's something to know how to listen! ... In this case it was not in vain; I'm very proud of it! And I felt the need to tell you about it now.[5]

Obviously, however sincere and earnest Christine appears in this speech, there is no way to verify the truth of her assertion. What we see, however, is at least as important as what we hear. In this respect, we might discern behind Christine's words, "It's something to know how to listen," Renoir's own voice proclaiming, "It's something to know how to observe!" – his signature statement. As in the airport scene opening the film, our position as spectator is established as one of the invited guests. Immediately prior to Christine's confession, just to our left, we see and hear a quick conversation in which "the homosexual" and Charlotte speculate on whether André and Christine "have or haven't" had sex. But again there's no verifiability. Instead, as we look back at Christine during her confession, Renoir's camera picks up her husband and Octave situated directly behind the couple, but located *in between* the two "lovers." Their antics and spoofing create a commentary on Christine's actions that no dialogue could render. They nudge one another, smirk awkwardly and, at one point, Robert pokes his eye in a gesture that usually means in French "Mon oeil" or "Riiiiiight ..."

This "intrusion" recalls the airport scene where another couple involving André is visually disjoined by someone situated behind them, distracting our eye from events in the foreground. In both cases (the radio reporter who barges in between André and Octave and the couple, Octave and Robert, whose antics distract from Genevieve's performance), Renoir has resorted to what we call "deep focus" to make his point. Renoir wrote in 1938, just before shooting *Rules of the Game*, "The more I learn about my trade, the more I incline to direction in depth relative to the screen: the better it works the less I use the kind of set-up that shows two

Plate 2.2   Renoir's use of depth of field

actors facing the camera like two well-behaved subjects posing for a still portrait."[6] ... Already, as we have just observed, this use of "depth of field" has been established as the "signature statement" of Renoir in this film. In scene after scene, the director will film in very long takes (there are 15 shots of one minute or longer and 68 shots of 30 seconds or more) and using depth of field to offer his spectator a maximum of visual information from which to draw his or her conclusions. One has, for example, to think only of the hunting scene and the soirée in the chateau to appreciate the ways Renoir loads his scenes with too much information to incorporate into a single impression or interpretation. But this style is most evident in the confession scene which would normally be shot in close-up, isolating the speaker from their context, and allowing the film's spectator to make a reasonable interpretation of the scene's meaning based on close attention to the character's facial expressions and what they might reveal about intention, honesty, and what these attitudes may portend.

While Renoir was shooting *The Rules of the Game*, Jean-Paul Sartre was conceiving and writing *Being and Nothingness* in which he would argue that we are never able to define ourselves since our definition depends as much on how others see us as it does on our own beliefs and intentions. What's more, we can never "wrest" that definition from the other, but must always be subject to their freely held view of us.[7] What seems to result from Renoir's camera work here is a nearly identical conclusion. It little matters what Christine *intends*, it only matters how her words are received by others. In this case, Robert's immediate reaction is, "I think we should have a celebration. We'll put on a comedy and dress up in costumes!" Clearly the "rules of the game" imply that nothing counts but the roles played in this game, and thus Christine would be assumed merely to be playing her part with great panache.

In other words, depth of field for Renoir offers a far richer yield of meaning than any more limited view could provide. When André Bazin looked back six years later on this film, he discovered in it and in its signature stylistic trait not only a philosophy of perception, but the very ontology of film itself. There could be no clearer indication of the perfect harmony of these two men's views than Renoir's dedication of *Rules* to the author of *What Is Cinema?*

What Bazin would discover in this "simple" stylistic gesture was a manifold of cinematic, psychological, and even metaphysical implications:

> Depth of field is not just a stock in trade of the cameraman, like the use of a series of filters or of such-and-such a style of lighting, it is a capital gain in the field of direction – a dialectical step forward in the history of film language. Thus, depth of field not only affects the structure of film language, it also affects the relationships of the minds of the spectators to the image, and in consequence it influences the interpretation of the spectacle.[8]

In purely cinematic terms, he notes that "depth of focus brings the spectator into a relation with the image closer to that which he enjoys with reality. Therefore it is correct to say that, independently of the contents of the image, its structure is more realistic." But realism is hardly an end unto itself. Bazin sees in realism huge implications for the position of the spectator *vis-à-vis* the screen: Depth of focus

> implies, consequently, both a more active mental attitude on the part of the spectator and a more positive contribution on his part to the action in progress. While analytical montage only calls for him to follow his guide, to let his attention follow along smoothly with that of the director who will choose what he should see, here he is called upon to exercise at least a minimum of personal choice. It is from his attention and his will that the meaning of the image in part derives.[9]

But the implications don't stop there. In this shift from passivity to activity, Bazin sees more than psychology:

> From the two preceding propositions which belong to the realm of psychology, there follows a third which may be described as metaphysical. In analyzing reality, montage presupposes of its very nature the unity of meaning of the dramatic event, and thus by its very nature rules out ambiguity of expression. On the other hand, depth of focus reintroduces ambiguity into the structure of the image if not of necessity at least as a possibility. The *uncertainty* in which we find ourselves as to the spiritual key or the interpretation we should put on the film is built into the very design of the image.[10]

In short, depth of focus allows Renoir to "reveal the hidden meanings in people and things without disturbing the unity natural to them." And yet it would perhaps be more accurate to argue that depth of focus allows Renoir to reveal that people and things hold hidden meanings which we, as film viewers, must struggle to interpret.

Now, we would not expect Renoir's pedagogical demonstration of the implications of depth of field to be limited merely to illustrations of how depth of field produces a plethora of meanings available to the viewer. Any good teacher would want to expand his lesson to include evidence that the *opposite* of deep focus (i.e. the use of close-up) would limit, misrepresent, or otherwise distort the reality factor or truth of the world of La Colinière. Not surprisingly, then, Renoir offers just such an illustration during the hunting scene. At the end of the hunting scene, Christine, the General, Berthelin, Saint Aubin and Octave are returning to the chateau. Suddenly Saint Aubin notices a squirrel in the tree above them. While he fumes over his inability to shoot the animal, Berthelin offers his field-glass to Christine so that she may get a better view of it. "It's marvelous!" she cries enthusiastically. "I can see it as though I could touch it." Renoir now devotes almost 1,000 frames of his film to a discussion of the refinement and capabilities of the field glass, a conversation that would have no bearing on the narrative outcome of his film were it not for Christine's insistence on using the glass to scan the entire field before her.

Away across the marshes, at a distance that would normally hide them from Christine's view, Robert and his mistress, Genevieve, are making their final adieus. Rather than prolong the discussion, Genevieve asks Robert for one last embrace and Robert takes her in his arms for the last time. Had Christine the entire context for this scene, she might have been able to appreciate Robert's sacrifice for her and forgive him this affair. But no such contextualization is possible at this distance and she is allowed only this close-up – a snapshot (what the French would call an

Plate 2.3 Christine holding the field glasses

"*instantanée*") – of what can only appear to be a passionate kiss, here isolated in both space and time. This *misperception*, created by the specific *limitations* of close-up provided by the field glass, robs Christine of the contextualization that is offered by the use of depth of field. She naturally assumes that Robert is committed to his affair with Genevieve, rather than in the throes of ending it. Had she benefited from a larger perspective on this event, she doubtless would have acted with much more restraint (in keeping with her initial "confession" of her friendship with André), rather than falling entirely out of character, chasing after three different men during the carnivalesque gala, and ultimately agreeing to run off with André – a decision that directly leads to the "deplorable accident" that will result in André's death.

I believe that we can see in Renoir's otherwise gratuitous scene of the field glasses an example of a "counter-demonstration" of the failure of montage and the close-up to capture the larger ambiguity inherent in what Bazin calls the "unity of experience." Once again, as we watch one of the great French films, we become aware that it is not only the *events* of the film that give rise to an interpretation, but an entire *philosophy of cinema* that is being carefully elaborated just beneath the film's storyline, a philosophy that must be appreciated before we can grasp the film's deeper meanings. To be sure, Renoir's *Rules* does, as most critics agree, paint a devastating picture of French upper-class society on the eve of the Second World War. The director himself, when asked, "Did you discover only later all those things in *La Règle du jeu* which made one feel the approach of the war?" replied, "No. I thought of it then, but in an extremely vague way.... My ambition when I made the film was to illustrate this remark, 'we are dancing on a volcano.' "[11] But what emerges from Renoir's depth of field is a sustained, if entirely intuitive meditation on this particular social group and more profound sociological and anthropological questions.

So, how might our appreciation of the question of depth of field lead to this other, deeper understanding of Renoir's film as a whole? First of all, we've seen how depth of field allows Renoir to comment on others' reception of Christine's confession: Robert immediately decides that everyone must play and put on masks. The extent to which this invitation will subtly but surely invade every succeeding scene is remarkable. To appreciate just how extensive is this effect, let's look at the scene in which Robert tells Genevieve he can no longer be her lover. I suggest you put this book aside for a moment and look at this scene.

You will have noticed that, in their "face off," Robert and Genevieve stand addressing each other from opposite sides of a room. Each takes up a position adjacent to an oriental mask. As you look at their expressions, you will notice that at various times in his discussion with Genevieve Robert's expression takes on a pseudo-tragic look that resembles *exactly* that of the mask beside him. And when Genevieve says, "I care for you ... If you left me I would be very unhappy and I do not want to be unhappy," she turns her eyes down to the left, slightly closing her eyelids in an expression that *exactly* duplicates that of the mask beside her. And although there is not an extensive depth of field here, it is nevertheless evident that Renoir's use of these masks both anticipates his characters' need to imitate or replicate a model rather than act with any spontaneity – a *mise-en-scène* that subtly but assuredly questions the two characters' sincerity. Once again, the rules of the game serve to dictate established roles of a game so habitual that it goes *almost* unnoticed and is signaled only by two seemingly unrelated objects in our field of vision.

This use of masks also anticipates the gala soirée staged by Robert for all of his guests at La Colinière. This soirée is also one of the three scenes in the film in which Renoir uses depth of field to the most startling advantage. From the moment the scene opens, we are aware that Renoir is giving us altogether too much visual information to account for in any simple narrative fashion. For one thing, the camera's attempt to keep the theatricals

Plate 2.4 Robert and Genevieve imitate statues

limited to the improvised stage is frustrated when the actors rush off the stage and mingle with the "audience."[12] Any subsequent attempt to distinguish the theatrical comedy from the social one is vain. Renoir's camera gives so much depth of field as to insist on the interrelatedness of all the different plot lines. Here, depth of focus allows us to see just how completely each group of characters (for example Lisette, Schumacher and Marceau) enacts scenes that are replicated in the adjoining room (by, for example, Christine, Saint Aubin and Robert). Frequently Renoir enhances this sense of depth by shooting scenes in mirrors that signify no increase in space, but only a sterile replication of actions already witnessed. No one seems capable of an original or truly spontaneous act; all are caught in a hall of mirrors of their own making. Even when Octave takes Christine outside of the chateau to express his love, Renoir's camera pulls back to reveal that he has only succeeded in placing her on the proscenium-like terrace (more mere theater!) – a stage to which Robert will later return to play out the film's final piece of hypocrisy. So, the use of deep focus in this scene allows us to see how tiny is each individual's share of spontaneity and/or originality. Everyone seems "destined" to replicate the actions of those around them.

We must not fail to notice, amidst all of this chaos, chasing and gunfire that there is another sort of depth of field operating in this film. It is almost as if Renoir has taken the flow of the events of his narrative and turned it ninety degrees so that we can look down along the whole course of the narrative as if it were one of the long hallways in this prison-like chateau.[13] In this other notion of *temporal* depth of field view we can appreciate the way in which events situated at different moments in time look increasingly like mere repetitions of each other. Thus the gala is but a replay of the long hunting scene that precedes it – or, to put it another way, the hunting scene is but a dress rehearsal for the tragic evening party that follows. Renoir himself notes, "I had the idea for the death of Jurieux just the way it plays out – Jurieux was condemned well before I had begun the film – but the idea of having him die as he does came to me when I shot the death of the rabbit. My idea was that the entire hunting scene primitively prepared the death of Jurieux."[14] This phenomenon of repetition in time seems uncannily connected to the notion of Renoir's use of depth of field: the twinned hunting and gala scenes, despite occurring at different moments in time, end up evoking the sensation of déjà vu in much the same way Renoir collapses each of the different events of the gala into a single field event occurring claustrophobically in a single field of vision.[15]

The hunting scene occurs outdoors in the woods and marshes of La Colinière to be sure, but a number of the party wear special costumes anticipating the stage costumes in the gala's theatrical piece. These specially dressed actors, like the ones in the following scene within the chateau, make a strange music, beating sticks on trees like so many drumbeats. Death is certainly the central character in both performances, and it is his appearance that seems to unite all of those who sit waiting for the "play" to begin in a frenzy of violence enacted without regard for the innocence of those who must die. All of the players in both of these dramatic events are spread out across a single landscape participating in a startlingly bloodthirsty drama as if it evoked no particular horror. Both scenes succeed in uniting through depth of field the entire *dramatis personae* (with but two exceptions) in their indifference to the blood of the innocents they are slaughtering, and in their inauthenticity *vis-à-vis* each other.

By telescoping the hunting and gala scenes, we can appreciate the sense that Renoir has simply recast the primitiveness of the venery to a location inside the chateau where different members of each class hunt each other down, where all the fine elegance guaranteed by their attention to social rules is shed for a more animal-like brutality and sexuality. Octave struggles in vain to shed his bear costume and resume his civilized form at the very same moment that the rest of the players seem to be moving in the opposite direction. The "pure" Christine runs from one lover to another with indiscriminate abandon. Schumacher hunts down his rival Marceau, who pulls Lisette along behind him like the proverbial caveman. Fistfights break out between gentlemen and catfights between women. In this pandemonium, all the normal differences between the characters are dissolved into a generalized violence. Need I insist? It is Renoir's depth of focus that renders all this visible.

But mightn't we say that this erosion of differences has been visible from the very beginning? Indeed from the very outset of Renoir's film the blurring of separate identities into series of doubles is breathtaking! When Robert, for example, makes his grand entrance into *The Rules of the Game* he is proudly displaying his latest triumph: a *mechanical bird*. But didn't André make his grand entrance via the same device, a *mechanical bird*? Surely there can be no coincidence in a film so carefully constructed. This odd doubling is matched by many other examples. In a society as apparently close-knit as this one we nevertheless discover a rather unusual number of "outsiders." Robert himself is an outsider – a Jew occupying uneasily the role of a French Marquis – a circumstance that provokes some commentary in the servants' hall downstairs (and one that produced a storm of anger from the right-wing press in France at the release of the film).[16] Another "outsider," Marceau is discovered and arrested by the game warden, Schumacher, for poaching, yet we cannot fail to notice Marceau's striking physical resemblance to Robert when they are first paired on the screen. Both are swarthy, are of somewhat diminutive stature and easy smile, and are dressed identically as if two twins on parade. Robert instinctively and immediately allies himself with this alien presence by standing up to his very Germanic and militarily garbed warden. Thereafter, Renoir often pairs these two unlikely "brothers." During the chaos of the gala, Robert and Marceau will steal a few moments of calm, hidden among the leaves of some potted plants (recapitulating their first meeting in the woods) to lament their common troubles with women. Robert shares with this *doppelgänger* his complaint that he always seems to make everyone unhappy, but then aids and abets his lower-class friend in outwitting Schumacher. Robert and Octave are also paired in odd but significant ways, to wit: Robert introduces the gala by presenting his new acquisition, a beautifully baroque mechanical organ, as if he were the musician about to play it. Octave, who ends by courting Robert's wife, Christine, ends the evening on the terrace with her, acting out his own version of a *chef d'orchestre*. Even Robert and Schumacher share a common condition: that of cuckold.

It is as if, between the organized chaos of the hunting scene and the chaotic carnival of the gala, the various individuals undergo a fundamental loss of difference. In the depth of field of Renoir's camera, they seem to appear, disappear, and reappear in a myriad of configurations through which each ends up occupying physically or symbolically the position others had just taken. Nor are Renoir's women exempt from this absence of differentiation: Christine, Genevieve, Lisette and Jackie all move in constellations of interchangeability.

The most dramatic and visibly tragic of these interchanges provokes the denouement of Renoir's film. Although Octave and Christine plan to run away together, a double quid pro quo occurs to plunge their happy plans into tragedy. First, Lisette lends Christine her cape, causing Schumacher to assume that Octave is running off with his wife. Second, Octave relinquishes Christine back to André, who, in his eagerness to join her, runs toward the greenhouse in the dead of night where he will be shot "like an animal" by the game warden. All of this is termed "a deplorable accident" (Sc. 168) by Robert, but Renoir gives it a very different spin.

We remember that Renoir wanted to presage the death of Jurieux by the death of the rabbit in the hunting scene. Renoir goes on to add:

> Jurieux was the innocent one, and innocence can't survive in such a world –
> a romantic and rotten world. So we have two extremely innocent beings,
> Christine and Jurieux. Had to have a sacrifice. If you're going to go on, you
> have to kill one of them, since the world survives through sacrifice. So we
> have to kill people to appease the gods.[17]

So clearly Renoir felt some larger purpose at work in his film.

The problem on the face of this explanation is twofold. First, André's sacrifice does not seem to change anything. Robert glosses over it; two servants are reluctantly let go, and the weekend's guests re-enter the house as if nothing had been disturbed. Second, the classic notion of sacrifice to which Renoir appears to be alluding simply does not ever depend on such "deplorable accidents." Aristotle's celebrated definition of tragedy speaks of a "tragic flaw," a rigorous process of discovery that "through pity and fear leads to a catharsis." In Sophoclean tragedy, Antigone discovers that, when civic law clashes with family law, she has no choice but to bury her brother in obedience to the laws of family and thereby accept her death for the city. In Aeschylean tragedy, Agamemnon again confronts the double-bind created by a conflict of civic and family duties. In sacrificing Iphigenia for the good of the Greek army, he must incur his own death at the hands of Clytemnestra in order to expiate his infanticide. Clytemnestra in her turn must pay the same heavy price for murdering the father of her children.

There is one theory of tragedy, however, which brings all of Renoir's thinking into the sharpest possible focus. What we have seen at work in *The Rules of the Game* is, on the one hand, an *esthetics* of realism that allows Renoir to use deep focus to produce both an active role in his spectator and an interpretation which maximizes the world's basic ambiguity (as Bazin has suggested). On the other hand, we also see at work in this film a *thematics* of identity loss, role confusion and mistaken identity that all lead to a "deplorable accident." How might these two positions, the esthetic and the thematic, be reconciled?

In *Violence and the Sacred*, the French anthropologist René Girard suggests another way of looking at the notion of sacrifice. At their origins, Girard argues, so-called "primitive" societies encountered, among the many dangers of their world, one threat for which there seemed to be no solution. When violence broke out between members of their societies, it seemed to take on a life of its own, impervious to any attempt to stop it. Once initiated, violence seemed to necessitate a response, and this *reciprocal* nature of the activity caused it not only to continue, but to spread throughout the community like a contagion. "Vengeance," Girard explains, "is an interminable, infinitely repetitive process. Every time it turns up in some part of the community, it threatens to involve the whole social body … and puts the very existence of a society in jeopardy."[18]

Girard notes, "The more men strive to curb their violent impulses, the more these impulses seem to prosper. The very weapons used to combat violence are turned against their users. Violence is like a raging fire that feeds on the very objects intended to smother its flames."[19] (We see this at work, by the way, in the *Oresteia* of Aeschylus, where Iphigenia's death *necessitates* a response from Clytemnestra, and Clytemnestra's murder of Agamemnon *requires* Orestes to commit matricide.) Girard noticed that, in societies where violence occurred, there ensued what we might call "collateral damage": in the throes of the contagion of violence, differences between people began to break down until all were simply perceived as violent beings, unable to find any definition outside of that of revenge. Thus the "contagion" of violence risks decimating, even eradicating (as in the case of the Hatfield-McCoy feuds in early twentieth-century American history), entire societies. Against this danger of endlessly perpetuated reciprocal violence, primitive societies seem to have come upon a solution almost by chance. Any society that finds itself threatened by this contagion of violence "hurls itself blindly into the search for a scapegoat," someone whose faults seem to have caused the current crisis, yet who himself can easily be disposed of without fear of further reprisals.

> When a community succeeds in convincing itself that one alone of its number is responsible for the violent mimesis besetting it; when it is able to view this member as the single "polluted" enemy who is contaminating the rest; and when the citizens are truly unanimous in this conviction then the belief becomes a reality.... In destroying the surrogate victim, men believe that ... they are effectively doing away with those forms of violence that beguile the imagination and provoke emulation.[20]

Almost magically (or, eventually, religiously) the community discovers that, whereas previous acts of reciprocal violence *provoked more violence*, their violent unanimity has the unexpected but immediate effect of *banishing all traces of violence*. The scapegoat, selected for his marginal relation to the community (ensuring no reprisals) and for his malicious nature (ensuring no lingering guilt), is, almost magically, transformed from marginal to central (as bringer of peace and harmony) and from malefactor to benefactor. The blood of the scapegoat is immediately received as *pure* (given for the entire community, able to end the contagion of generalized violence), re-establishing the lost distinctions of pure/impure and re-establishing the notions of differences and values that had been submerged by the *sacrificial crisis*. The memory of this crucial event will be regularly celebrated in a ritual in which an animal (or other symbolic element) will be substituted for a human scapegoat. One such celebration might be the enactment of the death of the scapegoat in a theatrical arena (Greek tragedy, for instance). Another might take the form of a religious ceremony that would recollect/re-enact such a sacrifice. In either case, this commemoration of the death of the emissary victim is considered to be crucial to the health and continuation of the community.

Renoir's phrase, "Had to have a sacrifice," certainly communicates the director's sense that Jurieux's death is necessary in some way. And yet, for all the theatricality of Robert's announcement – he stands on a kind of proscenium as he addresses his audience – nothing seems to have changed. This is most likely because Robert insists on labeling this event as an accident. Certainly no community practicing a sacrifice would call the death of the victim an accident. Antigone's death is no accident; it represents a conscious choice to die for a set of values in which she has invested every fiber of her being. To label it so in either case is to strip the event of its fundamental importance and consign it to the status of news item.

And yet, even if the characters within the film fail to perceive the emissary value of André's death, we as spectators can appreciate the forces that produce it. Just as Girard would have predicted, the members of Renoir's microcosm enter into a classical "sacrificial crisis." As the distinctions between truth and falsehood and between authenticity and mere role-playing begin to dissolve, so too do differences between individuals. The Marquis and the poacher exchange roles in what amounts to a carnivalesque overturning of the world as we know it. We become unable to distinguish between hero and mere dilettante, between spouse and lover, between upper and lower classes, between insiders and outsiders, between private and public spaces and, frequently, between men and women. In this topsy-turvy world, violence is first introduced as a game to be played, but then spreads rapidly, like a fire or a contagion, throughout the community. It is remarkable that Girard's metaphor of contagion (that violence spreads exactly like the plague and produces the same fear) is anticipated by Renoir when he reflects that "When I made *La Règle du jeu* I knew where I was going. I knew the *malady* that gnawed at the contemporary world…. My awareness of danger furnished the situations and the lines in my film."[21] Elsewhere, Renoir took up René Girard's other metaphor – the "raging fire" – to describe in symbolic terms the progression of his film:

> I would like to make a film that would take place on a roof. Let's imagine a fire: three or four people have, below them, a fire which has begun in the stairwell on the first floor, is raging out of control and climbing slowly but surely toward the inhabitants of the building… But our people up there aren't the least bit disturbed by the smoke since there's a good wind…. Among them would be played out another drama that would have nothing to do with their imminent danger, but rather a kind of great love romance… and, at the moment that virtue would triumph and the wicked punished, the roof would cave in and they would all fall into the inferno. My ambition in beginning this film was to illustrate this historic phrase: We are dancing on the edge of a volcano.[22]

We should not lose sight of the fact that it is precisely Renoir's use of deep focus that allows us to perceive the "contagion" that gives rise to these multifold confusions. From the outset, the director's camera allows us to perceive together in the same field of vision the coexistence of two radically different interpretations of the same event. At the landing field, André's exploit is initially broadcast to the French as a great act of heroism, but the projection of the radio announcer into the private conversation between André and Octave allows an entirely contrary explanation of the event. Christine's explanation of her "friendship" with André cannot withstand the comedy enacted by her husband and friend captured by Renoir's depth of field shot. Whether this depth of field is presented vertically, within a single segment (as in the two cases just mentioned), or horizontally, as connected moments along the narrative timeline of the film (as in the perception of similarities between apparently opposed figures), the result is always the same: we recall André Bazin's dictum that depth of field introduces "ambiguity into the structure of the image if not of necessity at least as a possibility. The *uncertainty* in which we find ourselves as to the spiritual key or the interpretation we should put on the film is built into the very design of the image."

Renoir's realism allows us to perceive the real tragedy underlying the superficial frivolity of the Colinière society: *their* spiritual uncertainty has produced a breakdown of the old system of values and of differences that makes for the kind of sacrificial crisis in which violence becomes the inevitable result.

Renoir's courage in displaying this kind of realism (both stylistically and sociologically) earned him the immediate opprobrium of his countrymen. For the film's spectators understand immediately what the film's characters do not: the violence will not end until some means is found to stop the erosion of values and the surge of hypocrisy that characterizes France of 1939. No one goes to the movies to see themselves ruthlessly exposed for what they are. Or rather, perhaps, only the French do – but only when they enjoy enough historical distance on their problems to permit them to see them without too great a degree of discomfort. As Renoir himself remarked, "The audience recognized that their society was defeated at the outset.... The truth is that they recognized themselves. People who commit suicide do not care to do it in front of witnesses."[23]

Throughout this film, the storyline has been shadowed by Renoir's theory and practice of deep focus in ways which allow us to reconsider a "deplorable accident" in terms that are newly tragic and of much wider import than we might otherwise have thought. Once again, we are faced with a French cinematic masterpiece that demands that we become conscious of much more than the story and that we appreciate Renoir's practice of intertwining theory, style, and the question of sacrifice in subtle but forceful ways.

What we might take away from this experience is a new appreciation for cinema's ability to portray the discomfiting ambiguities of our world. We might (like Renoir's first-night audience) prefer to use the movies to escape from such unpleasant truths but, alas – or thankfully – the French cinema all too often holds such a mirror up to nature as to offer us little way to avoid seeing ourselves in its stark images.

Suggested Further Reading

Bazin, A. (1958), *Qu'est-ce que le cinéma?* Paris: Editions de cerf. Trans. H. Gray (1967) as *What Is Cinema?* Berkeley, CA: University of California Press.
This book deserves to be read in its entirety. Bazin's essays on "The Ontology of the Photographic Image," "The Myth of Total Cinema," and "The Evolution of the Language of Cinema" are dazzling.

Girard, R. (1977), *Violence and the Sacred.* Baltimore, MD: The Johns Hopkins Press. Girard's study deserves to be read in depth. We will come back to it in later chapters as well.

Sessonske, A. (1980), *Jean Renoir: The French Films 1924–1939*, Cambridge, MA: Harvard University Press.
Perhaps the best overview of Renoir's work with a chapter on each of his films through 1939.

Cinema and/as Crime
Breaking the Law in
The Children of Paradise,
Pickpocket, and *Breathless*

> *"Crime is originally natural.... Evil is accomplished without effort, almost by fatality; the Good is artificial."* (Charles Baudelaire, 1964)

As the sound of the gunshot that kills André Jurieux fades away, we watch as Robert de la Chesnaye takes center stage and theatrically declares that this cold-blooded murder was a "deplorable accident." We may sense, as Jean Renoir did, that this social group "needed a sacrifice," for their confusions, loss of difference, and violent behaviors all suggest that they are mired in a "sacrificial crisis." But Renoir offers us little or no catharsis, and the trappings of tragedy feel devoid of the seriousness Aristotle had prescribed as a condition of this high art. The formality of Robert's exit from this stage does more to highlight the insufficiency and pure theatricality of his gesture than to reassure his audience of his authority. After all, it was he who had proclaimed at the outset, "Let's play! Let's put on masks!" Our sense that it is precisely his sense of "play" that has led to the death of an innocent is more likely to leave us feeling that the world has been turned upside down than that it has been "righted" by Robert's final words of "reassurance."

Three years later, another shot would ring out in the midday silence of an Algerian beach and another innocent life would go unpunished. This second murder occurs in Albert Camus's *The Stranger*, arguably the most famous novel of mid-century France. Although Meursault will go to the guillotine at the end of the novel, the murder of this Arab boy will be largely forgotten and his murderer will be sentenced for another "crime": failing to cry at his mother's funeral. We come to understand that Meursault's murderous act has been "staged" in order to allow Camus to rail at the hypocritical theatricality of French legal and social mores, and to set the stage for the discovery of the beautiful absurdity of life which offers to Meursault his ultimate freedom and to Camus his justification for *revolt*.[1] The cold-blooded homicide at the center of Camus's story is committed, then, not to provide the reader the suspenseful thrill of the whodunit or to convince us that crime does not pay. Instead it stands as a grand gesture to remind us of society's obeisance to mere role-playing and hypocrisy and the need to revolt against this absurdity. That Camus saw this story as theater was confirmed when he "translated" *The Stranger* into a play about the mad and murderous Roman emperor Caligula, for whom all the world is a very bloody stage. No doubt the "funny war" that opened the theater of France's engagement with Nazi Germany, and the moral and political confusions of the subsequent occupation, had a great deal to do with Meursault's and Caligula's theatrical and criminal gestures. Debates about values and roles had been roiling French historians, sociologists, and artists for most of the first half of the twentieth century and it was perhaps inevitable that they would come to the fore in the late 1940s and 1950s.

Cognizant then of the timeliness of both Renoir's and Camus's *mises-en-scène* of the histrionics of crime, I would like now to turn our attention to a series of three films about criminals that punctuate the French experience of the occupation and postwar years in order to appreciate the ways in which a small group of directors pursue these particular themes as calculated acts of cold-blooded transgression against the traditions and practices of the seventh art itself.

Carné Storms the Stage: The Assassination of an Idea

One of the great debates that animated French critics and filmmakers throughout the twenties and would continue well into the fifties centered on the relationship of film to theater. (Indeed, the cinema began by borrowing stage actors for film, though many disdained it). Should films be "improved" by presenting great dramatic literature, critics asked? *Could* they be improved in this way? This was not an easy question to answer. André Bazin, for example, noted that "a filmed play can show due respect to the [dramatic] text, be well acted in likely settings, and yet be completely worthless."[2] The real question that seemed to provoke endless debate in France was this: Given that both stage and screen are essentially theatrical conventions, employing actors and decors in service of a plot that generally leads to a dramatic climax, what are the specific differences between them? To some (e.g. Leo Braudy) it was the presence or absence of the actor that signaled this difference,[3] to others (e.g. Bazin) the essential question lay in the way film handled décor, and to a third group (e.g. Susan Sontag) everything came down to the way film guided our eye toward specific details through camera movement and editing.

These questions of film's relation to the stage were evidently paramount in Marcel Carné's mind when he set out to direct what was to become the most celebrated film of the 1940s – and possibly of the entire corpus of French cinema: *The Children of Paradise*. His interest in the confrontation between these two media was evident in the title of the work, which alluded not only to the Garden of Eden but also to the cheap sets in Parisian theaters of the mid-1800s. In the opening images of the film we see a painted representation of a theatrical curtain "open" to reveal not a stage, i.e. a circumscribed, raised platform set before an audience, but instead a "real" décor, set on a busy Paris boulevard. Carné's camera emphasizes the apparent "realism" of this space by providing a deep-focus shot taken from a position both "in" and above the crowds of people who throng the streets. The camera pans across this carnivalesque chaos, catching momentarily in its viewfinder a makeshift stage on which a monkey demonstrates its prowess on a tightrope as if to re-articulate the contrast between the mere "aping" and monkey business of staged representations and the realism revealed by Carné's art. The camera then voyeuristically "enters" a peep-show tent, where a naked woman immersed in a well of water is exhibiting her charms to a group of four men.

Were we to stop (as we must) and ask, "What is Carné up to here?" we would be hard-pressed to find an easy answer. On the one hand the realism of the film shocks us by its implied contrast to the stage we expected when the pictured curtain "opened." The scene may thus be said to enact cinema's violent pre-empting of the space that was "announced" to be theater by the opening of the curtain. On the other hand, the entire décor could not be more artificial. It has been reported that 350 tons of plaster and 500 square meters of glass went into the construction of this long *façade* of buildings which were constructed at a cost of five million francs and then used only for this five-minute scene – a cost which led Carné's critics and admirers alike to parody Descartes's famous adage, "Je *dépense* donc je suis" [I spend therefore I am]."

The title of Carné's first "act" of *Children*, "Le Boulevard des crimes," alerts us, however, to the fact that this "faux" realism represents precisely that group of nineteenth-century edifices known to have housed Paris's most celebrated "boulevard theaters" where hundreds of crimes were staged each year. I would like to suggest that the nickname of this boulevard and the title of the first "act" of this film "innocently" announce the underlying theme of this entire work *and* allude to the film's violent dénouement. In other words, what Carné will display in his *Paradise* is not just the romantic tangles of a series of well-known nineteenth-century thespians, but also and more importantly the staging of a symbolic battle between the cinema as an art form and the theater from which it is said to have sprung.

In this opening scene, then, we see at work the first elements to be woven into an allegory of the struggle for independence of the cinema from its "aged parent," the theater. Throughout his film, Carné will depict the theater as engaged in a life-and-death struggle to maintain its integrity. Indeed, in *every single case* in which we are meant to be spectators at what we might call a *legitimate* theatrical production, that production is undermined when elements of the off-stage, everyday reality burst unwanted onto the stage (exactly as they do when the opening "curtain" is raised to reveal a film). In our first night at the theater, for example, the play is interrupted by a feud between two families of actors that erupts onto the proscenium. In another performance, Frédérick Lemaître will play havoc with the script and jump into the audience, sabotaging the entire dramatic effect and revealing the play's artificiality. In yet a third, Baptiste will be so distracted by Garance's presence in the wings that he will cry out in violation of all rules of miming. Everywhere we turn in this film, the staid traditions of the theater will be unexpectedly shaken by unwanted intrusions from off-stage.

Understanding this film as an allegory of the epic struggle between these two arts allows us to discern even in this first scene some central elements of that "other" story. After tracking over the boisterous crowds, the camera pauses before a sideshow tent, where a hawker invites us in to see "The Truth!" He assures us, that when we have seen her, "We'll think about her all day long and will dream about her at night!" What we discover upon "entering" this tent is a platform on which a naked woman holding up a mirror is immersed in a "well" of water, rotating around so that the spectators can get a full view of her "charms." As we watch, four different men approach this seductive spectacle and direct their entire attention to the woman immersed in the bath – near enough to touch yet clearly inaccessible.

It is worth remembering that the cinema began in France as a fair-ground attraction, usually projected in tents, whose primary appeal was that of a peep-show.[4] In this tent, Garance is spinning round, recalling the early *phenakistoscope* or a reel of film, and the men are "condemned" to watch but not touch this luscious body. It was Shakespeare, of course, who envisioned the theater as "a mirror as it were held up to nature," but Carné seems bent on appropriating the bard's looking-glass to his own (cinematic) ends. This mirror at first seems to reflect only Garance, but cannot help also throwing the reflection of each of these spectators back on themselves. You will recognize then that basically all of these details confirm this 15-second scene (5:23–5:38) as emblematic of the history and conditions of the cinema. That Garance is "cinematic" rather than "theatrical" is confirmed when, in a matter of only 60 seconds, she has magically emerged from this water, dried, dressed and is strolling happily through the crowd (a fold in time only the cinema could manage). When Lacenaire asks why she's left her job, she complains that the spectators were "really too ugly." Indeed, her disgust with these conditions of view-ing suggest that Carné is reminding us that both the subjects proposed and the conditions for viewing the early cinema were considered so vulgar that the seventh art had, under the tutelage of a group of French intel-lectuals, to reclaim its right to be called an art by moving away from such vulgarity.

We may well ask, then, what Carné would propose as an alternative vision of the cinema. To respond to this question, we might well return to the well to observe that there are precisely four men observing her – the exact number of men who will become her admirers in Carné's film: Frédérick, Edouard, Baptiste and Lacenaire. I would suggest that we look at Garance's relationship with each of these four as symbolic of one or another aspect of the cinema versus theater debate. One will attempt to woo, one to possess, the third to merely idolize, and the last to free this iconic woman from the constraints of her situation.

Let us review each of these "suitors" in turn to better understand the "allegory of cinema" that Carné is proposing in *The Children of Paradise*.

Frédérick Lemaître's relationship to Garance (and to the world) is the most obvious of the four. His ambitions, clearly stated the minute we meet him, are to become synonymous with the very idea of theater in Paris. Unfortunately for him, he is not just good at acting; he is unable to do anything else. However much we may be charmed by his seductive approach to Garance in the crowd, we are quickly appalled to discover in his second approach to a woman that he is but a poor player who struts and frets his hour on *and off* the stage and then is heard too much. He seems wholly

Plate 3.1   Garance as a mirror of the cinema

unable to escape from playing a prepared set piece. He does this not only with Garance and the anonymous woman in the crowd, but again with the landlady at the rooming house he frequents. It is abundantly clear, then, that his allegorical role is that of theater itself, caught in its own artificiality and traditions, unable to transcend them since everything is based on previous writing rather than on fresh observation of reality. The closest he ever comes to authenticity is the jealousy he feels while playing Othello but, even there, the script belongs already to tradition and he can only repeat another's words. However much Garance finds him diverting, she ends up by rejecting his tiresome and uninspiring behavior. He can never really exercise any influence over her. The ultimate irony for Frédérick is that he himself is so bored with the theater that his antics risk destroying the very medium on which he depends for his identity. (Indeed, the theater in the second half of the nineteenth century had become a tradition emptied of social importance or poetic beauty). From this allegorical demonstration, we would conclude that Carné's position on the place of theater in the development of film is that it remains *inessential* in the seventh art's evolution.

Baptiste, who appears to be Lemaître's "colleague" in the theater, really isn't. Notice, first of all that Baptiste begins by exercising his talents outside rather than inside the theater because, as his father, Anselm, so nastily observes, "he's a sleep-walker" who has "fallen from the moon" and is "good for nothing" in the "legitimate" theater inside. There is something about Baptiste's miming, moreover, that powerfully suggests his connection to the cinema. Let's take a look at Baptiste's first mime. When Garance is accused by her neighbor of pickpocketing her, the policeman asks if there are any witnesses. "I'm a witness," answers Baptiste, "I saw everything!" But when the officer asks for a report, Baptiste, unlike his colleague Frédérick, answers not in words, but in a perfect *representation* of the crime. This time, the crime portrayed is not some melodramatic invention of a bad playwright, but one taken from a "real" event, one we have just missed witnessing and need Baptiste's eyewitness representation to catch. The mime's account is not verbal but a very nearly *cinematic* – i.e. a visual replication of the events he has focused on. Indeed, Carné insists on Baptiste's eyes in two close-ups that precede his "witnessing" of this event. What Baptiste produces is as accurate as any six o'clock TV news report of a crime. Unlike the journalistic versions we are used to, however, it is also highly *artistic*.[5] In Baptiste's version we "see again" as if it were a video playback of the events that he has witnessed. The key pieces of Baptiste's performance are thus: (1) inspiration taken from daily life; (2) a faithful (almost mechanical) reproduction of the witnessed events; and (3) a representation that is also highly artistic. That this representation is mimed suggests further that Baptiste may represent, in this allegory, the influence of *silent* cinema on Carné's vision of the seventh art.

There is one other thing about Baptiste's performance that bears mentioning here: his art replays the perpetration of a crime, or rather two crimes, one committed by Lacenaire against a rich bourgeois rubber-neck and a second one committed by those who would falsely accuse Garance of that crime. In short, Baptiste replays a crime in order to free Garance from false arrest. Inasmuch as *The Children of Paradise* culminates in Lacenaire's murder of Edouard, we should pay particular attention to the role of crime in this first instance as well. In allegorical terms we might say that Baptiste represents a version of early cinema that introduces a kind of poetic realism that liberates cinema from accusations of vulgarity on the one hand and, on the other, from Hollywood's interest in "picking our pockets."

Despite Baptiste's witnessing for Garance (which in the immediate liberates her), he seems too caught up in dreamy idolization of her to inspire her lasting involvement. When, alone in a hotel room with her, he has the chance to go beyond this dreamy idealization, he seems unable to embrace the woman as she is, and fades back into his world of fantasy and longing. This is clearly not what Carné intends for the cinema either.

When Marcel Carné set out to direct this film, in 1943, French cinema was hugely constrained by the German occupiers and their puppets in Vichy. Alfred Cobban has suggested that the ease with which the Germans managed the invasion and occupation of France had something to do with the belief among many right-wing and aristocratic families that the Germans would rid France, once and for all, of leftists, Jews, and homosexuals.[6] That Carné attempted to shoot this film in the Free Zone of France, far from the centers of censorship and control, suggests that he intended the film to be subversive. Its subversiveness is nowhere more evident than in the character of Edouard: Stuffy, prepossessing, certain that his aristocratic origins entitle him to lay claim to Garance, Edouard becomes at one and the same time the personification of the stultifying influence of the occupying forces and a return of very traditional and hierarchic tendencies in French society and in the French film industry. So complete was the domination of the studio system in France during and immediately after World War II that it would take the "revolution" of the New Wave to undo that system. Edouard's approach to Garance is, first of all, to overwhelm her with so many flowers that she exclaims, "What on earth are all these flowers? I don't believe it. Someone must be dead" (Sc. 105). Ironically (and prophetically) Edouard responds, "Yes, Mademoiselle, someone is dead … and you have killed him!" His love is a kind of death. He exercises that love as a form of capital, hoping to purchase Garance's love at the cost of her freedom. His most active form of loving her consists in the murder of those who would threaten his control. But Garance will have the courage to tell him that, though she would publicly profess love for him if so required, she does in fact love another more than him. If he has an allegorical role to play here it is as the double vise of Occupation censorship and a failing studio system in which hierarchy and stale theatricality are dominant.

But exactly how to undo this potential death-grip on French cinema?

There can be no doubt that Lacenaire is the most intriguing, if far from the most appealing, of Carné's quartet of Garance's admirers. The first glimpse we catch of him is, significantly in a dissolve, in which his face emerges from the signboard announcing "*Ecrivain public.*" What catches our attention immediately is Lacenaire's overly manicured appearance. A row of curls festoons his forehead and his clothes are too refined to fit his situation as an underpaid, undervalued writer of love letters for the illiterate. There can be no doubt that his appearance marks him as a dandy, a figure celebrated by the "*poète maudit*" Baudelaire. For Baudelaire, the dandy was not simply a fop who developed an "immoderate taste in his personal appearance and material elegance," although these are necessary "symbols of the superiority of his mind." In keeping with his sense of his

Plate 3.2   Lacenaire as dandy

own superiority, the dandy holds that everything considered by the crowd to be beautiful and noble is merely the result of reason and calculation. "Crime," Baudelaire exults, "is originally natural…. Evil is accomplished without effort, almost by fatality; the Good is artificial." Baudelaire conceived of dandyism as an outlaw institution, but one that adheres strictly to its own rules. For Carné (and Lacenaire), the dandy follows first and foremost a "doctrine of *originality*, a cult of the self" which he practices "as a kind of religion."[7] In recognizing the figure of the dandy in Lacenaire, we encounter an eerie confluence of artistic originality and crime. Let's listen for a moment to Lacenaire's philosophy and ambitions. He tells Garance, "I declared war on society a long time ago," and when she asks "Have you killed many people lately?" he responds:

> Look, no trace of blood … only a few *ink stains*. But it shouldn't surprise you, Garance, to learn that I'm planning something quite out of the ordinary … and I am certain of myself, absolutely certain. Petty thief from necessity … murderer by vocation, my way is already *marked out* … My road is straight ahead, and I shall walk with my head held high … until it falls into the bucket on the other side of the guillotine … I *write plays* when I've nothing better to do … (Sc. 32)

Much later, after Frédérick's performance in *Othello*, Edouard will taunt Lacenaire by asking, "Might one be permitted to ask how you are utilizing your talents at the moment?" Lacenaire explains:

> I am about to put the *finishing touches* to something quite fascinating, which will be a resounding success…. In the end, gentlemen it really doesn't matter what type of play my little piece is, the important thing is that it should be amusing …
>
> But I warn you that there are murders in it, and that when the curtain falls, the dead won't get up to take a bow. (Sc. 203–4)

Notice how much, in Lacenaire's words, the notions of revolution and art are mixed. Instead of blood stains, there are ink stains in the first speech and, conversely, in the second is the idea that his "play" will end not with ink stains but blood stains. And when the curtain goes up on Lacenaire's dramatic piece, we discover that he has "composed" it in two acts, neither of which is written but each of which blurs the boundaries between the theater and the real world. In the first act of his "little drama," Lacenaire goes directly to the curtained window in the theater lobby and draws back the curtain. In an exact replication of Carné's opening shots of *The Children of Paradise*, the curtain opens not on a stage but on the reality *outside* the theater. What Edouard experiences is a re-visioning of the *Othello* we have just seen performed *in* the theater, here conceived by the outlaw Lacenaire with Baptiste and Garance *outside* in fond embrace. This violent intrusion of an unwelcome reality into the space of the theater recapitulates Carné's entire allegorical trajectory in this film. Lacenaire's second act is even more violent. In the graceful architecture of the municipal baths, Lacenaire confronts Edouard with a knife. Avril's horrified look and the sound of a body splashing lifeless into the bath tell us that Lacenaire has literally put the "*finishing touches* to something quite fascinating" – i.e. both Carné's film and Edouard's possession of Garance. In the end, this man who tells Garance that she is the only woman he's ever approached "without hatred or contempt" is responsible for planning the "something quite fascinating" that combines elements from the real world, from drama, and from his ideas of revolution against the accepted order of things. As such, he functions as a double of the film's director, Marcel Carné, who had once complained that he couldn't look at the current cinema without irritation, that it seemed complacently confined in a closed vase, instead of going into the streets to storm the barricades. By identifying himself with Lacenaire,[8] Carné suggests that both film director and character are criminals by virtue of their violent desire to bring about a revolution in the artistry and political engagement of the seventh art. We may or may not feel that on the whole *The Children of Paradise* accomplishes this vision, and yet everywhere we turn in this film, we see Carné's tendency to effect the unexpected intrusion of images of everyday reality into the spaces traditionally reserved for the theater. It remained, however, for two other directors to complete this initial identification of the film director as criminal.

Bresson Picks Pockets

When asked about the role of actors in his films, Robert Bresson once said, using a metaphor we shall explore further in the next chapter, "An actor in cinematography might as well be in a foreign country. He does not know how to speak its language."[9] I wonder if you didn't experience a similar degree of what the French would call *dépaysement* [disorientation] as you viewed *Pickpocket*? Certainly, we sense from the opening images to the final kiss through Michel's prison bars that we are not watching a typical film. Bresson's characters walk through his film as if in a slow-motion daze. They speak to each other without emotion, careful never to betray any of the typical expressions that communicate their underlying intentions. As spectators we quickly grow impatient and want to reach through the screen, take hold of the actors and shake them into some sort of responsiveness.

If we are uncomfortable watching them, Bresson's actors in *Pickpocket* report that they too felt entirely out of their element. Marika Green reports that she had constantly to repeat the same line in order to "expel all the psychology from the character ... to wring out every little bit of personal interpretation."[10] She recalls that Bresson exhausted Martin Lasalle to breaking point in order to get him to the point of "*pur automatisme.*"[11] Léonce-Henri Burel, Bresson's cameraman for *Pickpocket*, went so far as to say, "I didn't understand what he was trying to say. As a matter of fact I don't think anybody has ever understood really. Who is this pickpocket, why does he steal and so on?"[12] (It's perhaps a bit comforting, isn't it, to see that sometimes even the French don't understand French cinema!)

Actors and spectators are all caught up in a remarkable experiment, launched by Robert Bresson as if he were taking up the challenge Carné had laid down to expel once and for all every trace of the theater from the cinema. Indeed, Bresson explains:

> The truth of cinematography cannot be the truth of the theater... Nothing rings more false in a film than that natural tone of the theater copying life and traced over studied sentiments... The photographed theater or *cinema* [as opposed to Bresson's term *cinematograph*, a word that emphasizes the

aspect of *writing* in the seventh art] requires a metteur-en-scène or director to make some actors perform a play and to photograph these actors performing the play; afterwards he lines up the images. Bastard theater lacking in what makes theater: material presence of living actors, direct action of the audience on the actors.[13]

Clearly, so committed is Bresson to ridding the cinema of any trace of the theater that he is willing to take the risk of robbing his actors of any semblance of traditional acting styles. In his book, *Notes sur le cinématographe*, he refuses them even the label "actors," preferring instead the term "models." His theory of the "model" culled from this volume can be synthesized as follows:

- No actors (no directing of actors)
- No roles (no learning of roles)
- No staging (*mise-en-scène*). But the use of working models taken from life
- *Being* (models) instead of *seeming* (actors)
- Model. Reduce to the minimum his consciousness of playing a role. (See NC 1/10, 26/58, 29/63, 31/67)

This effectively *absent presence* was to be accomplished by a rigorous training requiring repetition of the model's lines until all theatricality had been eliminated:

> Your models, pitched into the action of your film, will get used to [*apprivoiseront à eux*] the gestures they have repeated twenty times. The words they have learned with their lips will find, *without their minds taking part in this*, the inflections and the lilt [*la chanson*] proper to their true natures. A way of recovering the automatism of real life. (NC 32/70)

Thus the model would become a kind of blank slate that would draw its meaning from its context rather than from itself: "Model. Enclosed in his mysterious appearance. He has brought home to him all of him that was outside. He is there behind that forehead, those cheeks…. Over his features, thoughts or feelings not materially expressed, rendered *visible* by intercommunication and interaction of two or several other images" (NC 7/21).

We can appreciate how subversive Bresson's idea of the model is when we compare it to the standard of Hollywood films. David Bordwell notes that:

> The classical film relies for its sense of realism upon individual characters each of whom must be defined as a bundle of a few salient traits, which usually

depend upon the character's narrative function.... The importance of character consistency can be seen in the star system. The star, like the fictional character, already had a set of salient traits which could be matched to the demands of the story.... Their traits must be affirmed in speech and physical behavior, *the observable projection of personality* ... Hollywood cinema reinforces the individuality and consistency of each character by means of recurrent motifs (e.g. a craving for tomato juice) ... For major characters the motif serves to mark significant stages of story action.[14]

We begin to see that what Bresson is about is nothing less than an assault on the entire bastion of Hollywood cinema, and yet one carried out with such subtlety that one hardly knows that the castle is under siege until the enemy is well within the gates.

When Bresson moves from the idea that his actors should be vacant ciphers rather than characters to the idea that the film communicates not through storyline and dialogue but rather through a language that is not "*materially* expressed, but rendered *visible* by intercommunication and interaction of two or several other images," he is extending his critique of Hollywood into a much larger realm.

To understand the enormity of Bresson's project, let us look at the opening scene of *Pickpocket* to attempt to understand what he might mean by the phrase "rendered visible by intercommunication and interaction of two or several other images."

A disembodied hand writes in what is presumably a diary as the voice-over of Martin Lasalle remarks, "I realize that usually those who have done such things don't talk about them, and those who talk about them haven't done them. And yet, I have done them." Although we might be lulled by our previous experience of the use of extra-diegetic narrative voices into easy acceptance of the authority of their pronouncements, especially when combined with a written text, we need to be wary of this one. Indeed, later in the film, Bresson will introduce an element of the journal that will entirely undermine our faith in Michel's journal writing.[15] Bresson quickly moves us from the journal-as-unreliable-writing to the more solid domain of the film's images. We see another disembodied hand passing some 500 franc notes through a ticket-window in exchange for some sort of tickets. This transaction cannot be placed without recourse to other images. We could be at a train station or a race track (and the ambient noise throughout this opening scene allows for either possibility, given the indecipherable nature of the words we hear over the loudspeaker and, later, a roar of sound that could either be horses passing or a train entering the station). Bresson will keep us guessing about this partly because the film's images (not its narrative "logic") tell us that there is an important

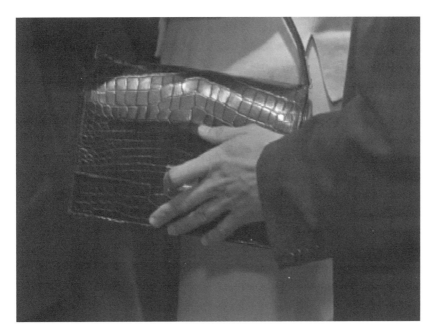

Plate 3.3   Michel's first crime

connection to be made between this scene at the racetrack and a later scene at the train station.

As the man who has just purchased these tickets leaves the window, he passes another man, who looks him in the eye. The same voice-off we heard earlier is now "attached" to Michel, who 'thinks,' "For several days now my decision had been made. But would I dare to do it?" In other words, what was assumed to be a narrative authorial voice now becomes entirely subjective since it is linked to a single point of view *within* the film's diegesis. Michel turns and follows the ticket holder and his female companion through a gateway and into a crowd. He positions himself directly behind the woman and the two exchange looks. For the next 30 seconds (what seems like an eternity), Bresson's camera is focused directly on Michel's blank face. Another quick voice-off tells us "I should have left." A sudden cut takes us to a third disembodied hand, this time placed against an alligator purse. We move back and forth between this hand as it works to undo the clasp of the handbag and Michel's blank expression. Finally the clasp snaps open and Bresson cuts quickly to Michel's face. We now witness the most dramatic expression we will see on this face for the entire film: Michel blinks in what might be an ecstatic reaction. Then again the blank stare. In another quick cut, the hand removes some large bank notes from the purse. There is a sound (of horses passing?) and then everyone turns and walks back toward the gateway. This single scene has lasted one minute and 25 seconds. There have been about twelve seconds of action. The camera follows Michel as he leaves the crowd and passes through an iron gateway. The voice-over says, "I was walking on air with the world at my feet." He continues to walk and two unidentified men fall into step behind him. As the voice-off says, "But a minute later I was caught," Bresson does an overlap dissolve from Michel walking to Michel sitting in a black sedan between two men. Another overlap dissolve finds Michel in an office saying to another, as yet unidentified, man, "You can't prove anything. You're not certain." This other man, now recognizable from the context as a plainclothes police inspector, rises and says, "We won't keep you any longer, sir. You're free to go."

The pattern in this scene (as in so many other scenes in *Pickpocket*) is almost a kaleidoscope of fragments[16]: long takes of faces, groups or walls that seem to offer little or no information to the viewer, followed by cuts to other locales with scant or no information as to where we are or how we got there. In this first segment Bresson leaves out the very shots that Hollywood would consider central. In this case, we would expect to see the arrest and hear the accusation. But no, we get only the connecting bits to these actions. It is almost as though Bresson chose to write sentences with only adjectives and prepositions, leaving out seminal verbs and nouns. We are being asked to "fill in" or infer an unusual amount of information all the while the camera lingers almost absentmindedly on blank faces. No wonder Bresson's cameraman, L.-H. Burel, felt confused!

It is not just the theatricality of traditional cinema that Bresson has chosen to contest in this film, it is the entire grammar of "classical Hollywood cinema."

It is important to remind ourselves that, beyond the question of theatricality and rational character development, Hollywood cinema relies for its success and its dominance on what David Bordwell defines as the "classic Hollywood style," one relying on the principles:

> that telling a story is the basic formal concern; that unity is a basic attribute of film form; that the Hollywood film purports to be "realistic" in both an Aristotelian sense (truth to be probable) and a naturalistic one (truth to historical fact); that the Hollywood film strives to conceal its artifice through techniques of continuity and "invisible" storytelling; that the film should be comprehensible and unambiguous; and that it possesses a fundamental emotional appeal that transcends class and nation.[17]

Such a grammar of continuity allowed filmmakers to concentrate on the significant actions that moved the story along, and also to manage an economy of gesture without any apparent discontinuity in our experience of that story. Bresson's work, on the other hand, seems dedicated to maximizing our sense of discontinuity to the point of disorientation. This is reflected not only in this opening sequence, but in many others as well. Perhaps the most glaring of these occurs in the sequence when Michel accompanies Jacques and Jeanne to an amusement park. After his two friends leave him at a café table to enjoy an amusement ride, Michel stands. Bresson's camera fails to follow Michel but instead remains focused on the empty table. A dissolve moves us away from this scene to an empty staircase. Michel passes through the frame and enters his room, obscured by shadows. He takes up a pitcher of water and the voice-over announces, "I had run and fallen." It is only later that we discover from other pieces of this "absent" narrative that Michel has stolen a watch, presumably been pursued, had fallen and cut his hand in his flight. Again, Bresson gives us only some disconnected images, leaving us to make sense of these elements as best we can.

Both the opening sequence and this second example are illustrative of Bresson's theories on film. Not only is the director of *Pickpocket* rejecting the idea of the image as referential and substantial (i.e. containing all by itself enough information to communicate its meaning), he is suggesting that any given image is really a neutral element belonging to a system of relations from which it draws its meaning. In proposing what he will call simply the *cinematograph*, Bresson is proposing a new *language* of film

> where expression is obtained by relations of images and sounds, and not by mimicry done with gestures and intonations of voice.... One that does not analyze or explain. That *recomposes* ... An image must be transformed by contact with other images, as is a color by contact with other colors.... No art without transformation.... Cinematographic film, where the images, like the words in a dictionary, have no power and value except through their position and relation.... No absolute value in an image. Images and sounds will owe their value and their power solely to the use to which you destine them.... In this language of images, one must lose completely the notion of image. The images must exclude the idea of image. (NC 5/16, 5/17, 11/28/ 33/71)

We can easily imagine a Hollywood director scratching his head in bemusement over this! But we should remember that Bresson made this film in 1959, when he was already in his fifties. By then he had been working for sixteen years, had made four feature-length films and had been enshrined in François Truffaut's pantheon as "one of the three or four greatest film directors."[18] Thus, although he was already established, he found himself in the midst of the maelstrom of what was to become known as the New Wave. Jean-Luc Godard and François Truffaut were not only waging open warfare on the French film industry by their virulent attacks on the "*tradition de qualité*" published in *Cahiers du cinéma* but would take the bastion of studio production by storm with the success of *The Four Hundred Blows* and *Breathless*. Bresson was thus exposed afresh to debates about the definition and meaning of the cinema and had begun to be exposed to Claude Lévi-Strauss's ideas on structural anthropology. Lévi-Strauss was himself hugely influenced by Ferdinand de Saussure's theories on language. Although Saussure never published his ideas, his students gathered his writings in the posthumous *General Course in Linguistics* (1916). By the mid-fifties, Saussure had become one of the major influences on French thought, and is today thought of as one of the greatest influences on French philosophy after 1950. It is thus worth pausing just a bit to get the gist of his theories. Saussure's biggest break with the traditional linguists of his day was to propose that linguistic signs were purely arbitrary, that is to say, had no possible grounding in a substantive connection between words and things. (It does not take much to realize, then, that his thought went counter to the entire classical French belief that, as God's gift to mankind, language could not conceivably be arbitrary). Having argued for the arbitrary nature of the linguistic sign, Saussure went on to propose that individual units of language had no intrinsic *value*. Language, he claimed,

> is a system of interdependent terms in which the value of each term results solely from the simultaneous presence of the others ... The value of any term is determined solely by its environment.... Concepts as well are purely differential and defined not by their positive content but negatively by their relations with the other terms of the system. Their most precise characteristic is in being what the others are not.[19]

Sound familiar? It is abundantly clear that Bresson has simply borrowed Saussure's theory and substituted "image" for "linguistic term." To wit, "The most ordinary word, when put into place, suddenly acquires brilliance. That is the brilliance with which your images must shine" (NC 56/116). And elsewhere he adds, "See your film as a *combination* of lines and of volumes in movement apart from what it represents and signifies ... To move people not with images likely to move us, but with *relations of images* that render them both alive and moving" (NC 44/92, 43/90). He insists: "Cinematography: the art with images of representing nothing" (NC 59/120).

Such a theory runs counter to everything that has been theorized about the ontology of the photographic image.[20] Because the camera replicates mechanically the reality that stands before its aperture, it has a relation to things that words cannot have. This being the case, we must consider that Bresson's decision to strip individual images of their normal narrational and/or cultural meanings is both fundamentally *transgressive* and yet paradoxically creative in a life-giving way! "Montage [editing]. Passage of dead images to living images. Everything blossoms afresh." (NC 43/91).

Faced with this conundrum of transgression and creativity we must stop and ask, "What *does* the story of a pickpocket have to do with Bresson's project to undo almost fifty years of the dominance of classical Hollywood style?"

Certainly Bresson provides a clue to his approach by quoting lavishly from Fyodor Dostoyevsky's *Crime and Punishment*. We are surprised to see the police inspector who interrogated Michel after his racetrack caper enter the café where the pickpocket and his friend Jacques are enjoying a drink. Rather than avoiding him, Jacques and Michel join him at a table. Jacques makes polite conversation about types of thieves the inspector must encounter, then asks, "Aren't there crimes that the police would close their eyes to?" When the inspector hesitates, Jacques turns to Michel: "You have a theory on that." Prompted by the inspector, Michel admits that his theory is "not new" but nevertheless wonders whether "certain skilled men, gifted with intelligence, talent or even genius and are thus *indispensable to society* should be free to disobey the law in certain cases?" Despite the inspector's skepticism, Michel insists, "Society could only gain from it." The inspector objects that such a possibility would "turn the world upside down." Michel corrects: "It's already upside down. This could set it right." We cannot fail to recognize this "theory which isn't new." It belongs, in fact, to Raskolnikov, Dostoevsky's indigent student, who lives alone in a room at the top of his building, who, when prompted, will tell another police inspector, "I simply hinted that an 'extraordinary' man has the right ... an inner right to decide in his own conscience to overstep certain obstacles, and only in case it is essential for the practical fulfillment of his idea (sometimes, perhaps of benefit to the whole of humanity)."[21] Raskolnikov goes on to propose that all great leaders, by virtue of the fact that, in making a new law they had to transgress an established one, must by their very nature be *criminals*.

Later, Bresson adds a second major quotation from his Russian model just to make it clear that *Crime and Punishment* is the novel with which *Pickpocket* must be compared (or against which his film must be read).[22] Once we see the parallel between the two works, we find allusions to

Crime and Punishment everywhere in the film. Both artists recount stories of men who commit crimes, are "cornered" by a sympathetic police officer and end up in jail, where they are comforted by a woman to whom they had confessed their crimes. Both protagonists are students living in squalor. Each receives an important letter from his mother and, as a consequence, grows increasingly estranged from her. Each decides as an act of will to commit a crime against a woman and each entirely disdains any financial gain, hiding his ill-gotten gains in a hole in the wall rather than enjoying his plunder. Each will return to the scene of his crime (Michel to the race-track) where he will be trapped. Even the ending of Bresson's film seems to mirror the religious ambiguity of Dostoyevsky's novel.

One of the effects of these many similarities is to place into stark relief the dramatic difference in the mode of transgression chosen by each of the protagonists. Raskolnikov, we remember, pays a visit to the apartment of the old pawnbroker and, while her back is turned, pulls an axe from his coat and bludgeons her to death. Then, rather than hurry purposefully about the business of robbing her, he loses himself in useless blundering, wasting just enough time to ensure that the old lady's younger sister, Lizaveta, will return to their rooms. Hearing her in the living room out-side the old lady's bedroom, he confronts her and, taking up his axe again, drives the blade into her forehead. Dostoevsky provides a banquet of hypotheses as to why Raskolnikov should need to commit these two mur-ders. A long and dreadful dream, his mother's highly manipulative letter, his sexual confusions about his sister, all suggest that Raskolnikov is acting out some revenge fantasy that he is powerless to understand or avoid.

Michel, on the other hand, has, from the very beginning, been stripped of all psychology. We get very few clues as to why he should take up a life of crime. In all, what we must focus on is the fact that between the double murders and the relatively non-violent act of picking a pocket, there is an ocean of difference. As Jacques points out, picking pockets is merely a socially reprehensible and cowardly activity. So why would Bresson have shifted Dostoyevsky's ethical register downward in a way that apparently trivializes Michel's status?

If we look again at the scenes in which Michel is at his best in the prac-tice of this activity, the answer to this question will become altogether clear. After several pretty awkward practice runs at his new profession, Michel decides that he needs instruction. Bresson provides as his instruc-tor a professional pickpocket, Kassagi. When the student and teacher meet in a café, Bresson, for the first time, moves his camera in close and focuses directly on the series of moves that are required to be successful. What we see are two bodies and four hands which, with consummate dexterity and

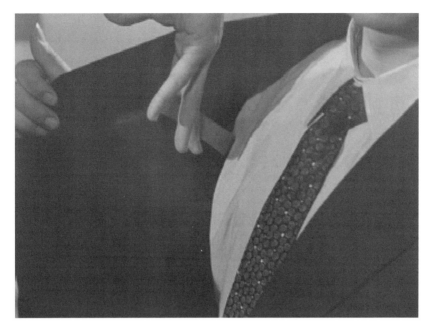

Plate 3.4   Michel learns his trade

art, penetrate the seemingly impenetrable, use every form of legerdemain and split-second timing to achieve seemingly impossible results. There can be no doubt that this fundamentally transgressive activity has been elevated to the status of high art.

And, when Michel is finally ready to practice this art at its most balletic and harmonic level, the team of pickpockets moves to the Gare de Lyon. Here, amidst the crowd of travelers, the team reaches the apex of their talent. We watch spellbound as, with utter sureness of touch, newspapers are substituted for purses, wallets, watches, valuables of all kinds are whisked away, passed from hand to hand in a spontaneous explosion of talent that looks as though it took weeks of rehearsals to perfect. It is a performance reaching levels of bravado seldom seen at the Paris Ballet – including in one case a wallet that is removed from a man's pocket as he moves down the train's corridor and then, emptied of its contents, replaced in that same pocket on the man's return.

Here, transgression has met high art. This work of hands is important to Bresson, for he wrote in *Notes sur le cinématographe*, "Your film, let people feel the soul and the heart there, but let it be made like a work of hands.... The things one can express with the hand, what economy!"

(NC 12/30, 64/127). And, explaining the scene in the Gare de Lyon, Bresson crowed:

> They told me, "Hide, it's easy." I hid. I was soon discovered. We had to employ ruses. Shots made from hiding are not very precise. Crowds are chaotic. I used this chaos in certain scenes. The sequence in the station was shot entirely in the crowd, during the month of July as the rush was on to leave for vacation. It required an enormously mobile camera and the rapid deployment of our material. In short, I heaped difficulties on myself, not the least of which was working in all that bustle and noise.[23]

It is not hard to grasp to how great an extent Bresson is identifying with his character as criminal-artist. Elsewhere, in another moment of cinematic bravado, Bresson writes, "Your camera catches physical movements that are inapprehensible" (NC 53/110). Ultimately he seems to be playing the same game as his pickpocket when he says, "For me, the word 'shot' (*prise de vue*) signifies capture. One has to catch the actor under the play of lights and surprise him and *seize from him* the rarest and most secret things he can produce."[24]

Once again, to capture the degree of transgression necessary to break free of the bonds of tradition, a major French filmmaker ends up identifying with the criminal he has invented. Clearly Michel does not pick pockets to make a profit; he appears to us rather as an inspired artist, interested only in the creativity of his work. As proof of his artistry, he several times holds up a copy of George Barrington's *Prince of Pickpockets* as though to brag to us that he can match talents with the most famous of the practitioners of *le vol à tir*. But Barrington turns out to serve as a model for Bresson himself as much as for his fictional character Michel! After a celebrated trial and subsequent conviction in London, Barrington was exiled to Australia with other men of his ilk. There he founded a theater company, and to celebrate their opening night, composed a poem of introduction to herald the ex-convicts' newly discovered artistic talents. In doggerel, he admitted that he and his fellow prisoners had "left our country for our country's good" but were now imbued with a "new passion of Theatric fame" and dedicated not only to improving their dramatic skills but to making a profit at this new enterprise and thus "*in an honest way, still pick your pockets.*"[25]

In subtly stripping the cinema of all of its useless theatrics and outmoded grammar, by daring to break all established rules and display his own (outlaw) artisanry, Robert Bresson, in homage to George Barrington, has himself become the *Dauphin* of pickpockets – picking not so much *our* pockets, since his films have never done particularly well at the box office, but, more subtly and surely, the pockets of resistance to a profound transformation of the dominant cinema.

Stealing from the Americans, Godard Style

Godard's Michel Poiccard (Jean-Paul Belmondo), the hero of *Breathless*, comes by his thieving ways honestly. In the treatment that Truffaut gave to Godard for his first feature-length film, the main character was to be the now grown-up Antoine Doinel of Truffaut's first major success, *The Four Hundred Blows*. In that earlier film, pursued by bad parenting and bad luck, Antoine steals a typewriter from his stepfather's office and, when he tries to return it, is arrested and sent off to reform school. Truffaut himself had seen time behind bars and had been rescued by none other than André Bazin, the founder of *Les Cahiers du cinéma*. Truffaut became a film reviewer for *Cahiers* and quickly got the journal into trouble because he was so virulently critical of what he called "la tradition de qualité" and "le cinema de papa." Truffaut was convinced that the studio productions in postwar France had become nothing more than "three hundred continuity shots stuck together a hundred and ten times a year" by professional rule-bound hacks.[26] Truffaut's attacks on the industry were so vitriolic that he was expelled from the Cannes film festival in 1958 and told to stay away. Instead, inflamed by this rejection, Truffaut promised he'd toss off something so fresh and exciting that it would shake up the whole industry. The result was a film that broke all the rules of studio filmmaking. Shot in the streets of Paris using actors who'd never been "trained," preferring ad-libbed dialogue to the elaborate scripts of the Albatross writers, Truffaut single-handedly turned the industry on its ear and his film made the first splash of what would become the New Wave. No doubt, the stealing of a typewriter was Antoine Doinel's (that is to say Truffaut's) revenge against the screenwriters Jean Aurenche and Pierre Bost whose "well-made" scenarios had exercised such a stranglehold on postwar French film.

Now grown up, however, the Doinel, rebaptized as Michel, was ready for more serious crimes, and Godard was going to aid and abet him. In the first five and a half minutes of *Breathless*, Michel steals an American army officer's spanking new Oldsmobile, heads north to Paris, breaks every traffic rule in the books, plays with the gun he finds in the car's glove compartment, is pursued by two motorcycle cops and shoots one of them dead. Not a bad start to a career as a car thief! And we soon learn why. Michel is wild about American movies and idolizes Humphrey Bogart.

Once in Paris, Belmondo will stand staring at a publicity photo for *The Harder They Fall* and unconsciously imitate Bogart's characteristic tics. He will chase after the very American Jean Seberg in other stolen American cars, and will ultimately die a very Bogart-like death, shot down in a Paris street in a copy-cat version of Bogart's final moments in *High Sierra*.

But Jean-Paul Belmondo is no Bogart; he and his creator, Jean-Luc Godard, are French, and, however much they may enjoy the fast pace and fast cars of their American counterparts, they are more interested in breaking rules than breaking attendance records. In these first five minutes of *Breathless*, Godard manages to break more rules than Michel does. As the credits fade we are confronted by an advertisement for ladies' intimate garments in a newspaper. A voice-off (Belmondo's) tells us, "After all, I'm an idiot. After all, if I must, I must!" and the paper is lowered to reveal Belmondo's face. Hollywood grammar dictates that when a character looks at something, there must be an eye-line match (shot counter-shot) to indicate what he is looking at. Not only does Godard not give us the counter-shot when Belmondo looks intently at something directly before him, the film director refuses to give us that shot when Belmondo suddenly catches sight of something off to his right, jerks his head around and peers at this new interest. When Godard does cut, the image that appears is that of a young woman's face peering intently to her right. There is no indication that she is (or has been) the object of his gaze. Now, in her turn, she catches sight of something interesting to her left, but we are not to be privy to this piece of interest either. Her eyes move back to her right and she gives a nod. At this point Godard favors us with what is presumably the person to whom she is nodding: Michel. He then looks to his right, again presumably to see what she has seen. But Godard still withholds this image from us. He looks to his left. Godard cuts to the girl. She looks to her left and then nods vigorously. A cut to Michel shows him looking left, then right. By this time we are hopelessly disoriented, for there is absolutely no way to establish either the positioning of either of these characters in relation to each other, or in relation to the point of interest that each seems to react to. Finally, 37 seconds into this series of cuts and glances, Godard provides a point of interest (though we still have no idea of the geometry and geography that may or may not link the three different points). An American military officer and a woman are shown from a medium close-up (another point of view that could not belong either to Belmondo or the girl) getting out of a new Oldsmobile sedan. Michel is ready to begin his career as car thief, but Jean-Luc is already a full minute into his career as a cinematic outlaw.

Later Godard was to exult:

I came along at a time when people were saying: French cinema doesn't say certain things or doesn't shoot in certain places, so we did…. In fact we dared go out into the street at a time when it was strictly forbidden to do so, if only for legal reasons…. In fact, *Breathless* came out of the New Wave; it's a film which had no rules and the only rule was rules are bad or badly applied.[27]

As soon as Michel hits the road, Godard races him to the next infraction. It is always the rule in studio productions to film people in cars on a stationary platform with the passing scenery projected on a screen behind them. Especially in 1959, when there was as yet no steady-cam (a device that kept the camera's own motion from blurring the image), to place a camera inside a moving automobile was unthinkable. Godard simply had to break this rule purely for reasons of economy. The entire film was shot for a fraction of the cost of a studio production. Into the Oldsmobile went Godard's cameraman behind Michel at the wheel. For perhaps the first time in a full-length feature film we are allowed to feel the motion of the speeding car and, consequently, may feel slightly dizzy or even carsick because of the swaying of the camera. This discomfort becomes quite intense as the ride goes on and the camera is literally bouncing up and down with the car's vibrations. Alerted to our own discomfort, we cannot fail to become conscious of the camera's presence.

Then, continuing his assault on proper editing etiquette, Godard throws into the first 45 seconds of Michel's trip no less than seven unnecessary jump cuts (cuts that make no attempt at spatial continuity, but move us abruptly from one point to another) to seven radically different landscapes along an unnamed road. It's as though Godard were proclaiming, "You didn't think I could include the entire trip, we had to cut it up into pieces! After all, cinema isn't a continuous, seamless flow of images, you know! It's a medium that is fundamentally discontinuous. There's no point in pretending otherwise!"

Yet another cardinal rule is about to be broken. No actor is ever allowed to look directly at the camera, much less address the implied audience behind the camera's lens. Audiences, like voyeurs, need to feel invisible in the darkened theater in order to ensure their ability to participate unselfconsciously in the story projected before then. Apparently someone forgot to tell Belmondo of this rule. In the third minute of the film, he turns to face the camera (now situated in the front passenger's seat beside him), and says, "I love France. If you don't like the sea, if you don't like the

Plate 3.5   Michel tells the film's spectators to "get stuffed!"

mountains, if you don't like cities …" and then with a big smile, "go get stuffed!" Not only has our anonymity been violated, the main character has insulted us!

Not content to have broken rules about perspective, editing, and spectator address, Godard now focuses his attack on the soundtrack. Michel has turned on the car radio, but from the second to the fourth minute of the film, we move back and forth between the sound of the radio and the extra-diegetic jazz theme that opened the film. In case we missed this infraction, Godard gives us another example. Finding a gun in the glove compartment, Michel starts playing at shooting passing motorists, saying "*Bang! Bang!*" like a comic-strip character. But suddenly he points the gun at the (closed) passenger's side window and we hear two loud gun shots. Presumably they are not shots from this revolver, for the window glass remains intact and there is no smoke from the gun. The soundtrack has become "unreliable": Godard can add or subtract anything from the "realism" of his character's story according to his own whim. "After all," he seems to be reminding us, "I'm the director. I can do whatever I want!"

These "outlaw" tendencies begin to multiply when Michel sees the motorcycle police and begins to speed up. Godard matches his speed with the speed of cutting. When Michel says, "Oh shit, the cops!" Godard proceeds to make a series of cuts that include: (1) the left front fender of the Oldsmobile (one second); (2) a shot from the passenger's seat through the car's windshield of the truck Michel is passing and of the police (two seconds); (3) an exterior shot from the right side of the highway of the blurred form of the Olds speeding by (one second); (4) a panning shot from the back seat of the Olds back to the motorcycles following the car and then forward to the road ahead (seven seconds); (5) another shot of the exterior from the left side of the road of the car speeding by from left to right (one second); (6) an exterior shot of the motorcycle cops *moving right to left* (one second); and finally (7) an exterior shot taken from 30 yards down a dirt road as Michel's car, moving from right to left, swerves off the highway onto this road. No doubt this spatial disorientation and radical discontinuity communicates better than classical editing might have done the sense of panic and confusion of our main character, but it is nonetheless highly idiosyncratic for both Godard and his character.

Godard saves the most radical of these infractions for the climactic moment of this segment, when Michel shoots the policeman. Now we see a long shot of the motorcycle speeding down the dirt road toward Michel. Godard cuts to Michel, who runs to the car and leans in the passenger-side window. The soundtrack emits a disembodied voice (Michel's or the *gendarme's?*) saying, "Don't move or I'll shoot!" Godard blithely ignores the source and menace of this voice to do a slow pan in a close-up of Michel, now apparently standing outside the car in the morning sun, moving from the right side of his face slowly down the length of his torso to his hand, holding the "found" revolver. As the camera reaches the weapon, we see Michel's thumb cock the gun, and, now in an extreme close-up, the camera pans along the gun's barrel (as if recording in slow motion the passage of the bullet). As we hear the sound of a shot, Godard cuts to a uniformed body already midway in its fall, and dropping, quite unexpectedly into the woods by the side of the road some distance from where we last saw the policeman. There is no way accurately to reconstruct either the time line or the spatial coordinates of this event. According to the editing, the officer began his fall before the gun fired and was now located far from the position on the dirt road he had seconds previously occupied. In short, there is no more logic to Godard's fractious cinematography than there is to Michel's crime. Both activities appear to be unmotivated and betraying an addiction to speed.

Later Godard would say, "In *Breathless* I was searching for the subject throughout the shooting of the film. Finally I got interested in Belmondo. I saw him as a kind of opacity that I had to film in order to find out what was behind it."[28] And finally, Belmondo tells Jean Seberg exactly what *is* behind it. In the exceedingly long scene in her hotel room, she takes up William Faulkner's *The Wild Palms* and quotes, "… if I become not, then all of remembering will cease to be. – Yes, he thought, between grief and nothing I will take grief." Then she asks Michel, "What would you choose?" Michel answers, "Grief is idiotic, I'd take nothing."

However much Michel and Godard had emulated fast American cars and American movies, there is a point at which this fascination comes face to face with their Frenchness. When Patricia (Seberg) quotes Faulkner, Michel responds with a virtual quote from Jean-Paul Sartre's *Being and Nothingness*.[29] Michel will spend the rest of the film madly stealing cars and evading arrest. The real reason for his eventual arrest, however, comes in the 52nd minute of the film when, parked in his stolen Ford Thunderbird, Michel orders a copy of *France-Soir* from a passing newsboy. A bystander then also orders a copy of the same paper and takes up a position, just to the right of Michel's car, to peruse it. The camera shows us a close-up of an article that contains Michel's photo and the words "The assassin of Route Seven remains at large [*insaisissable*]." Evidently looking at the same photo, the pedestrian looks pointedly at Michel in his car. The two men, dressed similarly and both wearing dark glasses, exchange looks. After Patricia joins Michel in the car, they drive off. The pedestrian, however, after a last exchange of glances (one might say of deep recognition) with Michel, crosses the street, encounters two policemen and points toward the departing convertible. Here, significantly, Godard uses an iris fade-out identical to the one used after Michel has "traded looks" with a poster of Bogart. The pedestrian in this scene is, you will have noticed, none other than the director, Jean-Luc Godard. However much Godard's cameo role seems to be a faithful homage to Hitchcock, the French director breaks with Hitchcock whose cameos never involved direct action in his films. This "*insaisissable*" criminal can only be seized by his director, who denounces him to the police. I believe you will agree that this scene is uncanny for the way Godard dresses himself to look like a *double* of the character he is sending to his death. He seems to be saying, "Look we're both criminals, but in denouncing my character I am both drawing attention to and justifying my lawlessness." For in every case in this film, breaking the rules has been so blatant as to cause us to question the rules. In the end, Michel will run melodramatically the length of an entire Paris street after (purportedly) having received a .45 caliber bullet in the lower back. He dies with equal theatricality by imitating facial gestures that he once shared with his moll, and carefully closes his own eyes with his left hand.

Plate 3.6   Godard denounces Michel

Moments later, Godard fades to black, effectively closing his and our eyes on this adventure that has joined character and film director in the most lawless spree since Jesse James.

This single film was to become a tremendous success at the box office even while it attacked the very Hollywood system it seemed to pay homage to. *Breathless* paves the way, I believe, precisely because it set the stage for the flood of cinematic experimentation that was to follow, for the entire New Wave. In his "assassination" of all the rules of Hollywood's classic style,[30] Godard was to prove, Biro's famous Comic Books notwithstanding, that crime *does* pay.[31] Godard's success as a cinematic outlaw reminds us of Raskolnikov's theory in *Crime and Punishment*:

> The extraordinary man has the right ... to overstep certain obstacles, and only in case it is essential for the practical fulfillment of his ideas.... All legislators and leaders of men, such as Lycurgus, Solon, Mohamet, Napoleon and so on, were all without exception criminals, from the very fact that making a new law, they *transgressed* the ancient one, handed down from their ancestor and held sacred by the people. In short, the majority of these benefactors and leaders of humanity must from their very nature be criminals. (C&P 254–5)

Marcel Carné, Robert Bresson, and Jean-Luc Godard should then be welcomed into the pantheon of French cinema for the revolutionary criminals they are. Upon reflection, however, we must admit that they are not so different from all of the other film directors discussed in this volume. Their quest for the new leads them inevitably into conflict with every major rule of the dominant cinema, and so into studiously intentional acts of *transgression*. In rejecting what is, they invite us, each in his or her own way, toward a radically new understanding of the means by which we may represent and understand our world.

Suggested Further Reading

Kline, T. J. (1992), "The ABC's of Godard's Quotations: *A bout de souffle* with *Pierrot le fou*." In *Screening the Text: Intertextuality in the New Wave French Cinema*. Baltimore, MD: The Johns Hopkins University Press, pp. 184–221. Provides a larger context for understanding Godard's radical approach to the cinema.

Kline, T. J. (2004), "The French New Wave." In Ezra, E. (ed.), *European Cinema*. Oxford: Oxford University Press, pp. 157–75. Provides, in an overview of the New Wave, the historical context for both Bresson's and Godard's films.

Turk, E. (1989), *Child of Paradise: Marcel Carné and the Golden Age of French Cinema*. Cambridge, MA: Harvard University Press. A first-rate introduction of Carné's masterpiece, providing historical, biographical, and cinematic details of great interest.

4

Cinema and/as Mapping

Reorienting Ourselves Through Film

"Bazin's book is entitled What Is Cinema? *To ask* what *it is may be the equivalent to asking* where *it is."* (Tom Conley, 2007)

It can certainly be no accident that Godard chose to orient *Breathless* around a car thief whose nearly aimless itinerary begins in an unnamed city, careens onto a never-to-be identified French highway only to be violently sidetracked onto a dirt road in the middle of nowhere. Nor does it seem unintentional that, with several bullets in his back, Michel should lurch toward his death down Anystreetwhatever in the French capital. For Godard and most of the 162 new directors who stormed the barricades of the old guard of classical cinema between 1958 and 1962, their anarchic stampede, like Michel's headlong rush through the French countryside after the shooting, was intended to break down all the familiar signposts of the traditional cinema and set off into the uncertain light of uncharted territory. Maps are normally provided only *after* the flag has been planted on a new continent. And so, after the New Wave and this temporary "loss of bearings," then, maps of a very different orientation will be required to find our way. I would like then, to turn to a brief discussion of three different French films that take up the question of mapping as if to rechart the territory ahead after Godard's obliteration of the old cartography. And, true to their "Frenchness," we will discover that, as a group, these works serve to orient us to the ways in which filming itself *is* a kind of mapping. In its most general terms, as Tom Conley has noted in his study, *Cartographic Cinema*, this question is almost universal to films whether they display maps or not:

> As the person who gazes upon a map works through a welter of impressions about the geographical information it puts forward – along with his or her own fantasies and pieces of past or anticipated memory in dialogue with the names, places, and forms on the map – so also do spectators of a film who see moving pictures on a screen mix and shift through souvenirs and images of other films and personal memories. [So that] even if a film does not display a map as such, by nature it bears an implicit relation with cartography.[1]

In the what follows, then, we will take up three very different kinds of maps in three radically different kinds of films – a combination that will allow us not only to understand the relationship French cinema enjoys with the *meta-cinematic* question of maps (how they are like films and vice versa), but also to entertain some notions about how we might constitute the "map" of French cinema itself.

The Cartographic Map as Symbolic Orientation: Charting the Path of Malle's *The Lovers*

At the release of *The Lovers* in 1958, critics directed their attention primarily to two aspects of Malle's film that, by today's standards, might be considered marginal: first of all, the film's explicit sexuality (which led the reviewer in *Films in Review* to tell Louis Malle that "he should be ashamed"), and secondly, the heroine's decision to leave her daughter behind as she ran off with a lover she'd met only 24 hours before.[2] Indeed, the steamy scene of adultery, combined with the couple's flight from the woman's bourgeois Burgundy household, are certainly "anti-social" by almost any standards. It is not so much this woman's blatant sexuality and open disregard for social conventions, however, which should perplex us, but rather the deeper reasons which motivate her. However much we may be "seduced" by the night of love shared by Jeanne (Jeanne Moreau) and Bernard (Jean-Marc Bory), Jeanne's decision to drive off the next morning must strike us at first viewing as, to say the least, unfocused, unplanned, and unlikely to make her (and us) happy in conformity to most traditional cinematic love stories. When we replay this film, to better understand Jeanne's perplexing itinerary, we may discover we had overlooked the

Plate 4.1   The Map of Tenderness

map displayed behind the film's opening credits: a replica of the famous seventeenth-century *Carte de Tendre*. The connections between this map and the film are hardly evident, especially since the document does not remain in view long enough to read it thoroughly. In order to fully grasp the significance of this first map, then, we should study another "map" that Malle has placed in his film. This second map is not visible per se, but can nevertheless be seen as a kind of "writing on the wall" behind every moment of this film.

Malle's narrative involves the beautiful wife of the well-to-do owner of a country chateau. This woman *may* be having an affair with a man who has captured the attention of the news media for heroic exploits. When he guesses his wife's feelings for this man of the hour, the husband rather surprisingly insists that she invite her "friend" down to the country for a weekend of gaming. When this first lover does arrive, a strange evening occurs during which the wife moves among husband, official lover and another man. In the end, after a chaotic evening, she plans to run off with this second lover. She and the "official" lover are thus not destined ever to enjoy their affair ...

Have you encountered this story before? When presented this way, we cannot fail to see that Malle has self-consciously based his story on one we have already encountered: Jean Renoir's *Rules of the Game*. For students of Louis Malle, this comes as no surprise since he himself once said, "I conceived my desire to make films, like so many other French film-makers, after seeing *Rules of the Game* at a *ciné club*. Renoir's film made an enormous impression on me ... It's one of the most inspired movies in all its details I've ever seen.... I've seen it around fifteen times."[3] And once we see the overall similarity between the two films, we cannot help seeing Renoir's presence everywhere in *Les Amants*. As an exercise, I ask you to put the book down again, and see how many similarities you can list between the two works.

Certainly you will have noticed the similarities of settings: Paris and a chateau in the provinces. You will have enjoyed the way both Christine and Jeanne move among a series of men, initially unable to choose, but ultimately deciding to choose a less obviously romantic partner (Octave and Bernard) over the more spectacular man (André and Raoul). You will have appreciated the fact that both Robert and Monsieur Tournier are having affairs of their own. Both films, of course, produce a farcical moment as the evening's guests say "good night" in the chateau's hallways and each of the soirées end with the promise of gaming the next day. You will, no doubt, have noticed that the climaxes of both films occur in the dark of night.

Did you also notice that Malle employs the now much aged Gaston Modot, who played Schumacher in *Rules of the Game*, to repeat the greetings as a car rolls up to the door from Paris? Of course, in *Les Amants* the context of this greeting is remarkably less splendid. Indeed, at every level, Louis Malle seems to have reduced or trivialized the elements of Renoir's film. André's heroic landing in a twin-engine plane becomes, for Raoul (José Luis de Villalonga), a ride in a tiny replica of a plane in an amusement park. The remarkably brutal hunting scene in *Rules of the Game* is replaced by Raoul's exhibition of "prowess" at a shooting gallery in the same park.

The author of *Les Amants*, leaves little doubt that Renoir's film is to be considered a kind of map against which to "plot" his own film's progress, but he also makes it clear that Renoir's devastating social criticism has been replaced by other concerns. It is precisely because *Les Amants* does not "measure up" to Renoir's model that we discover that there must be another itinerary through Malle's world that we must heed if we are to arrive where he intended us to go.

You have, no doubt, found other examples of Malle's "reduction" of Renoir's film. You may have noticed, for example, that, just as Renoir's male characters all end up being merely doubles of each other, Malle's "lovers" (all three) participate in a strange kind of mirroring. Two of Malle's scenes of doubling seem particularly disturbing. We may remember that following their night of love, Bernard says to Jeanne, "Hurry up!" Only seconds later, Henri (Alain Cuny) pokes his head in at their door and, not noticing Bernard (Jean-Marc Bory), repeats, "Hurry up, Jeanne!"

Has this most steamy of lovers been reduced to the coldest of husbands so quickly? Ostensibly the opposite of Raoul, Bernard does not achieve as much distance from his more urbane predecessor as we would want in order to be convinced that Jeanne has made the 'right' decision. When we first see Jeanne with Raoul, he is sporting a white towel around his neck. Then, in the bathroom, following their night of love, Jeanne takes an identical towel and shrouds Bernard's entire head with it. The gesture evokes both the earlier moment with Raoul and, uncannily, René Magritte's celebrated painting, "Les Amants." We cannot doubt that Magritte's canvas is intended to *make visual* the old adage that *love is blind*. But in this context it has the power of undoing any faith the audience may have placed in the value of the particular lover Jeanne has chosen. We sense then, that Malle has chosen, subtly but forcefully, to undermine any romantic belief in the power of love and has simultaneously shifted the meaning of his title from a designation of Jeanne and Bernard to the *series* of men Jeanne will engage during these 90 minutes. This rather sobering "lesson" may already be announced the moment we see Jeanne in her Peugeot 203 for, in French, the words 203 pronounced *deux cent trois* are orally indistinguishable from another famous adage "*Jamais deux sans trois* [never two without three]," i.e. "accidents always come in threes." To imply such a cynical message repeatedly in this film is thoroughly to *subvert* our romantic pleasure in the film's presentation of love.

So, what is going on?

We are now forced to return to the other, more explicit, if less well-known, map that opens Malle's film. This "*Carte du pays de Tendre*" appeared originally in Madeleine de Scudéry's *Artamène ou le Grand Cyrus*, a novel of some 8,000 pages, written between 1649 and 1653. This map, like the novel that contained it, had a powerfully political agenda: the propagation of the new social ethics of the movement known as "*Les Précieuses.*" Although Molière's satire *Les Précieuses ridicules* succeeded brilliantly in undermining this movement, the "female assemblies" of the women who founded it "played a very subversive role in the political life of the *ancien régime.*" Joan de Jean, whose research has rescued the *précieuses* from Molière's ridicule, has written:

> Esteeming the [general social] level of politeness and wit unacceptable, the marquise de Rambouillet simply created an alternative space. Within her blue room, [she] created an alternative court, a new center of power, a place where power was exercised through conversation. The salons were a world presided over by women. *Préciosité* was much more than a literary moment of minor importance. It began as a feminist movement, and the *précieuses*

made demands of striking actuality: they sought for women what would be today termed control over their bodies.[4]

While the pertinence of *La Carte de Tendre* may not yet be apparent, we should think about the fact that the map is politically subversive and is linked to the way women will want to talk about the female body and, especially, will seek out a place in which they seize the *authority* to do so.

The very presence of this map, then, should open our eyes to several elements in this film that we might otherwise have missed. The first of these is related to the ways films express an authoritative voice. When we think generally about our experience of classical films we will remember that often they open with an authoritative voice-off who informs us of the geographical and historical situation in which the characters find themselves.[5] Indeed in the *vast* majority of voices-off in the history of cinema, the extra-diegetic voice-off that provides this information is the voice of a man. (Ask yourself how many pre-1958 films you can name that include a woman's voice-off in such an authoritative role.) It has been convincingly argued that, even without the presence of the male *voice*(-off) in a film, it is *assumed* that the film's authority is *male*,[6] a situation that exactly replicates the role of women in Scudery's times. We are accustomed to assume that it is a male voice that is "telling" the film in some way or other and that therefore the female voice is cut off from any ability to "make meaning." Suddenly, however, in Malle's film, it is a woman's voice we hear as the authoritative voice-off. To be sure, within the diegesis of the film, we see men undermining and attacking women's authority. Monsieur Tournier, for example, the first time we see them at dinner together, tells Jeanne that her way of speaking is merely the way women think and speak. Moreover, he tells her bluntly that, since she is married, she does not need to concern herself with having a particular style or social identity and, having thus demolished her, triumphantly blows cigar smoke in her face, nearly erasing her from our view. But the presence of Jeanne's voice-off reverses the roles when she announces belittlingly, "Henri had seen nothing, noticed nothing." Her words can be interpreted as a challenge to the male spectators of *Les Amants*, to pay particular attention lest they *fail to see* to real story. Since the voice-off belongs both to Jeanne Moreau, the actress who plays Jeanne, and the "narratrix" of the film, this voice also lays claim to a kind of transcendence, moving within and above the world of the film. No longer "trapped" within the diegesis of her film, Jeanne's voice begins to reorganize and reverse the locus and *focus* of control. Later, for example, at the dinner during which Maggie succeeds in rendering feminine discourse truly imbecilic, Henri intervenes devastatingly to reinstitute the authority of the husband to subjugate Jeanne's desire and romantic life to his own. Here, the voice-off intervenes again, from a position of authority greater than Henri's (because extra-diegetic) to comment on Jeanne's position: "Her universe was collapsing. With an odious husband, an almost ridiculous lover, Jeanne, who had believed in herself in a drama, now found herself in a mere vaudeville show. She had a sudden desire *to be someone else [d'être quelqu'un d'autre]*." This is a remarkable observation, for Jeanne now knows that her options are entirely closed off in her role as Henri's wife. *She must become someone else.* But how? What route can she take to discover this liberating transformation?

Perhaps the *Carte du pays de Tendre* will offer some clues, a strategy that has been offered since the film's credits began to roll across the scene over its mysterious landscape. The fact that this map does not belong to the film's diegesis (any more than Jeanne's voice-off), suggests that, as viewers, we need to step back and view Jeanne's voyage of self-discovery *through the grid of the map*. This map, we remember, was intimately connected to a revolution in discourse and specifically discourse about the feminine body. If that discourse was initially restricted to the salons run by the "*précieuses*," the map itself functioned (as did other maps of utopias of the period) to extend those restrictions outside of confined spaces, opening up new possibilities for women to become empowered. *The Map of the Country of Tenderness* may thus be read as an allegory of desire and power, but now reorganized as a desire with a difference and a power exercised by deference. One of most acute readers of this map, Claude Filteau, has argued that the map aimed ultimately at establishing a contract (named specifically "*Nouvelle Amitié*" on the map). The "precious" explorer's initial contact with the map, however, is perceived as "a sort of window ... that seems to organize the only possible opening into an inaccessible 'elsewhere'... In this sense, the map is a challenge laid down to men by the *précieuses*."[7] This map would, if correctly read, give women as much to gain as men from friendship. It is an egalitarian project couched in both cartographic and rhetorical terms: "Designed by women, the map of tenderness is addressed to men.... Its code, in fact is meant to imitate another code: that of 'la conversation spirituelle' to which women alone hold the key.... Thus, the essence of the code can be learned by men only by a sort of 'devenir femme [becoming woman].'"[8]

How might we understand the *place* of the map in *Les Amants*? Well, the transformation of Jeanne takes place at night, as she exits the space in which her husband has held sway, to venture into a more natural setting. Once she meets Bernard, it is Jeanne who very pointedly leads the way for her new lover through a terrain that itself has become doubly hers.

Plate 4.2   The lovers walk across the Map of Tenderness

The voice-off tells us that "Love can be *engendered* by a glance. Jeanne felt her discomfort and her modesty *dying* away. She could no longer hesitate. One should never resist happiness." The word "engendered" has a remarkable resonance, here, for, since Jeanne needs (like Juliette in *L'Atalante*) to become "quelqu'un d'autre [someone else]" she must *die away* and be re-birthed now. But "engendered" may also have the sense of "assigning a gender to" and if love is to be "re-gendered" as feminine, we must set foot *on* the map of tenderness. Indeed, Louis Malle was to say, "Our working relationships are extraordinarily intimate. We cross *La Carte de Tendre* with great strides, observation, *coup de foudre*, tenderness, quarrels, reconciliations … a passionate complicity."[9]

Following the voice-off's "authorization," Jeanne leads Bernard through a field that looks like nothing so much as the areas sketched on *La Carte de Tendre* to indicate as-yet-uninhabited terrain. Their subsequent itinerary could easily be mapped entirely on *La Carte*, for Jeanne leads Bernard to the banks of a river and then across a dam constructed to look very much like the bridge on the map located in the town of "Nouvelle Amitié." There they symbolically "undo" the aggressive violence of Renoir's hunting scene by liberating a basket of trapped fish. Next she leads him back across the river and into a small boat, in which they drift downstream, presumably towards "Tendre sur Inclination [Tenderness on the River Inclination]."

Their night of love is filmed in such a way that the camera for once does not begin by voyeuristically exposing the woman's body, but rather captures the man in the act of undressing. The scene's eroticism likewise focuses not on male satisfaction but rather on tenderness, laughter, and generalized touch leading to the woman's ecstasy. Most of the words in the scene are spoken by Jeanne not Bernard. All in all, then, the perspective and orientation of this scene do not fit the genre of romantic films but belong instead to that "tender space" imagined three hundred years before.

It is worth noting here that many readers of *La Carte du pays de Tendre* have tended to misread the proper direction of the lovers' progression. It is crucial, however, especially given the use Louis Malle makes of this map, to understand that the Inclination River flows *into* not away from the *Mer Dangereuse* [Dangerous Sea], a direction that would suggest how *uncomfortable, uncertain, and open-ended* Jeanne's itinerary must be. By drawing the map in this way, the *Précieuses* of 1653 clearly understood that it is *after* reaching the city of Tenderness that the real test of a relationship begins. Indeed, following their night of love-making, Jeanne and Bernard must set out again, stopping briefly at a café where, on a wall behind them, an advertisement for *Gitanes* with its logo of a gypsy prominently displayed, reminds Jeanne of her new status. Her voice-off comments:

> They were leaving for a long voyage they knew would be uncertain. They did not know if they would ever again regain the happiness of their first night together. Already at this dangerous hour of the morning [*à l'heure dangereuse du petit matin*] Jeanne had been plagued with self-doubt. She had brought little with her but she regretted nothing.[10]

At the far shores of *La Mer dangereuse* lie *Les Terres inconnues* [The Unknown Territories]. It is likely that in attempting to conceive a utopia of relationships in which women might stand to gain as much as men, the *Précieuses* felt unable to chart any specific course beyond the initial first steps. Beyond friendship, a woman's options seemed limited either to the confines of marriage or to potential social opprobrium, both entirely controlled by a patriarchal set of laws that clearly rejected the liberties sought in *Le pays de Tendre*. For Jeanne as well, her rebellion leads her only to the uncertainties of broken conventions, for, in seizing her place on a map readable only by those willing to "become woman," she has had to gamble on her partner's willingness to abandon his conventional masculinity. Louis Malle has already suggested his own skepticism on this potential transformation by creating the series of doubles that generally erode the differences between Jeanne's three men. No wonder, then, that Jeanne should burst into tears and, in response, that Bernard should lamely wish that it could be "night all the time."

Jeanne's penultimate line in the film is, "It's crazy but I no longer feel like myself." In this, she has not only courageously followed the challenges of the *Carte de Tendre*, but has embodied Louis Malle's greatest aspiration for the cinema itself:

> The cinema I love is not addressed to either logic or reason. It touches us, invades us, provokes us, it is a deforming mirror in which the spectator looks at himself. My characters ... no longer follow social rules and thus cast a new and lucid light on society, because they're *outside* it.... I have an intimate conviction that I will never be for established order.[11]

In respect to his oppositon to "established order," Malle joins company with the trio of "criminals" we've already encountered. And by providing a map against which to read the story of his film, Louis Malle has suggested not only a new way of being but, true to his Gallic origins, intimated that cinema itself represents the possibility of a reorientation of our most basic priorities. It is a challenging itinerary, but one he believes we must all dare to take.

Intertextual Maps

It is perhaps no coincidence that Louis Malle opened *Les Amants* with the display of a map, for he had already ventured under the sea as a collaborator with the oceanographer Jacques Cousteau, and was, some years later, to travel to India for a series of documentaries that were intended to put that country "on the map" for the French, much as the Lumière brothers' films had done for early film audiences. *Phantom India* he termed "a detour that became a quest" – a phrase that will have enormous resonance for the film we are about to discuss.

By 1992, Malle had traveled extensively throughout North America, and made a series of feature films there. His interest in the intersection of maps and films, however, was not limited purely to cartographic maps. When he made *Damage* in 1992, he seems to have come at mapping from another direction. In his adaptation of Josephine Hart's novel, *Damage*, Louis Malle took the geographic metaphor that opens Hart's text and adapted it specifically to the cinema in ways that provide us with another look at the connections between filming and mapping.

To appreciate the way Malle reworks Hart's idea in specifically cinematical terms, let's take a look at the way she opens with a metaphor that evokes many of Malle's most fundamental concerns:

> There is an internal landscape, a geography of the soul; we search for its outlines all our lives. Those who are lucky enough to find it ease like water

over a stone, onto its fluid contours, and are home…. For some the search is for the imprint of another; a child or a mother, a grandfather or a brother, a lover, a husband, a wife or a foe.[12]

For Hart, the cartography of the soul is thus often "traced" in the imprint of an(other) human being, and her novel will play this out in insistently geographic terms. The narrator, Stephen Fleming, tells us,

I had not found the key to myself in any area of service, medical or political….[Yet] I learned the public geography of my soul from television and newspapers. It was neither shaming nor pleasing, just another perfect set piece…. The passion that transforms life, and art, did not seem to be mine. But in all its essentials, my life was a good performance. (D 18–19)

That is to say, he begins with a *map that designates a purely superficial and dead geography*. Everything looks familiar enough when mapped on the "public" page, but this map remains unconnectable to any space that feels "real" to the narrator. In other words, passion does not occur within any of the recognizable maps we have just been shown, but seems only to occur on the other side of a bridge, across a "dangerous sea" in a *terre inconnue*. It will be the theme of Hart's novel that, for the most part, we live on continents of continence, containment, repression, superficiality. Paradoxically, however, by the very fact of being merely habitual, they are, to use Hart's own language, "deserts," dead and solitary places. Her geography culminates in the (somewhat hackneyed) notion of "a living death." When he looks at photographs of himself, he sees "the face of a man I no longer understand. I know the bridge that connects me to him. But the other side has disappeared. Disappeared like some piece of land the sea has overtaken. There may be some landmarks on the beach, at low tide, but that is all" (D 25).

Fleming thus personifies the dilemma of a map that does not link up to the geography of the "real" person. One wonders immediately what it would take to reach that "unknown region." Clearly Stephen is so completely an inhabitant of this dead landscape that he is no longer able to take an active part in his itinerary, but is shaped by it: "I always recognize the forces that will shape my life. I let them do their work. Sometimes they simply shift the ground under me, so that I stand on different earth … Then I start on my way again" (D 82).

Anna Barton, Stephen's son's fiancée, comes to represent such a force, not only a ground-shifting (this is both a geographical and a perceptual metaphor) that enables him to "stand on different earth," but one which will ultimately lead him to a kind of impasse. When Stephen meets Anna, he experiences a shock of recognition … Just for a moment I had met my sort, another of my species…. I was like *a traveler lost in a foreign land*, who suddenly hears not just his native tongue, but the local dialect he spoke as a boy. He … just rushes towards the sweet sound of home. My soul had rushed to Anna Barton. (D 31)

In other words, "home" is that which is recognizable to the *real* Stephen, yet home is unlocatable on any of the available maps! How to reach this uncharted, unknown region? Stephen notes of his feeling for Anna, "the outer reaches of our being are arrived at through violence … My life ended in the split second of my first sight of her" (D 46, 44). Of course he *thinks* he means that (like Jeanne and Juliette before him) his recognizable life ended and an *unrecognizable* life began at that moment, and yet "the unknown region" is, sadly, so common a euphemism for death that we do not really trust his euphoria. These mapping and violent vocabularies increasingly and unsurprisingly merge: "The new and strange shape I was assuming … would allow no return journey. My path was clear. I knew I was on a headlong rush to destruction" (D 62–3).

The rationale for this unlocatable geography becomes clear when it is linked to desire. Stephen notes: "Tales of ecstasy are endless tales of failure. For always comes separation. And the journey towards the essential, fleeting unity begins again" (D 82). Stephen's passion is no more localizable, Hart seems to tell us, than is utopia, the ultimately elusive object of desire.[13] In Hart's geography we are forced to realize that this *utopia* is simultaneously and necessarily a very oxymoronic *dystopia*. Stephen's oft-repeated oxymoron for this "place" is "Impossible/possible" (D 169). To be there is to exercise a self-eradicating form of violence, simultaneously and paradoxically life-creating and life-destroying. Hart's tragic conclusion is that one cannot really *live* in either place.

When Anna writes to Stephen, she instinctively (instinctively because she is presumably not privy to the geographic metaphors of his internal monologue, and therefore cannot be assumed to be responding to them) writes: "My Lord, sometimes we need a map of the past. It helps us to understand the present, and to plan the future" (D 85). Anna, too, has her special geography – but hers begins with her dead (suicided) brother, Aston, with whom she had shared an equally unmappable space:

You cannot imagine what such a closeness was like. When it starts so early you see the world always, and in every way, through twinned souls … In the mornings we gazed at each other and at each new day – together. Whether we were in Egypt, the Argentine, or finally in Europe, it *simply didn't matter*. The world was Aston and me. (D 86)

Anna concludes her *notional geographic* with the words, "And so here is my story, the map of my journey to you" (D 94). And immediately Stephen reacts, "Anna was right. It was a map. That was all" (D 95). The words, "That was all," are quite curious here. Normally, we would be grateful for a map. What Stephen suspects without articulating it explicitly is that Anna's map represents a world destroyed – utterly and forever unrelocatable – or else relocatable only through the *repetition* of the deadly scene that caused a *diabol-ic* (i.e. explosive – the opposite of symbolic) shift of her world.[14] He only vaguely understands that the dystopia he seeks (innocently enough) with Anna can, for her, only be arrived at through the reenactment of Aston's suicide by Martyn. In other words, the only way for Stephen's world to become real (linking his inner passionate world to a geography shared with others) is to violently follow a map that charts the "end of the line-age" in the death of his son.

In Hart's version, Martyn's death creates a fold in time into "a dangerous pattern [that] is being reworked" (D 149), and so it is that when he confronts his father and mistress in the act of coitus, Martyn "raised his arms above his head as if to ward off a terrible blow. Then, like a child moving backwards, robotically, step by step from undreamed-of evil, and gazing at the face that had destroyed him, he fell silently … to his death below" (D 169). This robotic movement has a regressive effect precisely because Martyn is being pulled backwards in time not only to his own childhood, but also to the moment of Aston's death. Just as there is no locatable geography for this journey, its temporality is only understandable as taking place outside the normal space/time continuum.

Anna's final letter to Stephen reintroduces the novel's dominant metaphor: "Like aliens on Earth, we found in each and every step the language of our own lost planet…. Remember … even if you found me, I would not be there. Don't search for something you already have" (D 211). *Don't search for something you already have*. And what might that something be? When he had once asked Anna, "Who are you?" she had answered, "I am what you desire" (D 41). If at first reading, we assume that by this response Anna refers to her own pliability, we can only conclude at novel's end that she means this phrase literally: "I am only the figment of your desire for what cannot be found."

No wonder that Stephen's efforts at mapping are so tortuous. There exists no external geography of desire inasmuch as desire is not what unites two separate beings, but rather desire is what one being projects onto another, whose very otherness condemns us to be other to ourselves. Stephen ends up with the unreadable map of his own psyche. There he has graphed coordinates that lead to a conclusion terrifyingly similar to the one Freud had reached in *Beyond the Pleasure Principle*, where we learn that "the object of life is death."[15]

Louis Malle's *Damage* takes place in the recognizable landscapes of London, Brussels, and Paris. There is very little evidence that any scene of the film has, per se, been set in an "unlocatable" geography that might match Hart's dominant metaphor. On the contrary, Malle seems, at first glance, careful to represent most of the "events" of Hart's text quite faithfully: Stephen Fleming meets Anna Barton (his son's fiancée) at a cocktail party. They meet again when Martyn brings Anna home to meet the family. Stephen and Anna quickly become embroiled in a violently sexual love affair and when Stephen asks Anna to break it off with Martyn, she refuses, arguing that Martyn offers her something fundamental to her and that Stephen will always have what he needs from her. Just as in Hart's novel, Martyn accidentally happens on Stephen and Anna in bed and, aghast, falls to his death from the third floor landing. Malle ends his film as Hart did her novel, with Stephen staring desperately at a photograph. If there *are* slight deviations in plot between novel and film, they may strike us as much less significant than the uncanny way Malle has rendered Hart's metaphor of "unlocatable geography."

Malle's geography must be termed insistently *cinematic* for what he has substituted for Hart's metaphor in his film is nothing less than an *intertextual map*: What Malle has produced are images not only of "real places" but more importantly ones that cannot fail to evoke a series of films, his own as well as others', each of which provokes a specific resonance with the scenes in *Damage* in such a way as to comment on the nature of film as a locus of unattainable desire.

Thus, despite an otherwise very high degree of what we might traditionally call "fidelity" to Hart's text, Malle's adaptation of that text produces a series of meanings which go well beyond those uncovered in Hart's novel to a fundamental statement about the relationship of space, mapping, incest, and cinematic experience itself. In so doing, Malle does not appear to "sacrifice" any of the meanings available in Hart's novel, but rather incorporates these, yet provides a context (film itself) which considerably transcends the context(s) established in the novel.

Let us explore, then, what possible meanings may be evoked by this other, specifically cinematic "geography." This "unlocalizable" geography of intertextuality (unrepresentable in any concrete images specific to the diegesis of Malle's own film) becomes sexualized once Stephen's and

Plate 4.3   Malle's lovers imitate *Last Tango*

Anna's bodies intertwine. It is curious that, when discussing his role in the film, Jeremy Irons articulated his own appreciation of the intertextual nature of the love scenes, for he stated, "Louis Malle fell into all the traps that difficult story of eroticism laid for him, not the least in the way he shot the love scenes," for "the way he shot the love scenes" was unquestionably by allusion. The first "space" they visit is a re-inscription of the Jules Verne apartment in Bertolucci's *Last Tango in Paris*, itself an interpretation of Cocteau's scenes of mirroring and death in *Orpheus*. Stephen's and Anna's bodies replicate the position of Brando and Schneider in that earlier film in ways that are so obvious as to require little reminder. This itinerary had, in a sense, already been evoked in *Phantom India* for, in the midst of that exploration of what is most hauntingly exotic in the Indian culture, Malle came across a kind of clown show that for him produced "a Fellini-like atmosphere." Suddenly over the map of India had been pasted a scene from another Italian film! *Damage*'s itinerary also has its specific code: Bertolucci's film is a remarkable "remake" of both Cocteau's *Orpheus* and Hitchcock's *Vertigo*. As such, it constitutes, as I show elsewhere,[16] a complex study of the short-circuiting of desire: the violent projection of the mother and father by each lover onto the other, culminating in desperation and death. *Last Tango* also, not coincidentally, constitutes a meditation on the way film (in the person of Tom, the character played by Jean-Pierre Leaud) sublimates the lovers' problematic desire for the viewer. Thus, Malle alludes to a film in which sexuality is tightly linked to a meta-textual code. And in one scene in particular Malle effects a collage of *Tango* and his own first film, *Les Amants*. As Irons and Binoche sit in the position of Brando and Schneider in *Tango*, each covers the other's eyes – a gesture that recaptures Malle's earlier allusion to Magritte's *Les Amants*. Indeed, Malle himself confesses that:

> When I read *Damage* there were themes, visual moments and characters that really intrigued me; I was very compelled. *Damage* brings back many things I've covered during my lifetime and in my work.... Reading it I thought immediately of *Les Amants*. It's about somebody discovering that his life is very empty; something happens which brings about the collapse of the conventional world in which he lives. It seemed interesting for me to revisit this theme.[17]

The "something that happens" is, in *Damage*, incest. Has been incest, or must be, because it seems to be that only by a repetition of a fatal scene that one seeks liberation from and simultaneously encounters death(!). Malle's previous encounter with the theme of incest (in *Murmurs of the Heart*) had left his viewers perplexed. Mother/son incest seemed to be, in that earlier film, a casual, almost natural event, from which no "damage" occurred, only a minor detour on the way to manhood. But his new film moves in a different space altogether. Now the motif of incest is filtered through a much more psychoanalytic and cinematic lens. And it is in this context that we encounter another intertextual avatar: Alain Resnais's *Last Year at Marienbad*.

When Irons and Binoche first make love in her apartment, she adopts a strangely passive position, throwing her arms out to each side as he exhausts himself on her all but inert body. To be sure, Malle's scene "faithfully" renders the following paragraphs of Hart's novel: "We went into her sitting room and lay down on the floor. She flung her arms out, each side of her, and she drew her legs up and we rose and fell, rose and fell into the wilderness" (D 37).

Again the metaphor of unidentifiable geography (the wilderness). But no such figure is directly filmed by Malle. Instead, his scene evokes a thoroughly unlocatable space: Marienbad, and a thoroughly problematic character named quite simply "A" (Delphine Seyrig), her arms spread against a mirror, waiting in fear for Albertazzi to enter her chamber. It is, incidentally, uncanny how thoroughly Juliette Binoche and Delphine Seyrig resemble each other in features, coloring, and hair style. Malle references *Marienbad* several times in *Damage*, but returns most obviously to that film in Martyn's fall over the banister. Those familiar with Resnais's masterpiece will recall that in *Marienbad*, there is an insistent fantasy that the narrator has fallen through the exterior balustrade to his death.

Why *Marienbad*? Because, first of all, it is a story that cannot be located in either space and time and thus constitutes a kind of hyperbole of Hart's metaphor of unlocatable geography. Second, because, as I have demonstrated elsewhere,[18] the entire film turns on a carefully placed allusion to incest, and ties incest precisely to *that which cannot be tolerated (the traumatic) and therefore cannot be located in memory*. Like Malle's *Damage*, *Marienbad* puts into play a triangular relationship which ends in a sense of immobility that is very much like Stephen's final position opposite the photograph of himself, Martyn, and Anna. Finally, Resnais's film provides a remarkable commentary on the relationship of these psychological traps to the act of film viewing itself.

The film's insistence on mirrors presents an identity formed of a self and an alienated other, as well as the traces of the incestuous father's pervasive presence in the fragmented self of the incest victim. Resnais's film insistently repeats itself, and these repeated images occupy the screen as a sign of our inability to distinguish between the reality and the fictive nature of the images we have witnessed. But Resnais (and in his wake Louis Malle) also evokes the danger of the repetition compulsion encountered in the damaged self that will tragically repeat the same thing over and over again.[19] The arrangement in both films is constructed specifically to deny visual pleasure and to substitute an unpleasurable experience of doubt, anxiety, and trauma.

If we do not observe the insistence on mirrors in Malle's film that we did in Resnais's, we can observe a similar insistence on mirroring. Note how much Jeremy Irons and Juliette Binoche resemble each other, in expression, hair color and hair style (cf. Hart (1991), p. 36; "In her I had recognized myself"). Remember that Anna has confessed that she chose Martyn because of his resemblance to her dead brother. Malle creates a nightmare of surface repetitions, the same endlessly projecting itself onto an alienated other, ending, of course, in a still photo in which each of the three figures in the triangle resembles each of the others. The photo is nothing but an objective projection of Stephen's desire. The term "projection" evokes the Freudian term designating a defense mechanism consisting in attributing to another representations and affects which the subject refuses to recognize as his own; but it also suggests the cinema: images which, when projected, allow us to identify with them, yet remain outside us.

And so the film ends with Martyn's horrifying glimpse of the primal scene (his father perceived in naked penetration of his lover) causing him to lurch *backwards* and fall to his death.

Malle seems to intend this primal scene to be a specifically oedipal fantasy, one which inevitably involves an incestuous and regressive desire ending not in development but in death (for Martyn), flight (for Anna) or a death-like stasis (for Stephen). The film's ending in which Stephen stands transfixed, staring at the photograph of himself mirrored in his son and his lover is particularly *cinematic* because it constitutes a freeze-frame of what is normally ongoing (the flow of cinematic images). And so, we might conclude that Malle's version of this story has rather weighty implications for the way we regressively identify with what we see on the screen.

Without explicitly articulating Hart's metaphor of unlocatable geography with its particular emphasis on narcissism, Louis Malle has rendered it in his own language: an intertextual "geography" of three films which open the following psychoanalytic and meta-cinematic commentary:

1   Desire is always in some sense incestuous and regressive in that it seems to be based on the child's first experiences, and seems merely projective: i.e. the discovery of one's own aims in an alienated "other";
2   Desire inevitably functions outside of any concrete space/time map by virtue of its tendency to re-enact a repetition compulsion which collapses the present and the past into a maddening sameness;
3   Film viewing repeats the features of desire in general, that is to say it engages the viewer in a mirroring and projective experience that is regressive and repetitive in nature and allows him to maintain the desired object at a distance.

What Malle seems to have achieved in *Damage* is nothing less than a profound meditation on the way film produces its own maps of our most basic impulses. Malle's complex edifice seems to be suggesting that film appeals to the Oedipus complex in its most incestuous (primal scene) and regressive form (fixing us in a frozen moment from which escape seems impossible).

Through his transposition of Josephine Hart's metaphor of unlocatable geography into the geography of intertextuality, Malle engages us in the quintessence of film viewing: mirroring, regression, a sense of fragmentation frustrating our desire for stasis. In so doing, he suggests the inevitability of the implied violence in fiction film. In other words, the damage in *Damage* is already there in all of us. Ultimately he suggests that the map on the screen is also a "deforming mirror in which the spectator looks at himself" – one that we have seen in many different films.

Mapping Against Geography in Kieslowski's *Red*

Louis Malle's forays into the streets of London (or New Orleans, Atlantic City and New York before that)[20] forced a native speaker of French to find his way through an English- speaking landscape and to make sense of it. Likewise, after nearly thirty years in his native Poland spent shooting some forty films in Polish, Krystof Kieslowski found his way to Paris to shoot *Blue* and *White*, and ultimately to Geneva, where he shot his final work, *Red* [*Rouge*]. Negotiating these French-speaking cities with very limited French must have posed serious problems for Poland's greatest filmmaker. One scene in *Red* speaks directly to these difficulties of finding one's way.

In simplest terms, the film portrays the parallel lives of Valentine (Irène Jacob), a model involved in a very destructive long-distance relationship with a man named Michel, and Auguste (Jean-Pierre Lorit), a young law student destined to lose his girlfriend, Karin (Frédérique Feder), who operates a personalized weather service. Valentine and Auguste live near enough to cross paths, but would never cross destinies were it not for the agency of a third character, a retired judge (Jean-Louis Trintignant), who lives near enough to Karin to "wiretap" her phone conversations by means of a very sophisticated short-wave receiver. Valentine meets this crusty old hermit when she returns his dog to him after "accidentally" running it down with her car. Appalled to discover his "voyeuristic" wiretapping hobby, she urges him to cease such a disgusting activity, and leaves (with the dog). She subsequently reads in the Geneva papers that he has been hauled into court by his neighbors. When she returns to assure him that it was not she who denounced him, he tells her he has denounced himself "in order to see what she would do." Later, he visits her at one of her modeling shows and learns that she is leaving for several weeks in England (presumably to visit her hysterically possessive lover, Michel).

Valentine boards the channel ferry unaware that she is embarking with Auguste (on his way to England in desperate pursuit of Karin, who has run off with another man). As he sits alone in his hermetic retreat in Carrouges, the judge watches a TV news report of the devastating news of the ferry's sinking. Only seven of the fifteen hundred passengers aboard survive, and Valentine and Auguste are shown consoling each other, presumably brought together by "destiny."[21]

The scene which most graphically communicates the director's own encounter with the "maze" of Geneva streets occurs immediately after Valentine has hit the judge's dog. She gets out of her car and painstakingly

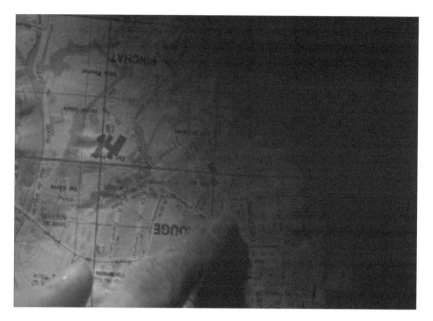

Plate 4.4   The upside down map

lifts and carries the wounded animal to her sedan and places her carefully on the back seat. After checking the address of the owner on the dog's collar, she pulls out a map of Geneva and studies it. Still unable to get oriented, she *turns the map over and studies it upside down*. Now, to be sure, we are all likely to copy her gesture when we need to drive south and to "correct" the map which, when right side up makes left-hand turns look like right-hand turns. The upside down map thus, ironically, provides a "corrected" orientation. One of the words appearing upside down on the map is Carrouges – a district of Geneva, but also by its obvious pun, a designation of something that is not on the map: Auguste's red jeep. This *inversion* of the map coupled with the *code* written upside down on the map and designating something that cannot be part of the map's cartographic function force us to think that Kieslowski's atlas in this film is going to be of a world "*à l'envers* [upside down]" and one whose itinerary must be followed by some other code that we must substitute for any known cartography.[22]

Evidence that this other code is, indeed, in operation will occur when, without ever asking for her name or address, Joseph Kern will have money delivered to her apartment. No explanation will ever be given for this mysterious knowledge.

But there is another mystery, closer to hand, which may help us discover one of the codes we must read to make our way through this maze-like environment. Again, I suggest you put the book down and watch the scene in which Valentine hits Rita. Listen especially for the sounds emanating from the car radio.

What did you hear? Just before her car strikes poor Rita and throws her limp body onto the street, Valentine has been frantically attempting to adjust her car radio, which has suddenly gone haywire. Indeed, it is precisely *because* she is thus occupied that she does not see the animal and runs into her. In other words, without this "accident," Valentine would never meet the judge and the rest would *not*, as we say, be history. How curious, then, that the signal we hear on the car radio is of a *short-wave* transmission, a frequency not normally accessible on our own car radios. You will have immediately recognized that this is the judge's "signature" sound. Immediately upon entering his house, she hears this same, very high-frequency modulation, and discovers that he is engaged in voyeuristically eavesdropping on his neighbors. It is, in short, his most obvious (and very likely only) connection with others. It suggests that this is one of the other "maps" at work in the film to which we may gain access by listening very carefully to the soundtrack.[23] I would like to come back to this subject at the end of our discussion of *Red*.

Rita, herself, may constitute another of these "orienting factors." She "brings" Valentine to the judge, of course, but it is her later itinerary that should give us pause. While walking her in a park near her apartment, Valentine unleashes her new pet and advises her, "Don't run off, now!" But Rita knows better. She is off immediately and heads for a nearby church. Valentine follows, and, unable to see Rita in the dimly lit interior, asks the priest presiding over mass whether he has seen her dog. He nods toward the door and Kieslowski's camera pans quickly to the door where we see Rita exiting. We have to wonder why the film's author felt it important to include a scene in which a dog leads his heroine to a house of god. Should this too be considered an orientation to the world of *Red* that we should heed?

Both of these possible paths are much overshadowed by the most significant mapping process in the film, this one announced by the film's title. Almost without exception, in order to move from one scene (locus of interest) to another, Kieslowski offers a simplified one-color map. It is enough to follow the "dots" of the color red to grasp the important connections between various scenes. As I have already suggested, Auguste's red jeep is a kind of station wagon (in the sense of constituting a movable terminus) for our attention. As Valentine stops for a coffee on her way to work, a bright red awning announces that she is entering "Chez Joseph" – an entry, as we will see in the next chapter, no less eerie than Adele's arrival into her film through her father's drawings. Joseph is, of course, the name of the judge who is to change her life. As these instances of the color red multiply, we might imagine a huge map of Geneva on which, instead of streets, parks and lakes, we would see a series of red dots, each of which would be connected with each of the others.

The French philosopher and film theorist, Gilles Deleuze, has suggested that there is something in cinema that goes beyond the colored image. He writes:

> In opposition to the simply colored image, the color-image does not refer to a particular object, but absorbs all that it can: it is the power which seizes all that happens within its range, or the quality common to completely differ-ent objects. There *is* a symbolism of colors, but it does not consist in cor-respondence between a color and an affect (green and hope, for example). Color is on the contrary the affect itself that is the virtual conjunction of all the objects which it picks up.[24]

This passage seems (although it was not written specifically with Kieslowski in mind) to capture the essence of how color works (much as do rhymes in poetry) to link up otherwise heterogeneous objects in *Red*. But, uncan-nily, in another passage (on yet another filmmaker) Deleuze discusses a concept that he terms (pertinently to our discussion of mapping and *Red*), the "any space whatever." As an example of the way this "any space what-ever" can be linked to color, Deleuze adds:

> The "any space whatever" takes on a new nature [with color]. It is no longer as before a space which is defined by parts whose linking up and orientation are not determined in advance ... It is now an amorphous set which has eliminated that which happened and acted in it. It is clear that the two aspects are complementary, and reciprocally presuppose each other: the amorphous set in fact is a collection of locations or positions *which exist independently of the temporary order* which moves from one part to the other, independently of the connections and orientation which the characters and situations give to them. The "any space whatever" ... no longer has co-ordinates, it is a pure potential, it shows only pure Powers and Qualities, independently of the states of things or milieus which actualize them.[25]

I would now ask you to go back to the film and make a list of these " red dots."

It will not have surprised you to see that the entire series of these ele-ments creates a huge web whose center is the enormous billboard standing

Plate 4.5   Auguste drops his book

at the intersection where Auguste and Valentine first cross paths, where he drops his book in the street, effecting an uncanny temporal intersection with Joseph Kern, who, years before, had dropped his law book in the very red theater where Valentine models on the runway. In this single instant in *Red*, Kieslowski seems to map a space that defies plane geography and linear chronology. The color red thus links up not only those events and characters chronologically connected in a linear arrangement of time, but those whose lives are connected outside of any concept we have of linear chronology.

The last and, in my view, most breathtaking example of the way color transcends space and time in this film involves three separate scenes from the film. In the final moments of *Red*, we see Auguste, Valentine, and four other actors from Kieslowski's other films, pulled to safety from the frigid waters of the English Channel. Suddenly we see Valentine's traumatized face against a red blanket – and immediately recognize it as an exact replica of her photograph on the immense billboard in central Geneva. I would ask you, however, to go back to the scene in the photographer's studio where this picture is taken. Please play this scene with the sound turned all the way up, and ask yourself what you hear. Uncannily, you report that, against all logic, you hear a foghorn as the fans of the Geneva studio ruffle the red material behind Valentine. Suddenly you realize in this return to the earliest appearance of this image that it is impossible to distinguish between the first and last iterations of Valentine's sad visage. We are, as Deleuze would phrase it, in "any space whatever" and beyond temporality.

We begin to understand that this particular system of connections has a remarkably archaic quality to it. Kieslowski's own statements about his life and work suggest such a matrix: "*Red* is really about whether people aren't by chance sometimes born at the wrong time. The quintessential question is, is it possible to repair a mistake which was committed somewhere high above? ... Has a mistake been committed somewhere? And if it has, then is there anybody in a position to rectify it?"[26] This desire for rectification seems to lead in *Red* to the person of the judge.

In reference to his earlier work, *Dekalog*, Kieslowski asked:

> What, in essence, is right and what is wrong? ... And what should one's attitude toward it be? I think that an absolute point of reference does exist. Although I must say that when I think of God it's more often the God of the Old Testament ... a demanding, cruel God; a God who doesn't forgive, who ruthlessly demands obedience to the principles which He has laid down ... The God of the Old Testament leaves us a lot of freedom and responsibility, observes how we use it and he rewards or punishes, and there's no appeal or forgiveness. It's something which is lasting, absolute, evident and is not relative. And that's what a point of reference must be, especially for people like me, who are weak, who are looking for something, who don't know.[27]

The more we think about the role of the judge the more uncanny he seems to be. On the one hand the judge seems to be an older version of Auguste, for, like the young jurist on whom he eavesdrops, he also once dropped his copy of the *General Penal Code* and stooped to read the passage that lay open on the ground. For both men, "it was exactly the passage they asked me on the exam." Like Auguste, the retired judge once loved a delicate blonde woman whom he caught "with her legs spread with a man between them." Like Auguste he catches a ferry boat to follow her to England, where, uncannily, she dies in an accident. (Although we do not know how the judge's lover died, we know that Karin will be lost at sea on her yacht during the same storm that capsizes the channel ferry.)

As Kieslowski himself says, "We'll never be sure whether Auguste really exists or whether he is only a variation of the judge's life forty years later."[28] This retired judge is not only the double of a man known to the viewer but not, as yet to Valentine, nor is he merely omniscient: he seems to enjoy what we might term "the omnipotence of thoughts." At various times in the film, the judge indicates that he has already decided how things are going to turn out. He laments early on to Valentine that when he was a judge he didn't know whether he was on the good or bad side and that he had retired after condemning a man he wanted to kill even though the judgment was "legal." Now, distanced from those he had formerly had to judge, he claims, "Here, at least I know the truth." Although claiming to have retired from his role as judge, he seems to have now become a supreme judge. "Sooner or later," he says of his homosexual neighbor, "he will throw himself out the window." Valentine, interceding for humanity, argues "People aren't bad, it's not true!" But the judge is convinced otherwise. Certain that Karin is not the right woman for Auguste, he tells Valentine, "It's almost over." "You provoked it?" she asks, and he responds enigmatically, "Because of my trial this girl met another man." This seems to be the way the "last judgment" of this film is initiated.

In their conversation at the theater, Valentine, awestruck by his seeming omniscience, exclaims, "I feel something important going on around me." Immediately a great wind can be heard beating at the windows of the theater.[29] "Who are you?" she demands.

Who indeed? When Valentine tells him she would like to go to England but is afraid of leaving her brother, he says to her, "Leaving is your destiny. You can't live your brother's life … Just be." And then he adds offhandedly, "You like planes. Take the ferry." "Do your dreams become reality?" she asks moments later. His answer can be deduced from his diabolical laugh when Karin tells him she is leaving her job and, as a last professional act, announces that the weather over the channel will be "fine." When the Judge takes leave of Valentine, he ominously asks for her ticket, insistently verifies it and then returns it. The sudden storm that bursts out of a clear blue sky capsizes the channel ferry, allowing only seven "chosen" people to escape its wrath: six of Kieslowski's characters from *Blue, White* and *Red* and the ferry's barman.[30]

Kieslowski once said:

> There's a need within us – not only a need but also a fundamental kind of feeling – to believe that those who have gone and whom we dearly loved, who were important to us, are constantly within and around us … I mean that they exist within us as somebody who judges us and that we take their opinions into account even though they're not there any more, even though they're dead. It's some sort of ethical system which exists somewhere within.[31]

It is precisely such a system, based on such a judge, which seems to function in *Red*. Not that it functions all that well. The Judge is, after all, something of a nihilist when we first meet him, insisting that he wants nothing and that people are just plain bad. But, as Kieslowski also noted, "As somebody once said, if God didn't exist, then somebody would have to invent him. I don't think we've got perfect justice here on earth, and we never will have. It's justice on our own scale: minute ... and imperfect."[32] And yet, a middle-aged judge in Carrouges, whose dreams have powerful prophetic properties, offers us a new path to the intuition that things might be otherwise.

When we reflect that the most prophetic and transcendent of the conversations between Valentine and the judge takes place *in a theater*, we can suddenly perceive the connections between the fictional figure of the judge and the real function of the director. Just as Joseph Kern has somehow to invent and "manage" a system of interrelationships that will "correct" Auguste's, Valentine's, and his own life, Krystof Kieslowski manages to invent in his "last work and testament" a new vision of the cinema – one that replaces geography and chronology with color, visual associations, and a transcendence of linear time. It is, after all, only in the cinema that these coordinates can exist to the degree they do to create a visual cartography as powerful as the one in *Red*. Polish though he may be by nationality, in adopting the French cinema, Kieslowski has adopted its most persistent trait. His film answers, above all, the question "What is cinema?" with the answer: It is a map without lines, the ultimate orientation to a world that has lost its bearings.

Suggested Further Reading

French, P. (ed.) (1993), *Malle on Malle*. London: Faber & Faber.
    Provides a wealth of material on Malle's films from the director's point of view.
Kline, T. J. (1987), "Last Tango in Paris." In *Bertolucci's Dream Loom: A Psychoanalytic Study of Cinema*. Amherst, MA: University of Massachusetts Press, pp. 106–26.
    Provides a context for the allusions to *Last Tango* in *Damage*.
Kline, T. J. (2006), "*Last Year at Marienbad*: High Modern and Postmodern." In Perry, T. (ed.), *Masterpieces of Modernist Cinema*. Bloomington, IN: Indiana University Press, pp. 208–35.
    Provides a context for the allusions to *Marienbad* in *Damage*.
Stok, D. (ed.) (1993), *Kieslowski on Kieslowski*. London: Faber & Faber.
    Provides a wealth of material on Kieslowski's film from the director's point of view.

Cinema and/as Dream
Truffaut's "Royal Road" to *Adele H.*

"It's the thing that annoys the audience the most; they'll accept anything except to be awakened from the dream they're having in the movie theater. Within this dream you can make them swallow anything, but if you tell them that the dream they're experiencing has a speed of 24 frames a second and that it comes out of an acid bath and the Technicolor labs [down the street], then they get angry and won't go along with it." (Bernardo Bertolucci)[1]

François Truffaut's representation of a map in the opening moments of *The Story of Adele H.* appears at first glance to be the most conventional geographic illustration of any we have encountered in this study. We should not, however, be lulled into believing that his map will bring us any closer to historical reality than any of the others we have discussed. On the contrary, as we shall see, *Adele* may take us farther from a locatable space than any of the films discussed so far.

By the time he began shooting *Adele H.* in 1974, Truffaut had spent three years in acrimonious negotiations with Frances Vernor Guille, the professor at Wooster College in Ohio who had unearthed Adele's private diaries at the Pierpont Morgan Library in New York and laboriously decoded them. There could be little doubt that Truffaut intended to make this narrative of the last years of Victor Hugo's younger daughter as faithful as possible to Adele's own journal records, and counted on this "translation" of her secret writings to provide that authenticity. Having finally gained access to Adele's own words and private thoughts, Truffaut made every effort to provide an historical decor so realistic that it might be mistaken for the Halifax of 1863, where the story is set. Shot on location in Halifax, with costumes and decors designed to copy the fashions of the day, the film seems at first glance to be paying homage to Renoir's (and Bazin's) credo of realism. And, as if these elements were not enough, we are informed by an insert at the end of the credits that "The story of *Adele H.* is true (*authentique*). It is about events that really happened and people who really existed." An impressively authoritative narrative voice(-off) goes on to inform us that we are to witness events that occurred in 1863 "in the Canadian town of Halifax, capital of Nova Scotia, formerly known as French Acadia." Thanks to these history and geography lessons, we are now perfectly situated to trust the historical "veracity" of what we are about to see.

Were this a Hollywood film, we could settle into this "biopic" genre, and expect that the authenticity referred to served as a guarantor of the historical accuracy of the events described. But this is, need I remind you, a French film and no such comfort will be afforded. From the first visuals of this film, Truffaut manages to create an uneasy tension between printed and voiced statements about "authenticity" on the one hand and, on the other, the film's images. Indeed, if there were ever a mistranslation that expressed the difference between French and Hollywood mentalities it is the use of the word "true" to "translate" the French word "*authentique*." "True" evokes the idea of historical accuracy, where as "*authentique*" suggests another possibility: what would be an *authentic* representation of Adele's point of view? Was she so concerned with history? Will her story have anything to do with the tensions created by the civil war occurring hundreds of miles to the south? Does the ethnography of Halifax really matter? If, perhaps, these are not her concerns, how will Truffaut get at what really animates his young heroine?

The answers to these last questions begin to emerge even as the credits unroll – a moment in most films that requires no attention from the film's viewer. Here, however, the film's title and subsequent list of characters are filmed against an eerie backdrop of watercolors and sketches of ruined castles, seascapes, including an enormous wave that seems poised to crash violently to the beach, carrying away everything in its path. Our awareness of these drawings, which serve as a backdrop to the words "The story of Adele H. is about events that really happened and people who really existed," creates an odd sense of dissonance – what one of my students labeled a nagging sense of "dysauthenticity." The gloom and foreboding communicated by these shadowy figures of decay and immersion is only

Plate 5.1   The Wave of Destiny breaks over Adele's actress

heightened when we realize that the author of these drawings is none other than Victor Hugo himself. Since Adele has come to Halifax to escape the influence of her father, and especially since she has changed her name to mask the identity of her father, Victor Hugo's foothold in the film – established well before Adele herself can make her own appearance – casts an enormous shadow over the film as a whole. His overbearing presence is only reinforced when we see the name of the actress who is to play Adele, Isabelle Adjani, written across the underside of that enormous wave. Not surprisingly Victor Hugo ominously entitled this drawing "La Destinée." Thus we *anticipate*, well before we catch a glimpse of her, Adele's stand-in's claustrophobic relationship to her father and we begin to sense how inescapable will be his hold on his daughter. What Truffaut has already accomplished here is a shift of authenticity away from the historical to the realm of creative expression and feeling.

Once alerted to this dissonant or "dysauthentic" element of the film, we begin to notice other signs of it in this opening sequence. The antiquarian maps that fill the screen as "evidence" that we are being directed to a Halifax of the mid-nineteenth century soon begin to lose their authenticity as guides, for we do not so much follow a direction indicated "upon" them (as we do, for example, by following the dotted line across the world map in the opening moments of *Raiders of the Lost Ark*) but, instead, plunge down *into* them. Rather than obeying its function as indicator of spatial relations, the map suddenly acts as a kind of magic carpet, transporting us to Halifax not across named spaces but by a vertiginous fall into a dot labeled "Halifax"! For geography, Truffaut has substituted a kind of time travel like that imagined in *Back to the Future*.

And this vertiginous free fall takes us not to the scene that the narrator describes as "passengers disembarking from the *Great Eastern*, a huge steamship also known as 'The Floating City,' " but rather to another drawing. This time, the drawing is engulfed in darkness and then gradually, thanks to the light of a "real" lantern attached to the bow of a longboat, we catch our first glimpse of the diegetic world of Adele, who sits huddled in the Canadian darkness aboard this landing skiff.

We begin to suspect, then, that the only real access to Adele's mind and story cannot be "officially narrated" by a disembodied authoritative male voice[2] but appears through this shadowy realm of night and fog, of the imaginary, of the shadowland imposed on her own imagination by her father's visions. But this conclusion itself will be further inflected by the unusual rendering of Adele's arrival on the docks of Halifax.

Suppose I were to ask you to look again at the scene on the quay, focusing on camera angles, the soundtrack, the presence of mist or smoke and Adele's particular itinerary through the customs check-point? Suppose as your assignment, I were to ask you, "What's wrong with this picture?"

Did you notice that when Isabelle Adjani makes her appearance, it is as though Truffaut's cameraman was never told who she was and failed to train his lens on her long enough to "single her out" from among the passengers climbing the stairs up out of the darkness of the water? When Adele does come into full focus, she still does not enjoy the central role in the drama. Some anonymous and very loud traveler has captured the camera and microphone's attention and argues heatedly with the Canadian border police over whether he has his identity papers. Why should we have to be privy to this dispute? We never see or hear of this man again. And yet, his voice will continue to occupy the entirety of the soundtrack even after Adele has left the area and climbed into a cab.

Might this have something to do with Adele's own situation? After all, if she presents her own papers (we realize only later), she will have a problem with the continued concealment of her identity and this she will not do. And yet the threat of discovery is so real as to entirely fill her and our hearing despite the presence of many other voyagers nearby. Here we might conclude that this sound is not "objectively" rendered, but instead what we hear is what occupies Adele's particular obsession. We would call this a very *subjective* use of the soundtrack. The "authenticity" of this scene has been shifted from the realism of the collective or historical to that of the obsessively personal. What is "real" here is not quite believable in any objective sense but rather what Adele herself is experiencing.

This said, we begin to see other signs of something gone amiss. If showing one's papers is part of the process of disembarking, why is it so easy for Adele to simply leave this post, and take a circuitous route around the customs barrier and out into the city? Can we find any rational explanation for this procedure? Why is there a mist blowing from the landside rather than in from the sea? Does the "fog" appear natural, then, or might it belong more to the state of mind of the character than the meteorological conditions obtaining in this scene? When Adele passes a large crate on her way out of the customs area, why do we see a huge letter "N" on one of the wooden boxes? Could this have anything to do with her father's own obsession with Louis Napoleon and *his* self-imposed exile from France? Might that be related to what we come to discover to be Adele's own self-imposed flight from home?

If I asked you, based on the camera angles provided, where the cab was in relation to the customs barrier, you would be obliged to conclude that it was situated on higher ground, since we are observing this entire scene from some three meters above it. And yet Adele ascends no stairs to reach the cab. She is suddenly and almost magically there. I will not speculate on the availability of cabs at moments like these when hundreds of passengers are debarking from *The Great Eastern*, but it is curious that this particular cab driver has selected Adele for his charge and, what's more, spends the entire rest of the film at her immediate beck and call at all hours of the day and night. Have you ever seen a portrait of Victor Hugo? Try searching on the web for a likeness of France's greatest poet. Whom does he resemble? Or more simply stated, isn't it surprising how much this particular cab driver just happens to look like one of France's greatest poets? (Might he also resemble another famous person?)

Under what circumstances might we undertake a journey, travel through a series of fantastic landscapes, debark from a boat, emerge in the darkness of night from a watery expanse, find ourselves wholly occupied with another person's struggle for identity with a representative of a soldiery who looks and dresses like our once and future lover yet then be able quite magically to walk around this authority figure and find ourselves lifted magically through the fog and mist of this nocturnal space into the waiting arms of a father figure whom we are both fleeing and seeking?

Might we not now hazard a guess that what Truffaut is telling us here is that he has elected to tell us the "authentic" story of Adele by means other than historical ones. Should we not conclude that instead of sticking to an objective rendering (remember the "referential" code in our discussion of journalism vs. poetry?) of her adventure, he has chosen to enter it through a much more subjective realm? Are we not, quite simply, accompanying Adele in one of her dreams?

At the risk of testing your patience and forestalling our interpretation of this remarkable film, I must again assume my French cap and ask, "So what is a dream anyway?" for remember that we do not dare take a step in this venture without doing as the French would do: define our terms. And if Truffaut has chosen to use cinema to represent the dream-life of Adele, is he not *also* asking to what degree cinema itself isn't akin to dream? Or even, isn't the connection between cinema and dream in fact more ontologically based than that between cinema and poetry or cinema and the real?

The following time-out is brought to you by *dreamworks* – not the company founded by Steven Spielberg, but the thinking initiated by a man whose work on dreams just happens to be coeval with the invention of the cinema. If we turn to the work of Sigmund Freud here, it is not in any way in a spirit of indoctrination, but rather with the notion that Freud's theories (and they are nothing more than theories) have been so influential in twentieth-century thought, and particularly in France's critical and theoretical thinking about the cinema, that French filmmakers themselves have often worked consciously or unconsciously in the aura of Freud's theories. We must remember that Truffaut himself said, "In relation to American filmmakers we French are all intellectuals."[3] Such a position certainly encourages us once again to explore the theory behind his practice.

In *The Interpretation of Dreams* (and in other related works), Freud proposed that our mental functioning is generally divided into conscious and unconscious processes. In Freud's "topology" of the mind, the unconscious was the "place" to which were relegated thoughts and feelings that were unacceptable to our waking mental operations. The part of the unconscious Freud labeled the id thus became the repository of all of those feelings and drives that were either condemned as being socially unacceptable (sexual and primitive drives, violent fantasies), or those feelings and memories that were too traumatic and painful to hold in our conscious memory bank (childhood molestation, for example). What makes Freud's theories so compelling, though, is that, working as he did in the light of contemporaneous work on the laws of thermodynamics, he saw the entire unconscious process in dynamic rather than static terms. Although the first and second laws of thermodynamics had been established by the late nineteenth century, what is called the "zeroth" law was developed during the first years of the twentieth century. This law dictated that when two systems enter into contact with each other, an exchange of energy will take place unless they are in equilibrium (that is, have the same amount of thermal energy). By adapting this idea to his model of the unconscious, Freud introduced a crucial concept. Rather than seeing the id as a dormant repository of buried material, the father of psychoanalysis believed that everything that was "contained" therein was charged with a kind of "thermal energy" that sought to be released. This in turn required Freud to posit that, since any expression of these drives had to be kept under control, then there must be another realm of the unconscious (that Freud will label the superego) whose role is to counter the force of the id's drives with an equal amount of energy. In this way, Freud arrived at the notion of repression. Hidden away from our conscious minds, a battle is constantly being waged by superego and id that requires the former to match the energy of the latter. If the superego is unable to match the energy generated by the repressed drives, that energy will escape and, depending on the amount of energy escaping, will cause a disruption of our mental equilibrium. The techniques of psychoanalysis were developed in order to deal with such disequilibria that might produce neurotic symptoms (for example obsessive-compulsive behaviors) or worse, psychosis, a breakdown of mental stability leading to chaos.

When Freud turned his attention to the phenomenon of dreams, he theorized that these nighttime visions occur because the superego tends to relax its vigil against the dynamic forces of the id and, as it devotes less energy to the work of repression, some of the contents of the id will work their way into our semi-conscious minds. Freud thus theorized that every dream represents in some way the fulfillment of a wish that is alien and felt to be unacceptable to our conscious minds. Given this belief in the dream's role as wish fulfillment, Freud baptized the dream the "Royal Road to the Unconscious." But the trip along this "road" was not to be an easy one. The author of *The Interpretation of Dreams* (1900) calculated that, were the wish to be represented in undisguised form, it would create so much disturbance that it would sound the alarm to the dormant forces of repression which, in turn, would wake the dreamer from his sleep. It is for this reason, Freud reasoned, that the dream must take on a disguise and present itself in costumes and false identities that are initially unrecognizable to the ego. If I dream, for example, that I am in bed with my mother, my superego will likely get me up and out of bed as quickly as possible! If, however, I disguise both characters in the dream so that my own self will be played by another, and my mother represented by some less incestuous figure, then I will likely sleep on undisturbed and enjoy the pleasures afforded by this more "innocent" scenario. The beauty of the dream's censorship is that it hides unacceptable wishes well enough to permit the dream to appear but not so well that we are unable to see the censorship at work. It both masks and reveals itself.

The more he thought about this process, the more Freud discovered about what he called the dreamwork. He saw in the dream that we report upon awakening a "manifest content" that seemed to tell a story, but that was full of gaps, inconsistencies, and odd juxtapositions. When properly analyzed (using the technique of free association), the dream offered up a "latent content" that revealed the set of wishes that were seeking expression (what Freud called the "return of the repressed"). All the "distortions" of the manifest dream seemed to Freud to belong to a type of thinking that was older, more primitive, more imagistic, less rational than the thinking we do in our conscious state. These "distortions" Freud called "primary process thinking," and he included as fundamental to this process three types of mental activity: projection, displacement, and condensation. Projection does as its name suggests: it projects our own feelings, desires, and intentions onto another person in order to free us of the guilt or embarrassment of "owning" them. Thus, we may see Glenda in our dream as extremely angry, but the anger is really in us. In the work of displacement, we may take sexual or hostile feelings that are secretly directed at our mother and redirect them onto a more innocent object. The work of condensation allows a desire or impulse to be joined with a less threatening idea and be represented in what Freud called a "compromise formation." I remember when I sang for a chorus years ago that the director who was quite wary of us "back-row basses" nevertheless felt he had to applaud our singing of a particular passage from Bach's "*Jesu, meine freude.*" "Basses," he crowed, "that was perfectly inspiratorial!" It doesn't take much sleuthing to figure out that he had managed to express his hostility to our bumptious back-row behavior by including in his praise the unlikely suffix "-atorial" – syllables that normally conclude the word "*con*spiratorial." This "compromise" between the disguised but ever-present hostility and the need for praise was "perfectly" expressed in this "Freudian slip." In a dream, the work of condensation may be seen in such blendings of words, but also in the conjoining of two different places or two different people in one. How often have you tried to tell a dream in which you find yourself saying, "Well, the person in my dream was like Ned, only he was also sort of like my brother, Michael ..."

The primary processes, Freud contended, were responsible for the particularly oneiric nature of dreams – principally their "overdetermination": "Dreams frequently seem to have more than one meaning. Not only ... may they include several wish-fulfillments one alongside the other; but a succession of meanings or wish-fulfillments may be superimposed on one another."[4]

To these primary processes, Freud added a few other observations about the dreamwork. Noting the very unusual chronology of our dreams, he theorized that the reason for the gaps and jumps in time is that all dreams

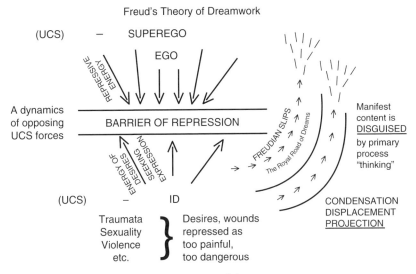

Figure 5.1   A diagram of Freud's theory of dreams

are using events of the very recent past as points of departure, yet inevitably go back to include elements from our earliest memories. Dreams are inevitably "timeless" because they are condensing different pieces of our past into one short narrative stream. And, because of the way primary processes work, Freud concluded that all of the characters of our dreams are but versions of ourselves. To unravel the meaning of the manifest content of the dream, Freud proposed that, rather than treat the dream narrative as an allegory (the way, for example Joseph interprets Pharaoh's dreams), we should rather take each detail of the dream and mine it for its associations. Thus, it may often be the almost unnoticed or marginal element in the dream which hides (and eventually renders up) the most important lode of psychic material.

To sum up, we might use the following diagram to show the way unconscious impulses meet the barrier of repression, and, instead of storming the barricades, simply disguise themselves as innocent travelers and circumvent the "night watchmen on duty."

I suggest you look carefully at Figure 5.1. Just stare at it for a few moments. Now, turn the book over so that the diagram is inverted. Does anything strike you about it? Does it look familiar in any way? Have we not just watched Adele emerge from the deepest watery night, awash in the fictions of her father's fantasies? Have we not seen her approach the customs barrier and, rather than attempt to show her identity cards, simply take a circuitous route instead, moving ever upward into visibility, yet carefully disguised as "Miss Lewly." And does she not enter a hansom chauffeured by a man who is a condensation of cab driver and father? Certainly Mr O'Brien is but a marginal figure in this scenario – or is he? And the paperless traveler caught by the Customs Officers will never reappear in this film, and yet he occupies a primary place: that of a double of the film's heroine. Onto this man, all of Adele's anxieties about her identity have been conveniently displaced. And when O'Brien stops at a hotel that seems too bright and too noisy to Adele, does she not project onto the group off-screen some hostility that we cannot yet understand? Truffaut once said, "Le cinema est l'art du petit detail qui ne frappe pas. [The cinema is the art of the little detail that almost goes unnoticed]."[5] Uncannily, in response to her refusal to stop at the hotel, O'Brien says, "If you'll take my advice, you'll go to a boarding house" (Sc. 24). Freud noted that "nothing in the dream is a matter of chance or of indifference and it is precisely by enquiring into such trivial and (apparently) unmotivated details that we expect to arrive at … the meaning of the latent dream thoughts."[6] Now in a bi-lingual film, a bi-lingual pun is quite "at home." If she stays at a "boarding house," Adele will be a "border": i.e. on the boundary again, where we spied her for the first time. For does she not perfectly *represent* the borderline between waking and dreaming?

There seems little doubt that we have been introduced by Truffaut not to an "authenticity" guaranteed by the geography of Halifax and the history of the American civil war, but rather to a symbolic landscape, itself representative of the civil war that is taking place in Adele's increasingly chaotic mental state. Moreover, Adele's specific itinerary in this opening scene not only places her within a particular dreamscape, but also, and quite uncannily, suggests that she is the personification of the dream state itself! In this way, once again, we see a French film whose real – or should we say authentic? – subject becomes a meditation on the nature of dreams and the relationship between dreaming and filming.[7]

Now it is no great work to perceive how closely the *structure* of films replicates that of dreams. First and foremost, films, like dreams, are primarily pictorial events. True, since 1929, films have had the capacity to accompany these images with sounds of all kinds, diegetic (or realistic) sounds of noises or the speech of characters, extra-diegetic music or voices, etc. Yet the language of cinema operates primarily through visual codes. The implications of this fact are enormous, but primarily center on the need for an act of interpretation that goes beyond the purely conceptual (the film's dialogue and narrative events) to include a whole range of visual and non-verbal cinematic communication.

Secondly, despite the grammar of continuity that has been pursued by the dominant Hollywood cinema practically from its inception, film is structurally a *discontinuous* event. Our eye may perceive a continuous series of movements within a given scene, but in actual fact, the projector lens opens and shuts 24 times a second, projecting 24 different frames. It is only because of the fact of retinal retention of the image that we gain the impression of continuity. This discontinuity was "tested" by the early poets of the cinema, such as Abel Gance, who shortened some of their segments down to two to four frames, segments that were "visible" but perceived primarily as highly discontinuous moments. Although almost never exploited by the classical Hollywood cinema, this discontinuity is nevertheless a feature of the cinema.

And discontinuity extends, as well, to film editing. If film, like dream, allows the possibility of reproducing images in continuous form from our daily lives, the norm is nevertheless for these events to be cut into discrete pieces, reassembled and displayed in an order that owes more to the filmmaker's (or dreamer's latent) desire for a particular meaning than to the order in which they were taken (i.e. experienced). (There is, in fact only one known fiction film that is not assembled from such disparate pieces, Hitchcock's *Rope*). Film's essential discontinuity allows, of course, for a non-linear presentation of events. Because both film and dream allow such discontinuity, older material can be introduced (either as flashback or as a chronologically unassimilable piece of the narration) into the "present" tense of the narrative. In both films and in dreams, time can be compressed or expanded in ways that defy rational explanation.

The implication of this understanding of cinematic structure is that, like dreams, films operate by means of discontinuous pieces whose relationship must be interpreted (reassembled) by an "analyst." In other words, the images processed by the film's viewer could be termed the "manifest" content of a work of art whose "latent" or metaphoric meanings are to be arrived at by an analytic work of association. And because these metaphoric meanings can be multiple, it can be argued that film is, like dream, potentially "overdetermined" in terms of its possible meanings. All of these elements of the common structure of dreams and the cinema have enormous implications for the language of film as well.

Inasmuch as cinematic images are representations of fantasy and function as displaced desire (either that of the director as author or that of the spectator as participant in the fantasies) it is arguable that displacement is an essential element of cinematic language. "The screen," corroborates Stanley Cavell, "makes displacement appear as our natural condition."[8] Cavell's comment neatly ties the production of cinema (as a conscious/

unconscious expression of the director's desire) to the consumption of cinema (as the viewer's conscious/unconscious identification with that representation). Not only is displacement a factor for the filmmaker (in displacing emotions from objects in his/her own life into representations) but it functions for the viewer via a strong projective-identification with the projected images themselves qua images.

But the coincidence of the language of cinema and dreams goes well beyond this remarkable double-entendre of projection. Cinema reveals its latent work in many other ways, most notably through the rapidity with which it is able to move from one shot to another, creating an effect of condensation.[9] It is by the juxtaposing of images that the filmmaker creates powerfully metaphoric meanings. But film need not operate with this degree of self-consciousness to produce the effect of condensation: Indeed, a single powerful image in an appropriately charged context may condense into a single moment many disparate and even self-contradictory or illogical connections.

Cinematic "language," then, must be understood, like that of dream, as an assemblage of visual elements, none of which "means" anything absolutely in and of itself, since there is no lexicon, but all of which must be studied together. Instead of a (rationally arranged) language, cinematic analysis makes use of many different codes whose arrangement in a particular scene operates by association to/with the various other cinematic elements at work: dialogue, diegetic sound, extra-diegetic sound (usually music), lighting, camera angles, camera movements, composition, editing, decor, period costumes, etc., few of which are codifiable as a fixed language. Of these, only dialogue could be assumed to operate at a "manifest" level of understanding. All of the others tend to be received at a "latent" level of consciousness and require the work of analysis (what Freud would call "secondary elaboration") in order to arrive at the meaning(s) of the work.

We might well ask, then, what might be the advantage of this analogy between dreams and films? Why should François Truffaut need to insist on it in this particular case? Our sense (given the "debate" between two notions of "authenticity" that figures so prominently during the credits of *Adele H.*) is that Truffaut wants his viewers not only to understand Adele as deeply as possible, but to understand that the cinema offers the best, most complete means for comprehending the pieces of her psychology (and ours) that are otherwise extremely difficult to grasp and to accept once grasped, and which, otherwise might remain inaccessible and incomprehensible.[10] But Truffaut won't leave it there: he wants us to understand in larger terms how the story of Adele (i.e. the psychology of the character) ends up being in some way the story of everyone who sits in a movie theater and *watches* her story (i.e. the psychology of the viewer). The first of these might be said to be thematic (related to the story); the second might be said to be meta-cinematic (related to a meditation on the nature of film). Once again we are face to face with the way a French filmmaker is going way beyond the "mere" story to propose a theory about the nature and possibilities of the medium itself.

I would like, therefore, to look at two scenes in this film, each of which develops one of these two "purposes" that Truffaut has set before us: the meta-cinematic (inasmuch as it comments on the nature of film) and the thematic (which links the nature of film to particular psychological states).

We learn, from their first encounter in the drawing room of the Saunders' rooming house, that Adele and Lieutenant Pinson had first met at Hauteville House on the island of Guernsey where Victor Hugo was serving out his self-imposed exile from the rule of "Little Napoleon." In that first conversation, Adele pleads for Pinson's love, and he does admit, "I did love you, Adele." And yet Pinson's love had withered, apparently because, as he says, "Your father despised me." Despite her entreaties, he remains stonily cold and tells her only, "You should not have come … I have only come to ask you to leave Halifax" (Sc. 71–2). The only "healthy" response to such a reception would be to pack one's bags. Adele, however, displays a series of reactions any one of which one might expect a rejected lover to express, but whose juxtaposition leaves us confused: she pleads, "Do with me whatever you want. I love you!" She bargains, "When I marry I'll have forty thousand francs." She tries to provoke his jealousy: "I have a proposal of marriage from Canizario." She threatens, "I will denounce you and have you thrown out of the army!" And finally she presses money on him "for your gambling debts." Ultimately we will come to understand that Pinson serves as the vehicle for the entire gamut of Adele's unavowed, unconscious impulses. Let's next turn to a scene that looks innocent enough – or rather seems at first glance to fit the logic of Adele's "love story."

The scene I'd like you to look at is entitled (appropriately enough) "Night Visions." The Saunders hear a thumping noise over their bedroom and Mrs Saunders mutters, "Poor child." Truffaut cuts to a view of Adele sitting at a small round table apparently having called up the spirit of her dead sister, Leopoldine. Now it is well known that Victor Hugo was an avid practitioner of this form of spiritism which had become all the rage in France in the mid-1850s. Sitting before a *table tournante* that mysteriously "levitated," Hugo had conjured up hundreds of spirits from André Chenier to Voltaire, and Adele had frequently been present at these séances, which in Hugo's case were limited to two participants only. The idea of communicating with the departed was naturally attractive even to the merely curious, still more to those who were in mourning for lost friends or family members. It should be noted that expectations favorable to the new idea had already been created by the interest in France in mesmerism and in the phenomena of the hypnotic trance. So epidemic was this practice that John Faraday and Michel-Eugène Chevreul were commissioned to make extensive studies of the phenomena, and both men concluded that the raps and elevation of the table were inspired by one of the participants, who was able, by the magnetic or hypnotic force of his character, to generate nonconscious responses in the other participant(s).[11] Faraday's and Chevreul's explanations of these phenomena suggest that the receiver(s) of the suggestions from this mesmerizing presence enter(s) into the production (or self-inducement in Adele's case) of an illusion that mimics a hallucinatory, trance-like state.

In this scene, Truffaut insists on the nocturnal nature of Adele's event, and, in a vertical pan that recalls the film's opening images (but in the opposite direction) the camera seems to move us from the Saunders' bedroom, up through the ceiling into Adele's room where she is indeed pictured in a hallucinatory trance. Her hands spread over a *table tournante* in imitation of her father, Adele addresses her dead sister: "Léopoldine, I know it's you. You must help me!" Now every student of Victor Hugo knows that he lost his older and favored daughter to a boating accident in the Seine, during which she drowned in the arms of her newlywed husband, who preferred to die in her drowned arms rather than outlive her. Students know this because Hugo dedicated to her "*Demain, dès l'aube*," considered by many to be his most beautiful poem. Thereafter, inconsolable at her death, he transformed their apartment on the Place des Vosges in Paris into a kind of museum in which to memorialize her. What many students may *not* know is that Léopoldine was not only Hugo's favored daughter, but may have been *his only* daughter since it was widely rumored that Adele was the child of an affair between Hugo's wife and his best friend, Sainte-Beuve. With this in mind, we may begin to understand Adele's fascination with her dead sister.

But we hardly have time to assimilate this first hallucinatory state before we have been transported with no transitional information of any kind into a nocturnal wooded landscape where a coach arrives in front of an isolated stone house. We watch as Pinson gets out of the coach to be met at the door by a woman of Adele's stature and coloring, who, smiling broadly at her visitor, advances to give him a passionate kiss and leads him inside. As the door closes, Truffaut cuts to the arrival of a second carriage, from which Adele emerges in a brilliant red gown, its scarlet coloring eerily matching Pinson's red coat. With her first steps toward the house, a nervous, suspenseful music begins and Adele seems to be running in time to this frenetic score. She enters a dark wood, and then emerges, captured in the light from the windows of the trysting place, face crosshatched by tree branches. After locating her in this hidden position, Truffaut gives us her view of the ensuing activities within. We peer, exactly as she does, through the bare branches, into the windows of the house, where Pinson and his paramour embrace, then, in a series of matching cuts (moving back and forth between Adele's face and the lovers inside) we watch as the couple ascends the stairs, followed by three small dogs.

Not to be outdone, Adele finds an old wooden staircase of her own, and, after peeping out between the steps, ascends these steps just as the two lovers have done. The insistently imitative nature of this scene cannot fail to impress us. Adele is, in some dark way, *participating* in Pinson's tryst by means of clothing that is certainly inappropriate to her activities and a set of stairs that, without any logical justification, simply emerges in the middle of the underbrush. This imitative stance, coupled with her voyeurism, culminates in one of the most uncanny moments of this entire film. As Truffaut notes in the French version of the screenplay, "Elle pourrait s'en aller, mais on la sent déterminée à alimenter sa jalousie. [She could leave, but we feel that she is determined to feed her jealousy]" (Sc. 20). As the lovers passionately embrace and fall onto the bed, Adele moves to a position inside this ruined structure she has happened upon, and watches through a window whose shards of broken glass mirror her own fractured state. Such a vision would normally provoke agonizing jealousy in the beholder. And yet, as the scene fades to black, her face half in light, half in darkness, breaks unmistakably into a smile. The last image we have is of her entirely disembodied smiling face, luminous as a half-moon (*une demie lune*), inevitably suggesting her lunacy.

There are simply too many unanswered questions for this scene to fulfill any narrative logic. How did Adele know when and where Pinson was going? How did she move from the hypnotic trance in her private room to the nocturnal adventure? Why does she so faithfully imitate the movements of the lovers, and then smile at their performance dramatically enacted before an uncurtained window? Our only recourse here, as before in the film's opening scene, is to understand this entire sequence as a dream. But if Freud is right about dreams communicating wishes, then how shall we understand the desire being portrayed here?

Consistent with his self-proclaimed role as an "intellectual French director," François Truffaut is not content merely to render Adele's story through the authenticity of her dreams, he must also comment on this oneiric version as being particularly cinematic. There can be little doubt that Truffaut's staging of this bit of voyeurism constitutes an allusion to the most famous of

Plate 5.2　Adele's disembodied smiling face

voyeuristic scenes, those found in Alfred Hitchcock's *Rear Window* (1954). Truffaut, as is well known, was an admirer and a disciple of Hitchcock. In his book, *Hitchcock*, Truffaut tells his mentor that "*Rear Window* is one of my two favorite Hitchcock pictures."[12] In describing this film in one of his articles for *Les Cahiers du cinema* in 1954, Truffaut had written:

> This film is one of the most important that Hitchcock made.... *Rear Window* goes beyond pessimism; it is really a cruel film. Stewart fixes his glasses on his neighbors only to catch them in moments of failure, in ridiculous postures, when they appear grotesque or even hateful.... *Rear Window* is a film about indiscretion, about intimacy violated and taken by surprise at its most wretched moments, a film about the impossibility of happiness, about dirty linen that gets washed in public; a film about moral solitude and ruined dreams.... To clarify *Rear Window* I'd suggest this parable: The courtyard is the world, the reporter/photographer is the filmmaker, the binoculars stand for the camera and its lenses. And Hitchcock? He is the man we love to be hated by.[13]

It doesn't take much to sense that Truffaut is *identifying* with Hitchcock in this eulogy. *Adele H.* cruelly catches Adele in moments of failure and is a film that catches her intimacy at its most grotesque, wretched moments. That François Truffaut himself *identifies* with Alfred Hitchcock is strongly suggested in a related scene. In that scene, Adele is walking in the street in Halifax and passes a soldier dressed identically to Pinson. She reverses direction, catches up to him breathlessly and touches his shoulder. The soldier turns, a look of surprise on his face. It is not Pinson; it is François Truffaut. Truffaut copies here one of the most familiar "trademarks" of the American master of suspense, a cameo appearance in his own film, and if he does so, it is to take up a position as close to the master as possible.

And, like *Rear Window*, Truffaut's film is also about the impossibility of happiness, about moral solitude and ruined dreams. But where this quote gets really interesting is the moment we realize that Truffaut is *also* identifying with Adele, for it is Adele who takes up the position of Stewart in her voyeuristic enjoyment of Pinson and his paramour. Adele and Truffaut collaborate in bringing us a French version of Hitchcock's parable of cinema! Why do we *love* to be *hated* by Hitchcock (according to Truffaut)? Because he has put us in the ugly position of being voyeurs rather than actors in the drama we witness. Because he reminds us that the pleasures of the cinema are guilty pleasures which we enjoy because, by implication, our superego prevents us from acting out such fantasies, so we are "condemned" to passively watch as the "dirty linen" of life unfolds before us. The more we think about the deeper implications of our position as filmgoers, the more we sense that Truffaut believes we secretly *suffer* from our voyeurism by being excluded from the field of action before us. Hence the curious phrase: "he is the man we love to be hated by." But look at how devilishly clever and complex Truffaut has made this scene. If he and Adele have taken up "condensed" positions as voyeurs, "the man we love to be hated by" is also Pinson. His sadism is directed not just against little dogs that he kicks pitilessly down the stairs, but repeatedly and mercilessly against Adele herself. But this is, remarkably, the position she *chooses*. As we watch a subtle smile spread over her half-lit face, we realize that Pinson is ideally selected to offer her precisely this kind of enjoyment. Pinson makes it clear from their first encounter that he is *not* interested, will *not* love her. But she persists. We must reluctantly conclude that she chooses Pinson because he does *not* love her. He is indeed the man "she loves to be hated by."

One word for the kind of pleasure that is derived from pain is masochism. Adele herself seems to conform to this "diagnosis" when a fadeout from the voyeurism scene brings us to her room where we hear her voice (-off) saying, "I am beyond pride and jealousy. Since love will not smile at me, I submit to its grimace. I want to think now of my sisters who suffer …" (Sc. 84).

The attempt to understand why Adele would make the choice to suffer will, I believe, lead us not only to a satisfactory explanation for the decisions

Plate 5.3   The portrait of Leopoldine

and actions of the heroine of this story, but also to an understanding of how this particular story (like Hitchcock's *Rear Window*) becomes Truffaut's retelling of the parable of cinema. We will once again see that a French cinematographer has chosen to tell a story that is, ultimately, both an allegory of the cinema itself and, within that allegory, a meditation on Bazin's question: "What is cinema?"

The scene we have just witnessed can only be understood as another of Adele's dreams. Here her mind lurches from an invocation of her dead sister to *another* nocturnal adventure in which she uses primary process thinking to project herself as both her lover and her lover's lover. In that process she condenses at least three different pairs of people and at least two different scenes in her own life.

Before we saw Adele invoking her sister at the *table tournante*, we saw her sitting with Mrs Saunders in the boarding house parlor, displaying an album of drawings. Mrs Saunders, seeing a likeness of Adele, exclaims, "Oh, what a lovely portrait. It's *as if you were alive*. Is it you?" "No," answers Adele, "it's my older sister," and she proceeds to recount the boating accident in which her sister drowned. One cannot avoid the obvious here: the uncanny likeness between sisters since Isabelle Adjani is clearly the model for both photographs and drawings. Clearly Truffaut has *condensed* both sisters into one person. Thus, if, as will be increasingly evident, we may suppose that the entire film is a series of dream episodes, this particular dream provides the fundamental thesis of the entire story: Adele wishes to be her older sister and does everything she can to achieve this identity, including always carrying her sister's jewelry with her. Why? Might it be because Leopoldine was the sister loved by their father and it was her death that produced Victor Hugo's greatest expressions of love for that daughter? "He nearly went mad with grief," Adele explains to Mrs Saunders. To evoke Leopoldine produces pain for the younger sister, not just the pain of grief, but another. "You don't know how lucky you are to be an only child," she blurts out to her surprised landlady (Sc. 51). The pain thus also derives from being the neglected, unloved daughter of the most famous man in the world.

To become Leopoldine, then, requires Adele to *die*, the only act that seems to Adele to be able to elicit her father's love. She is thus locked unconsciously in the most masochistic of all scripts: "I must die to gain what I most want." This, too, is portrayed not once but twice in the film in scenes which are the most explicitly oneiric (i.e. dreamlike) treatments of this entire film: "Adele, in bed, is having a violent nightmare. As she tosses back and forth in anguish, a superimposed image appears on the screen showing her in a desperate struggle to save herself from drowning. Adele wakes up screaming" (Sc. 53). This scene is repeated almost image for image later in the film and immediately after Mrs Saunders informs Dr Murdock that Adele has told her that "her sister was drowned at the age of nineteen" (Sc. 96–7). Truffaut's film flows more often than not by pure association rather than by any traditional narrative causality. In her nightmare, Adele clearly identifies with her sister, yet Truffaut's decision to superimpose the images of a young woman drowning over Adele, writh-ing, grasping at her throat, make it clear that this dream represents a *con-densation* of Adele and her sister.[14] By means of an economy of the type frequently at work in dreams (and the unconscious), Adele oneirically identifies with her drowning sister because that identification affords her the position as father's favorite. Yet the masochism at work here ensures that this identification can only be with her dead sister.

All of these considerations help us to understand why Adele has chosen Albert Pinson to be the focus of her attentions. It is clear from their first moments together that Albert does not love Adele, and can barely tolerate her presence. But she remains throughout the film in denial of a fact that he is happy to repeat every time they meet. Immediately after his first bru-tal rejection of her, she muses, "My love, I'm so happy we've found each other again … I am your wife forever more, till death do us part" (Sc. 83). No wonder that she has chosen Pinson as her "lover," for he allows her to perpetuate her masochism by treating her repeatedly in the same manner as her father has done. We should not miss the implications of Pinson's military rank: the word *lieutenant* means literally a "place holder" – in this case for Adele's father. He represents a figure so familiar in her life that one can only assume that Adele has chosen him in her compulsion to repeat her relationship with her father. The sad thing about this configuration is that Adele prefers a scenario that is familiar even if extremely painful to one that is unknown. The pleasure of the familiar – even when it is paradoxically painful – trumps the pain that it generates. This is, according to ideas Freud expressed in *Beyond the Pleasure Principle*, the very foundation and origin of masochism.[15]

Let us look quickly at one other scene in the film that brings all of these hypotheses together. In Chapter 8, "Her Parents' Consent," Truffaut provides us another uncanny juxtaposition of two scenes whose connection can only be associative (rather than narratively logical). We find Adele at the bank, easily receiving mail that must logically be addressed by her parents to Adele Hugo, despite the film's premise that Adele has successfully hidden her identity. And identity is immediately the central focus of this scene. Adele sees a small boy hiding under one of the tables in the bank and asks him his name. When, in return, he asks hers, she replies, "Leopoldine." In this instant we must understand that this scene represents a repetition in very different visual terms both of the discussion of the portraits with Mrs Saunders and the two scenes of drowning in which Adele condenses her own imagined death with that of her sister. After reading the letter from her father that contains his authorization of her marriage to Pinson, however, she returns to the bewildered child (a figure of her own childhood confusions?) and quite inexplicably and unnecessarily blurts out, "I lied to you, my real name is Adele" (Sc. 102). As in the voyeurism scene, there is an immediate and narratively confusing cut to another nocturnal scene in the woods. Adele, dressed in a man's formal attire and wearing a top hat, leaps over a stone wall, then passes through a stone archway. It is as though, in this piece of her dream, she has imported her condensation with the boy, David, from the bank scene, but we will discover a second, even more striking use of this gender switching only minutes later. Before her stands a "glass house" (a highly improbable structure in nineteenth-century Halifax) – more likely an architectural hyperbole of the house in which Pinson earlier displayed his love-making to the watching Adele. As she approaches, she performs two figures of repetition from earlier scenes. Rather than walking directly toward this building, she repeats exactly the pattern we observed on the quay in the film's opening scene: she moves forward toward a line of soldiers and then moves in a kind of circular pattern to make her entrance at a different point. There is no logic to this movement other than that it recalls her need to circumvent the customs in the first scene. (Perhaps the revelation of her real name in the previous scene causes this association?)

The second figure of repetition occurs when she glimpses, through the glazed wall of this building, Pinson openly embracing a young woman on the second floor. In this second version of her voyeurism, the scene does not fade to black until Pinson has descended the stairs to meet Adele. As soon as he touches her, the scene fades to black. When the image returns, we discover, without any logical explanation of how they have arrived there, the two lovers standing in the one place that best represents Adele's entire quest: a graveyard. (The headstones here also recall one of the earliest moments in the film. When Adele enters the Saunders' house for the first time, Mr O'Brien carries in a trunk whose position, size, and shape make him look more like a pallbearer than a coachman. Is this "coffin" a memory of Leopoldine or a presage of Adele's own demise?) The graveyard scene also anticipates the next to last image of the film: Adele's own gravestone, shaped in an arch that places her name in exactly the position Adele takes as she walks through an archway to begin this scene. Truffaut's "language" throughout this film works through many powerful visual associations of this kind.

Pinson dramatically removes Adele's top hat, a gesture that visually transforms Adele into his double: each has finely cut features, long black hair, and is identically dressed.[16] To emphasize the oneiric almost otherworldly nature of this entire scene, Truffaut has it bathed in a strange backlight that catches Adele's and Albert's hair in a halo of illumination. Adele's approach to her final "destination" is repeatedly prefigured here in two ways, Albert constantly (no less than five times) walks away in such a way that Adele is eliminated from the frame. When Truffaut relocates her, she is several times leaning wearily on one of the tombstones, as if yearning to enter the grave that awaits her at the end of the film. Finally, she manages to entrap him in a frame when she promises, "I'll leave and never see you again." At this moment, in a thoroughly dreamlike moment, Albert, who has throughout this film done nothing but reject her, takes her in his arms and kisses her passionately. Again we fade to black. Only in dreams do we get to enjoy such thoroughly opposite feelings condensed into a single moment.

I believe we may safely conclude that this scene provides the key to Truffaut's entire approach to *Adele*. Through it, we grasp that the entire film is composed of a series of recurring dreams, a set of variations on a single theme: Adele cannot find pleasure except through pain. She must invariably *repeat* a series of motifs each of which brings her closer and closer to a point of self-annihilation. It is no accident that the dream ends where it began, overwhelmed by the imprint of the father, Victor Hugo, with Adele posed perilously *and victoriously* (!) next to a body of water. I suggest that if you look at each of the major scenes in this film (the scenes with Whistler, the scene with the hypnotist, and the scene in which Adele claims she's pregnant and then runs after Pinson on the heath and throws money into the wind), you will discover a series of patterned elements (voyeurism, self-delusion, the enjoyment of disappointment). About many of these scenes we will have something to say in other chapters of this book, but what we should emphasize here is the binding of two crucial elements: the use of dreamscapes to reveal underlying patterns of voyeurism and masochism and the suggestion that these are not unique to Adele as character.

Indeed, François Truffaut has constructed a work of art whose story conveys through its narrative unfolding, through its structure of repetition and through its insistence on the meta-cinematic nature of both of the first two elements, the presence of something we wish we did not have to confront: our own *painful pleasure* of being voyeurs in a cruel drama. This entire film brings us finally to appreciate how thoroughly Pinson is "constructed" in Adele's unconscious wish to be both readily available to her, yet impossibly distant and cruel. He thus affords her the repeated and familiar "pleasure" of being rejected by her father. But he is also like the images on the screen we are watching: readily available yet impossibly distant. We inevitably must join Adele in the uncomfortable but inevitable realization that somehow we have wanted to be in this position as spectators, yet suffer both from the content of the film and our position as passive observers. It is particularly painful, moreover, to remember in this connection, that Freud theorized that all of the characters in our dreams are versions of ourselves. We end up in spite of ourselves identifying with Truffaut and Hitchcock and Pinson in helping to (self)-inflict this pain. Yet somehow Adele ends up, by dreaming all of these events, being the author of the pain she feels. Perhaps this is why she looks so triumphant in defeat at the film's end – her coded annals of misery have ultimately usurped the place of the Hugo novel she rejects: *Les Misérables*.

Bernardo Bertolucci was right. Certainly we would much prefer not to be awakened from the dream we are dreaming in the movie theater. Truffaut's genius, it seems to me, is to have succeeded in having us *understand* the painful consequences of such dreaming without ever really waking us up enough to object. What is particularly interesting, in view of our itinerary through the French cinema, is the way the notion of "authenticity" can be advanced to describe two such different films as Renoir's *Rules* and Truffaut's *Adele*. In the "debate" that is generated by the ongoing evolution of French cinema, we shall always have trouble deciding which version of authenticity leads us closer to the "true." That undecidability, I would suggest, is an essential element of our journey, for it continues to open the seventh art in France to such myriads of possibility.

Suggested Further Reading

Baudry, J. L. (1975), "The Apparatus: Metapsychological Approaches to the Impression of Reality in Cinema." In Braudy, L. and Cohen, M. (2004), pp. 206–23.

Baudry ties together the "sites" of Plato's cave, Freud's dreamer and the film's spectator in very surprising and provocative ways.

Freud, S. (1916), "Dreams." In In *Introductory Lectures on Psycho-analysis. The Standard Edition of the Complete Psychological Works of Sigmund Freud*, Vol. XV. London: Hogarth Press.

A more concise and straightforward presentation of Freud's theories on dreams than the earlier *Interpretation of Dreams*. The reader can appreciate the various aspects of Freudian theory in a fairly jargon-free presentation.

Kline, T. J. (2000), "Dreaming Up the Cinema." *Projections* 13(1): 18–37.

An overview of the various ways dream theory and cinematic theory overlap, suggesting the many parallels between dreams and films.

6

Cinema and/as Hypnosis

Jacquot's *Seventh Heaven*

"Our imagination, as the instrument of hypnosis, is alone capable of opening itself to the limitless variety of things and of beings, and their infinite connections, and of making possible a world in which they move." (François Roustang, 1994)

One of the more compelling scenes in *The Story of Adele H.* takes Adele to the theater in Halifax where she avidly watches a hypnotist at work. As we take up a position in the audience near her, we gaze at a stage where a series of strange objects surround a young Asian woman caught in the middle of a trance. A metronome ticks behind her while beside her a strange engine displaying smoke and mirrors (!) whirls on an axis. Suddenly our attention is distracted from the performance on the stage by an unruly Canadian Mountie, dressed in full uniform, who yells, "It's all a fake!" Calmly, the hypnotist invites the disgruntled policeman onto the stage and, to the delight of the audience, succeeds in hypnotizing him, making him row vigorously, and then remove his clothes. He claims, "Mesdames, Messieurs, Mesdemoiselles, if I wanted to I could force this man to leave the police!" Adele watches this transaction with intense interest and, now and again, takes notes on the proceedings. Indeed, it is as if she herself has entered a trance, so focused are her eyes on the stage. As the Mountie flees the stage in embarrassment, Adele touches her forehead and cheeks indicating that she herself has reached a feverish state.

Just forget about other things.
Listen to me carefully.

Plate 6.1 Adele spies on Pinson

Moments later, however, the entire exploit is exposed as a fraud. When Adele visits the hypnotist in his dressing room to ask whether he can use his talents to make a person fall in love, they are interrupted by the "Mountie" who barges in to return his uniform. Aghast, Adele storms out of the room.

In another context, we might discover that this scene too, has elements borrowed from many of Adele's other "dreams" – the ticking of a clock, the presence of a uniformed man who undresses in front of a voyeuristic audience, Adele's use of theater glasses to spy on Pinson sitting with another woman below her in the audience. What interests us here, however, is Truffaut's presentation of the practice of hypnosis. It should be fairly clear from our earlier discussion of this film that Truffaut has doubled his story of Adele's gradual psychological breakdown with a meditation on the relation between film and dreams. A first viewing of this scene might easily convince us that he has decided to underscore the film/dream analogy by debunking the entire practice of hypnosis. Subsequent viewings, in the context of the entire film, however, might lead us to a different conclusion. While it is true that the Mountie is clearly a set-up in a fraudulent practice, there is at least one person in the theater who *has* entered into a legitimately hypnotic state. Adele's glassy stare coupled with her feverish state make it clear that she has fallen under the influence of this powerful presence. We noted earlier, moreover, that Adele frequently puts *herself* in a kind of trance: in one case in front of a *table tournante* as she calls up her dead sister; in another scene, she goes into a similar trance while "praying" before a small altar she has erected in honor of Albert. In each of these trances, Truffaut gradually fades to black, cutting to a phantasmatic nocturnal encounter with the object of her "love." In other words, at the very moment the public performance of hypnotism is denounced as a fraud and delusion, Adele herself has entered one of her private trances that almost inevitably lead to close encounters of a weird kind.

While there is not enough evidence in Truffaut's 1975 treatment of Adele Hugo to suggest a strong parallel between cinema and hypnosis, we can turn to another film to examine this intriguing possibility.

Benoît Jacquot's 1997 film *Seventh Heaven* not only sets the stage for opening the inquiry into the place of hypnosis in film, but may suggest some unexpectedly intricate ways the two experiences may be connected.

Seventh Heaven is, from its opening images, a most troubling film. Jacquot introduces to his viewers Mathilde (Sandrine Kiberlain), a depressed beautiful woman, who suffers from fainting spells which seem to follow episodes of kleptomania. One evening at a party, she catches sight of an unidentified guest (François Berléand) and faints again. The next day, after another fainting spell, she regains consciousness to find this mysterious man beside her. At lunch, in a deserted restaurant, he fires a series of intimate questions at her and then abruptly hypnotizes her. The two begin a series of hypnotherapy sessions in a most unorthodox manner, culminating in a hypnotic trance, during which Mathilde becomes spontaneously orgasmic. The changes brought about by the mysterious therapist thoroughly upset Mathilde's relationship with her husband, Nico. Indeed, Nico himself seeks hypnotherapy after a sexually ambiguous encounter with a younger male colleague in a bar. Convinced that he must confront the doctor who has so profoundly upset the equilibrium of his marriage, Nico forces Mathilde to lead him to the doctor's office. Not a trace of the mysterious hypnotist can be found, however, and the film ends on a somewhat ambiguous note as Nico, having decided to sleep on the living room couch, is given motherly concern and care by Mathilde.

The film might thus be dismissed as merely one more example of a psychological family drama such as *Scenes from a Marriage* or *Ordinary People*. A closer look, however, makes us wonder about this hypnotist's relations to his patient as well as the orthodoxy of his hypnotic technique, and, as this *is* a French film, to wonder whether the film isn't also a meditation on the very nature of cinema.

The hypnotist (who is never named) first appears to Mathilde at a party – a most "weird and uncanny" affair with an eerily and insistently red decor.

While conversing absently with a friend, Mathilde suddenly catches sight of this man standing nearby, staring intently at her, though they have presumably never met. She looks away, then looks back. In the instant between those two looks, the doctor has vanished into thin air, and his exact location is occupied by a group of guests who are standing immobile in rapt and uninterrupted conversation. In the seven seconds between her two glances, it is highly implausible that this group has had time to move into this position. This uncanny disappearance of the doctor is surreal enough to evoke the effect in Magritte's painting, *L'Homme au journal*, of "Now you see it, now you don't."

Mathilde now moves into another room and has a second quite unexpected experience. She now catches sight of Nico, known to us as an ultraserious and dignified surgeon, standing on his head, a cigarette casually dangling from his lips. As he locks eyes with his wife, he gives her (and us) a very conspiratorial wink. In this we may see another allusion to a masterpiece of the early French cinema: in Jean Vigo's *Zero for Conduct* we witness a teacher in the extremely repressive boarding school do a hand stand on his desk in front of his class. Not content with this highly improbable act, Vigo next shows him drawing a cartoon with one of his hands while maintaining the balance of his weight with the other. And still not satisfied that this is sensational enough, Vigo makes the still drawing transform into an animated cartoon and the figure turn into a caricature of Napoleon! The allusion suggests just how surreal is this entire evening with its Inferno-esque décor and the disappearing stranger. Shifting her eyes away from her husband, Mathilde now encounters the mysterious stranger again, this time just slipping through the half-open door of the apartment into invisibility. As he departs, he turns and holds her in his look, a gaze that apparently has the power to make her faint dead away. We begin to wonder if this personage really exists or is merely a hallucination. A second viewing of this scene (in the context of the entire film) allows us to hear something in the soundtrack we might have missed in our first viewing: When she catches sight of the vanishing man for the first time, we hear a languid two-note musical phrase played on a flute. That exact musical phrase is repeated in our second encounter with the hypnotist, and will be heard in every subsequent appearance of this uncanny character.

Their next encounter only redoubles our uncertainty about the doctor's status. On what is presumably the morning after the party, we see Mathilde wandering aimlessly around her apartment. Then suddenly she is in the streets of Paris, hurrying down the stairs of a Metro station and onto a train. How coincidental! The by now familiar phrase on the flute announces a third appearance of our mystery man. On this occasion, he takes no

Plate 6.2   Mathilde enters Jacquot's Hades

notice of Mathilde, but when he gets off the train, she follows, as if by some invisible sign he has compelled her to come. They emerge from the Metro station, climbing the steps up to street level. As they emerge from the subway staircase, they pass under a shop sign that reads *Christian Hadès*.[1] No doubt, this shop is a well-known boutique, but here it has an entirely other valence: We remember that in *The Inferno* Dante presented a notion of Hell that exploited Classical notions of the afterlife in order to give his Christian poem the added authority of ancient beliefs. The river Acheron, with its "mournful shore," was said to lead to Hades because it went *underground* in several places. This Parisian underground leads to a place that is ultimately very difficult to locate on any map. (Mathilde's husband will, accordingly, experience severe mapping problems later in the film.)[2] *Christian Hadès* thus constitutes an allusion that leads us both beyond the "real" time and "real" space of Paris, and back to the film's title and the allusion it may make to medieval cosmology.[3]

When she again falls into a faint (a procedure that now seems to be a signal that she is changing worlds, or possibly falling into a hypnotic state), she finds her hypnotist magically waiting for her. He asks if she is hungry; she says no, but he whisks her off to a restaurant – yet another uncanny space, absent of any other clients. Suddenly he has hypnotized her, telling her she will no longer steal. But this is no ordinary hypnosis, for it is accompanied by a long demonstration of feng shui, an ancient Chinese art not usually associated with hypnosis!

By this time we are tortured with too many questions. How does she know how to find his office the next time? Why is it entirely vacant of any furniture? Why must she, as patient, remind the doctor that he hasn't col-lected a fee? Is it normal to pay with personal goods like a ring? Is it normal for her husband to find this ring on her closet floor after it has been "donated" to her doctor? And is it normal for the husband to assume that, because he has found her ring on her closet floor. she had given it to her doctor? (If so, why doesn't the doctor have it? And if he had, in fact, returned it, how would the husband know the hypnotist had once had it?)

These ambiguities might simply be accorded the status of postmodern paradox or of dream. And yet, the film does not remotely present itself as some sort of postmodern game, nor do the events conform to the characteristics of a dream.

Indeed, the ambiguous status of this character finds no explanation *within* the film. This ambiguity, then, forces us to seek some "way out" of this impasse. True to his Gallic traditions,[4] Benoît Jacquot offers us help in the form of two "guide" books which are pointedly foregrounded for the spectator.

Watching French films over the past forty years has taught me that the presence on the screen of a book is almost never an insignificant event. From the 1920s on in France, critics, theoreticians and filmmakers have carried on a debate on the relation of the seventh art to novels, plays, and poetry. For the most part, however, these discussions centered on the art of adaptation, whether it was the "calling" of cinema to bring great novels or plays to the screen. This debate changed pretty dramatically in the 1950s with the founding of *Cahiers du cinema* and the birth of the New Wave. From about 1955 on, filmmakers began to focus less on adaptation (i.e. the retelling of a story) than on what has been termed "intertextuality," i.e. the creative interplay between two different works of fiction. This new debate shifted the focus from whether Autant-Lara's film version of Stendhal's *The Red and the Black* was or was not a "faithful" rendition to the placing of books in films that would produce some commentary on the film's events or on the nature of film itself. With but rare exceptions, one cannot imagine this phenomenon in Hollywood cinema.[5] The idea that one would be required to read a book that had appeared in a given film in order to understand that film would be considered, in a deeply cultural sense, un-American. The opposite would be closer to the truth for French cinema. If a book appears on the screen, the strong implication is that we had better read it if we want to apprehend the full meaning of the film. Let us, then, armed with this cultural awareness, open the two books that Jacquot has offered up to his viewers.

The first of these, Selma Lagerlöf's *The Wonderful Adventures of Nils*, not only reinforces all the uncertainty surrounding the "nature" of the hypnotist, but strongly suggests an "other than dream" solution to the film.

Early in the film, we see Mathilde reading to her seven-year-old son from Lagerlöf's *Nils* and the more the film progresses the more we understand that this work enjoys a central place in the etiology (causes) of her neurosis as well as a significant role in her return to mental health. And beyond its role in the film's *plot*, the book may also be understood as connected to the very esthetics of our experience of this film and cinema in general. Lagerlöf's story introduces us to Nils, a fourteen-year-old who refuses to accompany his parents to church one Sunday and is left at home to study his Bible. Eager to finish his lesson, but bored into drowsiness by the text, "somehow he fell asleep. He did not know whether he had slept a short while or a long while; but he was awakened by hearing a slight noise back of him."[6] Such sleeping and waking indications create the conditions typical of a dream, i.e. often to "wake up" in such a setting is a code whose real meaning is "to begin to dream." In Lagerlöf's story this first oneiric element is doubled by another:

> On the window-sill facing the boy, stood a small looking-glass; ... He sat still and stared into the looking-glass ... and wouldn't believe his eyes. But the object, which at first seemed shadowy, became more and more clear to him; and soon he saw that it was something real. It was nothing less than an elf that sat there.... He felt that he had entered into an agreement with something weird and uncanny. (WAN 3, 4, 6, passim)

We cannot fail to be struck by the fact that this apparition first appears to Nils in a mirror – that it is "clarified" as some uncanny aspect of himself. This interpretation is quickly bolstered by another reference to the mirror:

> He would have been tempted to believe the whole thing a dream ... But then his glance fell on the looking-glass; and he cried aloud: "Look! There's another one! ... Why that one is dressed exactly like me!" ... and then he began to shake with terror. For now he understood that the ... creature whose image he saw in the glass was – himself." (WAN 7–8)

Lagerlöf places constant emphasis on the fact that this otherwise quite oneiric experience is *not* a dream for, except for Nils's relationship of scale to his surroundings, everything in his new world is in its proper place and time flows in its accustomed way. Indeed, "the intimate blending of fiction and fact is so subtle that one finds it hard to distinguish where one ends and the other begins."[7]

Both the book and the mechanics of its narration have too much weight in Mathilde's world to allow us to discount its explanatory value for the film, especially the parallel relationship between his (s)elf and her hypnotist!

Plate 6.3   Mathilde reading Roustang's *What Is Hypnosis?*

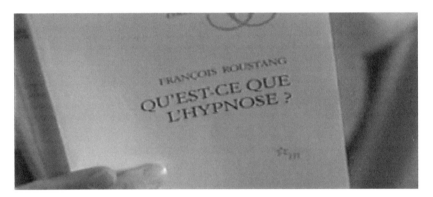

Plate 6.4   Close-up of Roustang's *What Is Hypnosis?*

Both Nils and Mathilde seem to "enter into an agreement with something weird and uncanny" that allows them access to an entire world they had hitherto unknown. Both Nils[8] and Mathilde (who is described by her mother as "on vacation," i.e. vacated) are, literally *nothing* until they join forces with powerful forces that transcend the ordinary limits of their respective worlds.

The other text cited by Jacquot is more direct and inescapable in its implications for the film than is *The Adventures of Nils*. When Mathilde awakens from her first fainting spell at the party, she wanders around her apartment in a daze and then pointedly picks up a copy of François Roustang's *Qu'est que l'hypnose? (What Is Hypnosis?)*, a title that, to the French film world, would evoke Bazin's famous *Qu'est-ce que le cinéma? (What Is Cinema?)* – indeed, given the parallelism of the two titles, the word "*hypnose*" feels like a kind of uncanny double of the word "cinema."[9]

Mathilde takes up Roustang's book at a moment of impasse. While she is reading it, the camera pans from a frontal shot of her reading to an increasingly blurred dark to light image that looks like nothing so much as a *screen*. And in the course of the film, each time this type of "transition" occurs, we hear once again the same uncanny musical motif that had accompanied the appearance of the doctor the evening before. This blank screen then gives way to her voyage toward her second encounter with the "hypnotist." Now, we cannot forget that his ontology is extremely problematic and that neither his hallucinatory status nor his methods are adequately explained at any point *within* the world of the film (what film theorists call the *diegesis*). If, however, we dare to read *Qu'est-ce que l'hypnose?* as a kind of "other script" of the film, some remarkable consequences emerge. The first is that Roustang's description of the hypnotic trance, its relation to the hypnotist and the metaphors that figure its powers provide a set of images that seem directly to influence, or even, we might say *produce* the experiences of Mathilde in the film.

Let's take another time-out to look at Roustang's description of the state of hypnosis to better understand how the French psychoanalyst's approach to this practice may be useful in understanding the French film-maker's visualization of it. I believe that we will discover in Roustang's study some implications for creativity that are extremely liberating for Mathilde and, at another level, for us as spectators. First of all, we should understand why hypnosis is even desirable or important.

Roustang's research on this subject led him to the hypothesis that we inhabit three different states of consciousness at different times. The first two (waking and dreaming) we mostly feel we are pretty familiar with. And yet the author of *What Is Hypnosis?* proposes an understanding of each of these that may surprise us. Dreaming he terms "paradoxical sleep," –paradoxical in that this state unites a high degree of cortical activity with a complete isolation from the exterior world. But the waking state is even more complicated. This is because Roustang believes that before each of us reached the age of reason, we passed through a stage of infancy in which we were overwhelmed by a surfeit of undifferentiated stimuli that assaulted our consciousness. On the other hand, Roustang theorizes, our powers of organization begin well before the acquisition of language as a means of keeping the world at a distance.

During this formative period, according to Roustang, the infant evolves a complete and very nonjudgmental relationship with the surrounding world, one in which she "plays with all the forms she receives, moving among beings and things and situating them relative to each other, finding limitless correspondences" – correspondences that she will later have to abandon as she is socialized (R 42). As she acquires reason and language, her waking world becomes limited to what Roustang calls "la veille restreinte" – a *limited* waking state. Roustang thus uses the concept of "limitation" in a way very similar to that used by the Surrealists, who argued that the waking state merely interfered with our access to an entire world of "knowledge" hidden from us by our too great attention on the practical problems of daily existence. As opposed to this "limited consciousness" of our waking state, Roustang proposes that:

> The unconscious escapes from consciousness by the very enormity of the number of connections which it brings to light and into action. It gives rise to too great a complexity for the conscious mind to grasp; we call it obscure, confused, unbound, and say that it expresses itself through very primary processes whereas it is really composed of over-connectedness and multi-connectedness." (R 47)

Roustang adds, emphasizing the positive aspects of his theory of the unconscious:

> We locate ourselves on the far side of the frontier and we retain but few traits from *this overwhelming lucidity which explicitly connects up to a thousand forms*, which we judge from our waking perspective to be too uncertain. Although our mind has at its disposition *a multitude of representations* such as we find in dreams, we are content to bring to consciousness but few of these…. *The realm of our intuitions is immense* in comparison with the few representations that reach our conscious minds. "*On the great map of the mind*," Kant muses, "but few points have been illuminated." (R 45, italics mine).

Hypnosis would give access to "a sort of natural potentiality" (R 11), where we perceive "a continuity between inanimate objects, animals and human beings … allowing … correspondences, variations and continuities … of every kind" (R 38–43).[10]

Roustang makes clear that hypnosis is but a specific type of a more *generalized waking state*, a kind of expanded consciousness allowing us not only to access but to retain the extraordinary riches of our imagination. In this domain of the imagination, he claims, we find solutions to life's problems, and, more significantly, enjoy a much richer life in general. To access this more generalized state, the subject has to "hold herself apart in space and time to prepare an action capable of remodeling reality" (R 55). Hence, no doubt, the sense that Mathilde is "en vacances" at the beginning of the film.

We noted at the outset that *The Wonderful Adventures of Nils* seemed to suggest a parallel between Nils's elf and Mathilde's hypnotist. What would it mean if this doctor (given his extremely shaky ontological position and uncanny ability to appear out of nowhere) occupies no space other than in Mathilde's imagination? How might we then understand the very notion of hypnosis if there is no hypnotist? Roustang's discussion of the hypnotic encounter directly answers this thorny question, for he repeatedly insists on the *disappearance* of the hypnotist in the hypnotic process.[11]

What is particularly important for our appreciation of Mathilde's inter-action with her own hypnotist is an understanding of this kind of *self-induced hypnosis*. Roustang assures us that "It is possible alone, without the aid of a hypnotherapist, either to concentrate on a fixed object, *to call up certain images that prepare the trance*, or to empty oneself of all preoc-cupations, of all thoughts, all specific emotions." Because, in the end hyp-nosis begins in a *relational state*, it is enough for the hypnotizing person to put herself "in contact with others, with her environment, with her world. In this sense, hetero-hypnosis and self-hypnosis are identical and no medium need be physically present to reach a trance."[12] After all, the hyp-notist, Roustang argues, is capable of suggesting only that which the sub-ject of hypnosis is herself already able to suggest to herself (R 76). In other words, "the hypnotist who does his work" merely "arrives at exactly the same moment as the subject of hypnosis in a place where things and beings are exchanged and correspond, and that their only concern is to give themselves over to each other" (R 143), and become interchangeable partners in the process (R 157).

When Roustang tells us that the hypnotist "inhabits the exact space occupied by his patient" (R 133), he is explaining how Mathilde's hypno-tist appears only when she is "ready" for him. It is mildly ironic, then, that "if the hypnotist tells her to see an individual seated on a chair even though there is no one seated there, the subject of hypnosis will not fail to do so" (R 75) for this appears to be precisely the way in which Mathilde creates for herself her own hypnotist!

So total is the effacement of the hypnotist in Roustang's scheme that we can now understand that his problematic status is the direct result *of her reading*. We could say that Mathilde could only achieve this erasure of the other-as-hypnotist as a direct consequence of reading Roustang's book.

It is also remarkable how many other apparently insignificant aspects of the book (for example metaphors that Roustang invents to render more vivid his principal arguments) find their way into the imagery of the film. Once there, however, they become elements of the hypnosis and its décor and we come to understand that their presence uncannily

Plate 6.5 Mathilde walks into focus

transforms Mathilde from mere character in the story into the film's *metteur-en-scène* – i.e. the source of authorial decisions of Jacquot's *explicit* and Roustang's *implicit* "scripts."

Thus, for example, Mathilde's first appearance out of focus and outside the range of the camera can be understood as a visual metaphor for Roustang's thesis that patients come to hypnosis because of "the state of confusion in which they find themselves" (R 75). "Often we are elsewhere [*ailleurs*]), outside of all that is imposed on us, trying to reconstruct in some other way the facts of our lives" (R 132).

Mathilde's mother's description of her daughter as "not here" or "on vacation" recalls Roustang's dictum that before the subject can be hypnotized, however, she must make herself entirely empty "by a kind of absence of concern, negligence, nonchalance, aimlessness, that is to say by a depreoccupation with the world" (R 127).

In such a state of dysfunction will she make her double "descent into the abyss" (R 70) – first into "Hades" and then into a fainting fit – exactly as Roustang's text suggests: "The hypnotic subject must be absorbed into images which correspond neither to real space nor real time" (R 71).

The scene in which the hypnotist takes Mathilde to an eerily empty restaurant can most easily be explained by Roustang's association of the hypnosis with "*foraging* in a previously unknown space"(R 153). The hypnotist's otherwise inexplicable presentation of feng shui in this scene (and Mathilde's subsequent rearrangement of her apartment) would only make "sense" if we understand them to be the residue of Mathilde's reading of this passage from *Qu'est-ce que l'hypnose?*:[13]

> When certain Chinese, who have maintained a taste for tradition, move to a
> new apartment or a new house, they call on the "master of wind and water"

who shows them the best arrangement of the rooms, the disposition of their furniture, especially the bed. We are not doing otherwise when we pay attention to the way someone sits, places her hands, takes her place in her family or in her group of friends, moves back or forward through generations, evokes places that are good or bad for her, situates herself in her work or in society. All that is full of meaning, not a meaning we must interpret, but an orientation that we must respect or modify (R 180).

When Roustang marshals this metaphor of hypnosis primarily to figure "the reintegration of the subject in a new relationship with her environment, not a meaning we must interpret" (R 178), he is certainly not proposing that his hypnotist practice feng shui! But we should pay particular attention to the last phrase in this passage – "not a meaning we must interpret" – because it orients us to Roustang's larger purpose in *Qu'est-ce que l'hypnose?* as well as to Jacquot's implicit redefinition of the notion of the cinematic apparatus in *Le Septième ciel*.

We might then see Jacquot's film as a kind of response to Truffaut's dreamwork in *Adele H.* Like dreams, the paradoxical waking state's contents are *fictions*, cut off from all exterior perturbations, and depending on the security of the hypnotic subject. Like dreams, too, hypnosis accedes to a "reservoir of possibilities," to the "matrix of thought," to the very "constitution of our individuality" (R 26–7). *Un*like dreams, however, the subject's hallucinations are conducted *in a waking state* and are not subject to the kinds of time/space distortions that we normally find in the dreamwork.

Roustang makes clear throughout his study that the (self)-induced hypnotic state is a kind of expanded consciousness allowing us not only to access but retain the extraordinary riches of our imagination. In this domain of the imagination, he claims, we find solutions to life's problems, and, more significantly, enjoy a much richer life in general. To access this more generalized state, the subject has to "hold herself apart in space and time to prepare *an action capable of remodeling reality*" (R 55).[14]

Far from being just another set of "scenes from a marriage," *Seventh Heaven*, "explained" by *Qu'est-ce que l'hypnose?*, allows us to view Mathilde as an agent of reconfiguration of the entire film: she seizes control of authority both within and outside of the film's narrative. Within the film, she rejects definitions of herself as a mere object, depressed and repressed. Her "cure" involves rearranging her space and her life, confronting her physician husband's medical authority, and challenging his diagnosis of her by openly expressing her desire and forcing him to confront his own homosexuality.[15] This move not only liberates her from his diagnosis, it liberates him from having to repress himself in order to accommodate and closet his own homosexual desires.

More significantly, as a reader of Roustang, she seizes control of the *mise-en-scène* of the film itself, and puts the very status of the "real" into question. Thus, not only does the film's plot derive from her associations with/to Routang's text, but she is able to create and animate the figure of the hypnotist to produce a "scenario" that only she can explain and that responds exactly to her own needs.

Mathilde's introduction of the hypnotist into her story does much more than just "fix" her broken relationship with her husband (an outcome the film does not in fact fully resolve). Her immense inventiveness allows us to see an entire system of connections we should not otherwise have noticed: Connections between the imaginative flight of the child (Nils) and the possibilities for such flight in the liberated adult; connections between the creative work of hypnosis and her reorganization of her world; and, most importantly, connections between hypnosis and the apparatus of cinema.

Her reading and subsequent reorganization of the world inside and outside the world of the film mirrors Roustang's theory of hypnosis as a movement "into images which correspond neither to real space nor real time" (R 71). Like the cinema itself, the site of hypnosis:

> is certainly in the space and time of our world. Yet it withdraws as far as possible from *this* space and *this* time to try to achieve a degree of concentration from which all forms produced in time and space are evacuated and then reorganized in such a way that none is privileged and all find a place. It is the ahistorical precondition which founds history as it configures space and time ... (R 181–6)

During her second hypnotic trance, the "hypnotist" asks Mathilde to focus her gaze on the wall "as if," he prompts, "it were a screen." The camera obediently pans to the wall and focuses on the white frame it provides, just as our eyes always do before the cinematic images begin to be projected on the screen. There, precisely where we are directing our gaze, she "sees" connections between her past and her present, mediated through the "reading" of Little Nils's marvelous adventures. But, in fact, we should realize that this is the *second* time in the film that we have experienced such a visioning, and Mathilde has not waited for the hypnotist to introduce her to this blending of the cinematic and hypnagogic experiences. The first of these experiences occurs immediately after Mathilde takes up Roustang's book. There, the camera pans, blurring the figures of reality into a white ground on which is projected ... *all of her experiences with the hypnotist*! It is

Plate 6.6   The hypnotist directs our attention to the blank wall

only retrospectively that we come to understand that he was *always already* merely a figure in her creative reorganization of her world and it is she who has seized this connection between hypnosis and the cinematic screen.

In this later scene, Jacquot makes a crucial shift of Mathilde's and our focus away from the (hallucinated) figure of the hypnotist to the cinematic screen. It is *there* that the subject must visualize her story and her cure. Indeed, hypnosis and cinema would seem to share equally in the production of fascination, paralysis, subjection and loss of subjectivity (R 105–6).

To use Roustang's terms, Jacquot allows us to wrap *la veille généralisée* ("the generalized waking state," a mental space generally located far from consciousness) *over* consciousness, the restrained waking state. Through film, Jacquot seems to be arguing here (with Roustang as a kind of "ventriloquist") that we can:

> enter into the essence of persons, of things and of the world, understand the directions that inhabit them, place ourselves within the flow of things. This new understanding will not be just an additional meaning superimposed with more or less elegance or genius. It is an orientation which can be received or taken and which, ultimately, doesn't need to be spoken because we are already there. (R 175)

As viewers of *Seventh Heaven* experiencing these connections both second-hand (watching Mathilde) and first-hand (by identifying with her), have we not in fact achieved what Roustang calls on us to attempt – access to a state of mind in which such connections become increasingly frequent and manifest and productive of solutions to the problems we face?

And is this not, as both Jacquot and Roustang seem to suggest, the very essence of poetry? "It is the essence of poetry that liberates us from the reality of the accepted and firmly established world, in which we believe we are living, to open up to us the multiform relations of other worlds which are possible, however evanescent."[16] It is in this respect, by the way, that *Seventh Heaven* most profoundly overlaps with the poetry of Vigo's *L'Atalante*.

The capacity to reach the point where "our generalized waking state can operate without interfering with our restrained waking state" (R 99) belongs to "artists, who transmit to us ways of seeing and understanding the world which have previously remained invisible to us" (R 128). Benoît Jacquot would no doubt agree that this is precisely the domain of film.

What is hypnosis? What is cinema? What is revealed in *Seventh Heaven* may tell us less about the particular characters and their immediate problems than about the nature of the medium in which they move. Jacquot illustrates this discovery in many ways in his film: by introducing a character whose very status lies somewhere between perception and representation; and by screening several texts which become important messages for his viewer. Perhaps the most subtle and remarkable of these strategies, however, can be detected in the way the film literally exceeds its own boundaries. The film alludes to a universe in existence before Sandrine Kiberlain walks into focus, and it alludes to another whole field of associations still going on well after the last image, as the final dialogue persists into the space normally allotted to the film's credits. Like Roustang's idea of the enormity of the generalized waking state, Jacquot's film spills over its regulated boundaries into unexpected and powerful spaces and meanings.

In *Seventh Heaven*, Jacquot has produced a meditation on the double question, "What is cinema?" and "What is hypnosis," which cannot fail to provoke some hard thinking about each one. And of course, since *Le Septième ciel* is really about what the French have labeled "le septième art" – the cinema – we, as observers, are invited to rethink our status as children of this paradise.

Suggested Further Reading

Fromm, E. and Nash, M. (1997), *Psychoanalysis and Hypnosis*. Madison, CT: International Universities Press.
  An excellent and accessible discussion of the relationship between hypnosis and psychoanalysis.
Lankton, S. and Lankton, C. (1983), *The Answer Within: A Clinical Framework of Eriksonian Hypnotherapy*. New York: Brunner/Mazel.
  The most straightforward presentation of Ericson's ideas on the effectiveness and value of hypnosis.

Cinema and/as Mourning

Anne Fontaine's
How I Killed My Father

"All photographs are memento mori. *To take a photograph is to participate in another person's mortality, vulnerability, mutability. All photographs testify to time's relentless melt."* (Susan Sontag, 1973)

Without Adele's report that her sister, Leopoldine, drowned in a boating accident and that her father "nearly went mad with grief," we might never understand the complex set of feelings that drives her increasingly toward her own "drowning" in melancholy. If the entire film may be interpreted, as we have suggested, as a series of Adele's dreams, then certainly the central motif (or, in musical terms, the theme and variations) of those dreams would be Adele's confused attempt to "become" her sister. When she shows Mrs Saunders portraits of her sister and herself, it is impossible to determine which images represent which sister. In her encounter in the bank with the little boy hiding under a table (as perhaps Adele had done when she learned the terrible news of her sister's death), she says, "My name is Leopoldine." In her repeated dream of drowning, she is most visibly enacting the single event that will merge her with her lost sibling. All of these behaviors suggest that Adele is not finished with her sister and that the work of mourning she has undertaken has become dangerous to her vitality. In his essay, "Mourning and Melancholia," Sigmund Freud remarked that "although mourning involves grave departures from the normal attitude to life, it never occurs to us to regard it as a pathological condition."[1] For Adele, something very pathological has happened, however, that leads us to suspect there may be other ways to understand the process of mourning. Why, for example, must Adele feel she has to "become" her sister? How are we to understand her entire process? We might also ask, since Truffaut's film is so resolutely "meta-cinematic", what might be the connection between the process of mourning and the work of the cinema?

Our discussion of *Adele H.* did not provide an adequate context in which to discuss the meanings of Adele's mourning per se. Nor could we, in that earlier discussion, legitimately divert attention from our discussion of the parallels between cinema and dream. When we step back, however, from that discussion, we may reflect that, just as Adele identifies with her dead sister, we as viewers are asked in some subtle, perhaps even perverse, way to identify with and mourn the by now long-departed Adele. We can think of many films that move us precisely because the main character must die, and so we mourn. In other cases, as in that of John Huston's *The Misfits* (1961) or in C. Nolan's *The Dark Knight* (2008), whose major stars died within a year of each film's release, our viewing often *becomes* a process of mourning actors who have died. But even without such specific losses, we must realize that cinema in its most essential form is an image of *something that is no longer there*. Like a cherished photograph, we can look at it over and over again, but we can never make its subjects return to the physical form they enjoyed when the film was made.

In the present chapter, I would like to explore with you the parallels that may exist between film and mourning as processes. By this time, you will not be surprised to learn that there is a French filmmaker who has used a story of loss to explore in all its complexity this potential connection between mourning as a process and cinema as a medium. I propose that we look at Anne Fontaine's *Comment j'ai tué mon père [How I Killed My Father]* (2001) as an example of such an exploration.

In the opening moments of Fontaine's film, Jean-Luc Borde (Charles Berling), a very successful Versailles gerontologist, enters his sumptuous living room and distractedly opens his mail. A voice-over – apparently "reading" the letter he holds – intones, "We regret to inform you of the death of your father which occurred last month. He was unable to return to France as he had hoped." As he finishes the letter, Jean-Luc sinks dejectedly onto the arm of a sofa, glances out the window at his wife, Isabelle, reclining in a deck chair, then lapses into a kind of trance[2] which is accompanied by lush but eerie chamber music. As we hear this music, Fontaine cuts from Jean-Luc's vacant expression to a gala soirée which Isa

Plate 7.1 Jean-Luc dreamily reads a letter

(Natacha Régnier) has organized to celebrate her husband's recognition by the Mayor of Versailles. In the middle of his speech thanking the town of Versailles for this honor, Jean-Luc realizes that the letter is apparently a terrible mistake, for there, standing before him, is his father, Maurice (Michel Bouquet).

Afterwards, rather than greet his father with happy effusion, Jean-Luc simply asks emotionlessly, "How long have you been in Versailles [and] what are you doing here?" Maurice happily answers the first question and ignores the second. His purpose will only gradually – and painfully – become apparent. Indeed, the film follows Maurice as he moves through the next few days as a guest of his son, wandering about the town, visiting Jean-Luc's clinic, getting to know Isabelle and Jean-Luc's brother, Patrick, and causing a rapidly escalating degree of discomfort for his son. What Jean-Luc's father discovers is that his son is emotionally dead, his outwardly happy marriage to Isa overshadowed by Jean-Luc's false diagnosis of Isa that purportedly prevents their having children. Maurice's presence also provokes Jean-Luc's brother to break free of his deadening enslavement to his brother, and Jean-Luc's mistress to end his manipulations of her. So angered is Jean-Luc by his father's intrusiveness in his life that he assaults him after dinner one night, throws him to the ground and chokes him to death.

Or does he? Leaving his father's dead body on the lawn, Jean-Luc retreats to the lavatory where he stares bewildered at his image in the mirror. Suddenly a knock on the door jolts him out of his reverie and he hears his

Plate 7.2   Jean-Luc kills his father

father's voice pleading, "Open the door! Don't leave me in this hole!" Jean-Luc opens the door to find his father undead. The scene fades out as Jean-Luc, standing directly behind Maurice, begins gently to stroke his father's right temple. Fontaine then cuts back to Jean-Luc sitting on the couch in his living room where we had left him at the beginning of the film, still holding the letter announcing his father's death, still staring out the window at Isa, reclining in a deck chair.

Certainly, Anne Fontaine is not the first director to choose to introduce into her film a character who is entirely the product of another's imagination. David Fincher's *Fight Club* (1999) and Ron Howard's *A Beautiful Mind* (2001) have used this narrative "trick" with enormous effectiveness. Both of these films catch us off guard at the end and cause us to re-evaluate what we have seen as the hallucinations of a schizophrenic (split personality). What makes Fontaine's film different, and very much worth our attention, is the fact that we are not dealing with a delusion, but a fantasy – what Anne Fontaine terms "a blend of dreams and memory."[3] The more we look at Fontaine's film, the more we realize that the letter Jean-Luc is reading produces a long fantasy involving his dead father – indeed a fantasy that is the product of mourning and what Freud would term melancholia.

Plate 7.3   Jean-Luc and Maurice reunited

This interpretation seems to have entirely escaped most critics of this film including such "stars" as Roger Ebert, Tom Dawson, Elvis Mitchell and Ty Burr, who either bemoan the film's flatness or, sensing that something is going on, resort to such unhelpful labels as "a Freudian self-help pamphlet."[4]

What is remarkable, then, in Fontaine's narrative structure is not the *fact* of dissociation per se, but the *process of mourning* in which Jean-Luc engages and *the interpretation* that this process elicits. Now that you're alerted to the unreality of Maurice, you might want to put the book down and take another look at this film, asking yourself, "What are the factors that clue us in to this situation?" and "What does the 'return' of the father accomplish?"

Let's look at the factors that determine the "unreality" of this film. Not only does Anne Fontaine employ a return to "the present" (Jean-Luc sitting, reading the same letter dressed in the same clothes with Isa in the same position, also wearing the same clothes as in the opening scene), but the director punctuates every one of its scenes with the same portrait of Jean-Luc, the same faraway look in his eyes that he displays at the fading of this first scene, accompanied by the same darkly emotive chamber music. We could use the evidence of this repetitive structure to conclude that Fontaine situates the point of view of the entire film in Jean-Luc's "imagined perception" of the events. Notice how often, for example, we will view a scene and then discover that Jean-Luc has magically materialized at a window or doorway or shadowy corner looking on.[5]

In other cases, Fontaine abandons the semblance of reality (e.g. Patrick's comic monologues presumably delivered in a comedy club in Versailles) for a dreamlike fantasy (e.g. all of Patrick's monologues after the first two are delivered in a dreamy tone against a blue backdrop without any of the audience responses we expect in a night club).

Notice also that from his first appearance, Maurice presents his status as existentially ambiguous. He makes no answer when Jean-Luc says, "I thought you were dead!" but confirms that he has been able to make this visit "à mes risques et périls." When his son guesses, "Are you retired now?" he cleverly equivocates, "Oh, not entirely, would you believe?" (Sc. 3). When asked if he'd like to try Jean-Luc's gerontological experiments, Maurice replies artfully, "Oh no, I don't want to delay the call … Perhaps it will surprise you but I don't think about death any more." At the restaurant, faced with another "guess" at his condition ("You're in very good shape"), Maurice allows that "The machine has had a few classical breakdowns" – quite an understatement from a man whom we may now presume to have died! And finally, in a highly ambiguous exchange with Jean-Luc purportedly about Africa, Maurice exclaims, Orpheus-like, "There are even people who are returning!" And to Jean-Luc's incredulous reply, "Don't tell me you're one of them!" Maurice intones with a sphinx-like smile, "Listen, I wouldn't have believed it, but it seems as though it *is* possible."

Maurice manages, moreover, to find his way into the lives of every one of Jean-Luc's intimates (wife, brother, mistress) in ways that defy rational geography or explanation. Even his old white Renault Dauphine makes an appearance in a purely associative way after Jean-Luc's own car has crashed and Jean-Luc is remembering a moment when his father's car had broken down in Spain.

In a film that is presumably about his father's effect on his life, it is astonishing that there is not a single flashback. Everything in the film has an eerily produced sense of present tense with no reference to any clock or calendar to situate present time. Alain Robbe-Grillet famously remarked that "The essential characteristic of the [film] image is its *presentness*. Whereas literature has a whole gamut of grammatical tenses which makes it possible to narrate events in relation to each other, one might say that on the screen verbs are always in the present tense: by its nature, what we see on the screen is *in the act of happening*."[6] In this case, we have a fantasy constructed like a dream, but clearly situated in the mind of a man awake. What is this fantasy – how would it be different from psychotic delusion and what implications does it have for our reading of this film?

We tend to think of fantasies merely as innocuous daydreams that we invent for our pleasure and over which we exert complete control. On the other hand, if we engage in fantasies, it's because we have unmet needs and desires that demand expression. We might say that the difference between a daydream and a night-dream lies in the amount of conscious control we exercise over the former.

Research on fantasies, however, suggests that the boundary between these two states is more permeable than we tend to assume. Perhaps you have had the same experience that I have had: after beginning a pleasant fantasy of some desired scenario, my mind may not cooperate in reaching that objective, but find itself spinning off in directions that are unwelcome. From her work with hundreds of subjects, Susan Isaacs discovered that fantasy often encounters (as it seems to in Fontaine's film) sudden *unintentional* representations that intrude on the conscious mind. She noted that for some people, a sudden break in continuity can lead to an incongruous shift from present conscious concerns, and signal that our conscious mind is no longer in control. Suddenly we may find ourselves in the role of *spectator* rather than that of the *director* of psychic images, and may experience unwanted images born of unconscious destructive instincts. In such cases, Isaacs notes, the fantasy becomes more a kind of call for help than a pleasant pastime. Isaacs makes it clear that such fantasies do not constitute anything like a psychic break from reality (as might be the case in a psychotic delusion in which a fictional person would be understood to enter the subject's real situation) but rather represent a kind of "time-out" from the real during which the mind may "work through" previously unconscious material.[7]

To understand quite suddenly, as we are forced to do at the film's conclusion, that everything that we had thus far imagined to be reality is but fantasy, is to necessitate a retrospective re-evaluation and re-interpretation of what we had believed to be simply "how things are." And as our (viewers') minds move backwards through the material represented to us (presumably by Jean-Luc Borde), we find ourselves combining the work of (at least) three important states: that of the mourner confronting a loss, that of the dreamer remembering the manifest content of his dream, and that of the film spectator attempting to make sense of a complicated plot.

Let us examine each of these three psychological moments. I would like to begin with Freud's work on mourning, not because he was infallible, but because he offers a good starting point for our thinking about this process. In the course of our examination, however, I would like to present you with some ideas that go beyond Freud's theories in order to acquaint you with the ways the French approach these questions. If Freud and

Freudianism was hugely influential in France through the mid-twentieth century, we need to understand how certain French tendencies modified his work in ways that came to have an influence on the seventh art. And again, I need remind you that, to understand French cinema we must confront a tendency to theorize in fields apparently unrelated to film that find their way into the very fabric of cinematic practice.

Let's begin then with Freud's thoughts on the subject. "Mourning," as Freud notes in "Mourning and Melancholia":

> is regularly the reaction to the loss of a loved person [and] although mourning involves grave departures from the normal attitude to life, it never occurs to us to regard it as a pathological condition … Profound mourning involves loss of interest in the outside world and the turning away from any activity that is not connected with thoughts of [the departed]… and can be so intense that a turning away from reality takes place and a clinging to the object through the medium of a hallucinatory wishful psychosis. [!] Normally respect for reality gains the day … bit by bit … but in the meantime the existence of the lost object is psychically prolonged…. Each single one of the memories and expectations … is brought up and [worked through], and detachment is accomplished in respect of it.[8]

Let's imagine, for a moment, that Jean-Luc's daydream constitutes "the turning away from any activity that is not connected with thoughts of [the departed] … and [is] so intense that a turning away from reality takes place and a clinging to the object through the medium of a hallucinatory wishful psychosis." Such would certainly be the sense of the second reading necessitated by the structure of Anne Fontaine's film for the conclusion of the film jolts us into the realization that what we have been watching is not a distressing reality to which Jean-Luc begrudgingly submits, but a self-punishing fantasy that he unconsciously creates. Now we are forced to attempt to parse out two Jean-Lucs: the one whose unconscious produces the images we see versus the Jean-Luc represented in his own fantasy.

What becomes gradually and painfully apparent in our rereading of the film is the massively deadening nature of this fantasized self. In Fontaine's presentation of Jean-Luc's father's imagined return, the director suggests two celebrated "literary models" to "explain" this deadness: Hamlet and Pygmalion. As he begins to make his speech accepting the honor that the Mayor of Versailles has just bestowed upon him, Jean-Luc suddenly catches sight of what we may now call "the ghost of his father" standing in the crowd before him. The apparition of his father's ghost leads Hamlet, as we remember, to his confrontation with a series of terrible truths about his

incestuous and murderous feelings about his mother and father that culminates in his conclusion that life is but "the heart-ache and the thousand
natural shocks that flesh is heir to."[9] Indeed, Hamlet asks "who would
fardels bear, to grunt and sweat under a weary life, but for the dread of
something after death?" (*Hamlet*, III, 1). As if on cue, Jean-Luc, faced
with his father's ghost, loses the thread of his acceptance speech and finds
himself intoning, "Mais tout le monde sait que la vie est tout de même un
fardeau ... [But everyone knows life is nevertheless a burden ...]" and his
voice trails off into perplexed silence. "Fardeau" is an exact "replica" of
Hamlet's "fardels" and this allusive lapsus unveils a side of this very successful physician we had not expected to see, the melancholic. In addition,
we may well wonder what Jean-Luc may have in common with Shakespeare's
more famous character.

From here on out, we witness a fantasy that puts into play a part of
Jean-Luc that is a kind of "life without feeling alive." As jargon-laden as it
is, R. D. Laing's phrase, "cathect[ing] his ego-as-object with mortido,"
really captures the way Jean-Luc's self-expression seems increasingly self-
annihilating.[10] Elsewhere Laing refers to this state in less psychoanalytic
terms as "petrification ... the dread of being turned from a live person into
a stone." In *The Divided Self*, Laing argues that such a feeling often results
in "the 'magical' act whereby one may attempt to turn someone else into
stone ... since the very act of experiencing the other as a person is felt as
virtually suicidal."[11]

As we come to realize, Jean-Luc is not only unable to express any feeling
for others, he is massively dedicated to transforming everyone around him
from living beings to statues – an uncanny reversal of Pygmalion's "birth-
ing" of Galatea from her stone statue, but one very much in keeping with
Ovid's more general tendency in *The Metamorphoses* to turn people into
objects, a rhetorical figure that the critic J. Hillis Miller labels "prosopopoeia ... the trope of *mourning*."[12]

In their first scene alone together, Jean-Luc's wife Isa mechanically takes
a smorgasbord of pills before going to bed, all presumably prescribed by
her doctor-husband to induce her *to sleep*. Later we are to learn that Jean-
Luc has also medically proscribed having any children, thereby depriving
her of her life's fondest wish and, along the way, turned their relationship
into what Isa will angrily denounce as "une vitrine [window dressing]"
and allowed her only to "recevoir, ouvrir la porte, faire des sourires, mettre
des fleurs sur la table [to greet the guests, open the door, smile, put flowers on the table]." And this accusation is accompanied by her realization
that he is "un homme sec, rétréci ... [qui] parle et ça ne sort rien. Il n'y a pas
de chair [a dried up man, all shrunk to nothing, who speaks, but nothing

comes out. There's no flesh and blood there]." To which Jean-Luc confesses helplessly, "Tout ça [the idea of raising and loving children] ça m'effrayait. Prendre en charge, élever, s'inquiéter, punir ... Pour tout ça je suis *inapte* [All that terrified me. To take charge, to educate, worry over, punish ... For all that I'm simply *inept*]."[13] Indeed, he has earlier confessed to Maurice that, "the truth is that nine out of ten times we screw alone [tout seul]."

Every shot of Jean-Luc up until this accusation fully corroborates Isa's fury: he treats his patients with undisguised disdain, as (largely unsuccessful) experiments. His brother Patrick is only good enough to chauffeur him from party to party or else "only stand and wait," a condition against which Patrick, like Isa, revolts – in his case by wrecking their expensive car and walking off into the night. Jean-Luc's associate and mistress, Myriem (Amira Casar), exists only as a puppet whom he can undress on demand and move about like a chess piece when it suits him. When Maurice first meets Myriem, he immediately guesses that Jean-Luc "l'a formée en quelque sorte [created her in some way]." And when Myriem seems to be too alive, Jean-Luc resorts to a prostitute to fulfill his sexual needs. Whereas Pygmalion wanted to turn a stone statue into the living Galatea, Jean-Luc is desperately trying to turn everyone around him (back) into stone!

When we enquire as to the reasons for this "deadness" in Jean-Luc, we find that it seems to result not from the news of the death of his father, but from some much more remote and troubled past moment. This moment *might* be the traumatic departure of his father when he was still but a child. (Indeed, Patrick will seem to recall being left behind at a department store, but the recollection is more likely a condensation into a hyperbolic single event of a larger sense of abandonment). Jean-Luc, too, will accuse his father of having "tout rayé d'un coup de crayon [having crossed everything out with one pencil mark]," and left. But some children successfully mourn their departed parents and subsequently, as Freud puts it, "regain the capacity to adopt a new [person to] love" (MM 244). Indeed, when Jean-Luc gets around to asking his father why he'd left, he listens to Maurice's explanation with a vaguely consensual interest and even asks, sympathetically, "So, what was it you couldn't tolerate?" And when his father answers, "I no longer knew who I was, I felt like I was part of another system," Jean-Luc wonders almost tenderly, "And did it work? Can one really forget?" This is hardly a subject that produces a violent reaction in the "abandoned child."

No, what seeps through this repeated and not entirely convincing reproach is another, more disturbing one: that on one occasion, Maurice gave up and talked of killing himself. "I can remember," Jean-Luc bitterly tells his father, "a man who could suddenly jump up during dinner and say, 'I'm going to put a bullet in my brain.'" And on another occasion, Jean-Luc tells Maurice that he has "the look you had when we were on a trip to Spain in the Dauphine. You had lost your wallet and all your money and papers and you stood by the side of the road moaning, 'We're screwed, we're done for!'" These two incidents seem to be the nexus of Jean-Luc's angry disappointment with his father. On the one hand, such crucial moments would have inspired a fearful rage that his father might abandon him. Simultaneously – and this would suggest Jean-Luc's deeper connections with Hamlet – he likely experiences "the guilty Oedipal complex of patricidal phantasies." And, not surprisingly, they also seem to be the point of intersection between father and son – a kind of Hamletian melancholia that feels like an unbearable burden, or fardel, for both men. But Jean-Luc's murderous fantasies include not only his father, but also his unborn children and in this way he seems to be both Oedipus and Laius, simultaneously patricidal and infanticidal, "something that returns like a ghostly apparition when his son curses his own sons."[14]

When we stop to consider that all of these traits are brought to us courtesy of Jean-Luc Borde's *own* extended fantasy, we are forced to conclude that he is tortured by self-loathing of the person he has unwittingly become. Why this self-hatred?[15]

Let's go back for a moment to Freud's thinking about mourning and see if he has anything to tell us about this aspect of Jean-Luc. Freud, of course, did not confine his thoughts on mourning to the death of a loved one. He also found the process to be at work when a patient was abandoned by someone she loved. He theorized that what happened to her emotional attachment to this loved one (what Freud ingloriously terms the love-object) was that she could not simply withdraw her attachment from the absent one and displace it onto another person. Instead, when this relation was shattered, Freud noticed, the abandoned lover withdrew this love-object into her unconscious where it served to establish "an *iden-tification* of the ego with the abandoned object" (MM 248–51). In plain words, this means that the mourner punishes herself with thoughts that she attributes to her rejecting lover and ends up directing abuse, debasement, and suffering on herself. This process produces "a self-tormenting melancholia that signifies that the sadism and hate" directed her way by the departing loved one have been "turned round upon the subject's own self." Instead of being able to scream "You're cruel!" at the departed lover, she ends up shouting "You're worthless!" at *herself.* Freud elsewhere calls this process the *introjection* of the lost object. But because Freud saw this as part of the mourning process, he felt that this element of introjection was temporary and that the mourner could gradually recognize that the destructive ideas belong to the mourned one and not herself, eventually freeing herself from his "power."

In Borde's case, we can imagine that, abandoned by his father, rather than hating his parent, he ends up identifying with the departed parent and feeling isolation, despair, helplessness, frustration, and rage.[16] But he seems implacably stuck there because, in the end, he attempts but cannot succeed in the elimination of this "loving hate."[17] His entire fantasy ascribes all of the evil to himself, and causes him to take the blame for the loss of his wife, brother, and mistress. In this scenario his father merely plays the role of uncovering the son's deadening manipulations.

Rather than understanding this as the gradual process of recovery that is implied by Freud's term "introjection," we are forced to see Jean-Luc's fantasy as obeying a force that is entirely unknown to him. In this, Jean-Luc seems to be obeying a French – rather than a Viennese – theory. In their own approach to the question of mourning, the French analysts Abraham and Torok suggested that some cases don't allow for a gradual process of introjection. Now, I want you to pay attention to the specific metaphors they use in developing this alternative to Freud's theory.

In the first place, Abraham and Torok argue that "incorporation is invariably distinct from introjection (a gradual process) because it is instantaneous and magical and implies the loss of an object before the freeing of the desires concerning that object":

> The object of pleasure being absent, incorporation obeys the pleasure principle and functions by way of processes similar to hallucinatory fulfillments … Incorporation is an eminently *illegal* act. It *must hide from view* and from the ego. *Secrecy is imperative* for survival…. Installed in the place of the lost object, the incorporated object continues to recall the fact that something else was lost: the desires quelled by repression…. *Like a commemorative monument*, the incorporated object betokens the place, the date and the circumstances in which the desires were banished from introjection; they stand like *secret tomb* in the life of the ego … and in this way the ego keeps alive that which causes its greatest suffering and is condemned to suffer the illness of mourning [or melancholia]. (my italics)[18]

Incorporation (as distinct from introjection) constitutes a *"refusal to mourn"* in that it is "the refusal to reclaim as our own the part of ourselves that we placed in what we lost"; a reclamation and a realization that would "effectively transform us." It reveals "a gap in the psyche that points to something missing where introjection should have occurred."[19]

This notion of incorporation of what he imagines to be his father's rejection would perfectly fit Jean-Luc's entire fantasy as a self-punishing revelation of his own deadness and his petrifying treatment of Isa, Myriem, Patrick – and even his father('s ghost). Abraham and Torok use the term *cryptophoric* to describe the images of the type produced by Jean-Luc, for it *entombs* him in its crypt-like design and because it is an *encrypted* text which he is unable consciously to decipher, but must blindly obey. Since Maurice secretly remains Jean-Luc's ego-ideal, it is *Maurice*'s dirty secret that needs to be kept, *his* shame that needs to be covered up in an endless repetition of acts that offer Jean-Luc's body as whipping-post for Maurice's failure. In a way, Jean-Luc might be said to be wearing his incorporated father's death-mask as his own![20]

Were this all that we could see of Jean-Luc's fantasy, we would no doubt find this film to be as dead as its subject, as devoid of development as *Memento* and just as fatally condemned to the uncertainty between what is real and what is merely a replica of the real. As such it would constitute a refusal to mourn and a shunning of the potential benefits of mourning.

Anne Fontaine's narrative purpose, however, turns out to be quite remarkably different. For if the self-portrait offered up by Jean-Luc turns out to be relentlessly "petrified" and a self-punishing entombment, the portrait of the father's ghost has a very different "agenda." Let's listen to Abraham and Torok again. They argue that "sometimes in the dead of night, … the ghost of the crypt comes back to haunt the cemetery guard, giving him strange and incomprehensible signals, making him perform bizarre acts, or subjecting him to unexpected sensations."[21] Anne Fontaine says of her protagonist, "He isn't part of his life and flesh…. It's as if, at times, you were a ventriloquist's dummy controlled by your father or your mother. You never know why but, all of a sudden, you feel your father or mother's expression on your face, overriding your own, as if there were someone inside of you."[22]

What is indeed surprising in Fontaine's arrangement is that this "ghost" who elicits from Jean-Luc bizarre acts and unexpected sensations is none other than the character of the Father in his fantasy. If Jean-Luc, as son, must continue almost to the end of this story, to wear the mask of the entombed memory of his father's deflating desire of self-annihilation, the Maurice of Jean-Luc's fantasy is revealed to be a wholly different figure – not the Oedipal father, but rather a figure we, as spectators, are allowed to see as vital, beneficent, paternally caring, loving, and concerned, able to elicit the best from his "other son", Patrick. Indeed, Patrick does a series of monologues at his night club which are masochistically "funny" and the invisible audience apparently enjoys them. But gradually, through the

Plate 7.4   Dialo arrives from Africa

repetition of these monologues, the audience disappears completely and we're clearly in an emptied-out space of pure fantasy. In some of these more obviously fantastic scenes, Patrick wistfully reproaches his father for abandoning him, but the last of the series involves Patrick humorously replaying his first monologue and receiving warm congratulations from his father. Maurice asks him about his prospects and Patrick confesses that he's thought of marriage and a co-ownership of a video store in the south of France, but doesn't dare leave his brother. Maurice plays paternity to the hilt here, questioning whether Jean-Luc really needs Patrick and telling his younger son, "You know, the years rush by. You can't get stuck in messy situations. If you've got a serious opportunity, take it!"

What is curious about this second scene is how subversive it appears toward Jean-Luc in Jean-Luc's own fantasy. What seems to be happening here is a huge battle going on between the incorporated image of the disappointing father and a newly rediscovered one in which the positive pieces of this incorporated object no longer fit the old dead image.

The most directly problematic sequence of this type occurs when Jean-Toussaint Dialo (Hubert Koundé) arrives from Africa to sing Maurice's praises: "C'est votre père qui m'a orienté. Il m'a changé la vie. Il m'a encouragé. Il était là tout le temps. [It was your father who got me started. He changed my life. He encouraged me. He was always there for me]."

Maurice's role in Africa exudes courage, devotion, dedication, and effectiveness.[23] One part of Jean-Luc (the incorporated dead object comprised of his father's impotent and suicidal words) openly disdains this possibility and sarcastically voices his suspicions that the whole African adventure is but a con-game to win his (financial) support. But the other part of Jean-Luc's fantasized father presents a loving, capable and vital parent – a much happier type of introjection!

Now, the battle rages. How can Jean-Luc maintain the incorporated image in the face of increasing "evidence" of his father's deeply sensitive paternal devotion? What is going on? Perhaps we may comprehend the character of Maurice in this film as a recovery of memories that begin to reintroduce his lost father into his consciousness in a form that can be positively assimilated as a life force able to counteract the incorporated tomb-like image that Jean-Luc has up until now worn as a mask. In Jean-Luc's fantasy, this new version of the father seems to be constructed out of long repressed memories of the positive aspects of the dead man, previously entirely hidden away behind a deadening incorporated image produced by an early trauma of disappointment. In other words, in Jean-Luc's fantasy, the vital character of Maurice ends up by dethroning his entombed double which has been masquerading as Jean-Luc!

Ironically, this new Maurice includes in his arsenal of qualities the ability to love – to love precisely that person whom the dead father inhabiting Jean-Luc has long forbidden him to love: Isa, his wife. This proscription is symbolized by Jean-Luc's prohibition of children – a circumstance that might risk resuscitating and unmasking the dead father. But clearly Maurice feels no inhibitions about loving this estranged woman.

The irony here is of course that such a fantasy brings up a host of old oedipal feelings that risk sending our Hamlet-Oedipus deeper into a murderous melancholy. This conflict is played out in the brilliant final scene of Jean-Luc's fantasy. Everything in this film prepares us for this violent eventuality, notably Jean-Luc's unremitting hostility to Maurice – a hostility doubly motivated by the son's belief in the father's betrayal, but also by the father's renewal of feelings of oedipal rivalry. Quietly, however, Fontaine has also laid the groundwork for the successful "resolution" of this impasse.[24]

She offers us the scene in which Jean-Luc readmits Maurice back into the space in which he is examining himself (for the first time in the film!) in a mirror. Their presence together in this mirror-image reawakens the realization that there was (or at least could have been) some original unity, whose wholeness, security or identity provided the son with enough ego strength to persevere. The father and son join (not forces) but *faces* and Jean-Luc's gesture of tenderness goes a long way toward welcoming this other piece of his father back into his sense of self. Jean-Luc will presumably now be able to don Maurice's vital, caring, and paternal expression.

By abjuring the incorporation of the destructive father image in favor of this recovered image of the beneficent father, Jean-Luc moves toward an active or generative position. Anne Fontaine suggests that:

> father and son live out the deep-rooted relationship that binds them beyond death itself … The film's denouement marks the birth of a being who had been living alongside himself until that point.... We realize that Jean-Luc will never be the same man again. He can move towards a new life at last. For the first time probably, the father has fulfilled his task as a father."[25]

But we must not forget that this *is* a *French* film. Anne Fontaine does not allow us any certainty about Jean-Luc's resumption of social life, ethical responsibility, and renewal. Because she withholds until the end the evidence that the entire film is Jean-Luc's fantasy, she forces all of us into the business of reworking what we thought we knew into new configurations. But isn't this the process we must engage in when we seek to interpret any work of art?

And because the necessity of rereading the past is inevitably common to both mourning and film, Anne Fontaine invites us, nay *provokes* us, to understand the deeper connections between film and mourning as psychological events requiring us first by *retrospection* and then by interpretation to re-evaluate bit by bit (these are Freud's terms for the process of mourning) the terms and figures of our own fantasies and dreams. Along the way, the work of this film implicitly argues for an extension of Freud's theory of *Trauerarbeit* (the work of mourning) into the realm of *Traumarbeit* (the interpretation of dreams) – to help us to see the way in which the dreamwork and mourning can resuscitate elements of our repressed unconscious desires into positive fantasies.[26] Fontaine would thus confirm Erik Santner's contention that "film turns out to be remarkably well suited to be the site of the symbolic procedures of funerary ritual because film is an inherently elegiac [meaning a nostalgic lament of past joy] medium."[27] Both cinema and the psychology of mourning would thus, in Derrida's words, be "phantom sciences," spectral (in the sense both of imagistic and ghost-like) discourses that constantly renegotiate the question of loss.[28]

We might never confuse the one with the other, but thanks to Anne Fontaine's film we may better understand how each endlessly reflects (in both senses of the word) and re-interprets the work of the other in us. Her film encourages us not only to take a second look at *Adele H.* and *Seventh Heaven*, but invites us to meditate on the losses we ourselves have sustained. Perhaps, like Jean-Luc Borde, we too will be better mourners and will learn how to use our experiences at the movies more creatively.

Suggested Further Reading

Abraham, N. and Torok, M. (1994), *The Shell and the Kernel: Renewals of Psychoanalysis*. Trans. Nicholas T. Rand. Chicago: The University of Chicago.

Despite its more psychoanalytic and French approach, Abraham and Torok's work is indispensable in understanding the notion of the "entombment" of the mourned "object."

Freud, S. (1917), *Mourning and Melancholia*. In *The Standard Edition of the Complete Psychological Works of Sigmund Freud*, Vol. XIV. London: Hogarth Press.

It is very much worth reading this fundamental essay on the psychology of mourning.

Kristeva, J. (1989), *Black Sun: Depression and Melancholia*. Trans. Leon Roudiez. New York: Columbia University Press.

One of the most intelligent and sensitive critics in France today, Kristeva is able to apply the question of loss to literary texts in a remarkably clear way.

Cinema and/as Terror

Michael Haneke's *Caché*

"My films are intended as an appeal for a cinema of insistent questions instead of false (because too quick) answers, for clarifying distance in place of violating closeness, for provocation and dialogue instead of consumption and consensus." (Michael Haneke, 1992)

Our discussion of cinema and/as crime focused on ways in which a group of particularly innovative French directors put into play characters whose criminality, be it staging a dramatic murder, picking others' pockets or stealing American cars, becomes a mirror for the director's own rule-breaking. You may be able to think of other films in which such mirroring occurs.

The twenty-first century brought with it another level of crime that, though alluded to in previous films, was never explored as a metaphor for the medium itself. The advent of sustained or what we might call state terrorism, coupled with the advances in internet imaging, brought with it an increased awareness of the ways in which the medium might itself become an instrument of terror. And by introducing the idea of *video and film* as forms of terrorism Haneke seems to be reopening another question, "What is cinema?"; the answer, "Cinema is a form of terror" (not the *Friday the 13th* sort of terror induced by ghoulish images, but a terror indistinguishable from the cinematic apparatus itself), seems a particularly twenty-first century phenomenon. And, since, the question and the answer are, as we have seen throughout this study, particularly French, it may come as a surprise that the most eloquent proponent of the idea that cinema *is* a form of terror is himself Austrian. It should not come as a surprise, however, that Haneke's cinematic icons are Robert Bresson and Krystof Kieslowski, nor that the films in which his most searching questions about the relation between cinema and terror were made in France.

Michael Haneke started out as a student of philosophy at the University of Vienna, gradually moved to film criticism, then play-directing, and finally began making films when he was already forty-seven. After completing three films in Austria, he moved to Paris, shot *Code Inconnu* in 2000, *The Piano Teacher* in 2002, and then *Caché [Hidden]* in 2005. For all its painful searching, little in Haneke's previous cinema prepares us for the exploration he would undertake in *Caché*.

Caché is a fictional account of a French Television talk-show host, Georges Laurent (Daniel Auteuil) who begins to receive videotapes of his house accompanied by grotesque drawings of faces vomiting blood. The series of tapes apparently leads him to an apartment on the outskirts of Paris. Believing "he knows who it is" but refusing to share his suspicions with his wife, Georges follows the clues to the apartment where he encounters Majid (Maurice Bénichou), an Arab man whom, it turns out, he'd known as a child. Upon entering the Arab's apartment, Georges will immediately accuse him of terrorizing the Laurent household with his videos and bloody drawings.

In the "present tense" of Haneke's film, then, Majid is now grown up and living modestly in Romainville with his teenage son. When confronted by Georges, Majid freely admits that he has recognized Georges on his TV talk show but calmly evinces stupefaction at the visit and is mystified by the accusation. Georges's (real or feigned) anger escalates rapidly and yet he ends up by admitting that he was the cause of Majid's forcible removal from Georges's parents' house. Georges ends his visit to his childhood friend by violently threatening that if Majid "continues to scare his family or damage him, he'll regret it." When Majid asks, "Are you threatening me?" Georges answers, "Yes, I'm threatening you and believe me, I mean it," then stalks out of the apartment. Curiously, Georges lies to his wife, Anne (Juliette Binoche), about this visit, telling her there was nobody at home when he went to the apartment! And even more curiously, this visit turns up on a videotape mailed to both Georges's wife and to his boss at the television station. What the video reveals in addition to the scene we have just witnessed, however, are the desperate tears shed by Majid after Georges's departure.

When Anne confronts Georges with this tape, evidence that he was lying, he responds, incredibly, "*I lied to save you more stress.* The world

Plate 8.1 The "terrorist" image

won't stop turning because of it!" This idea of lying for what the liar decides is to the benefit of the other is one we shall have reason to examine more closely in what follows. And then the bombshell, if I may be so aptly blunt: Georges confesses that the Arab's parents worked on the Laurent farm when he was a child; that his father liked them and that they were good workers. Then he says:

> In October '61 the FLN called all Algerians to a demonstration in Paris. They went to Paris. On October 17th, Papon, the police massacre. They drowned about 200 Arabs in the Seine. Majid's parents were probably among them. In any case they never returned. When my father went to Paris to search for them, the police told him that he should be glad to be rid of these "jigaboos." My parents decided to adopt the boy, I don't know why. They must have felt responsible in some way … It annoyed me. I didn't want him in the house. He had his own room. I had to share. I was six years old! … I told lies about him. [Je l'ai *cafté* – (literally, I denounced him)]. Afterwards he was sent away, sick, to a hospital or a children's home. I don't know which. I was happy. I don't feel responsible for it. It's all absurd!

It is perhaps a mere coincidence, but in the same year that Michael Haneke was shooting *Caché*, Alain Tasma was in Paris directing a docu-fiction film of the events that Georges is describing here. The two films share so many concerns that a comparison of their narrative structure and discursive origins seems imperative here. Whereas Haneke uses *Caché* to present a current (2005) perspective on events that happened almost a half-century previously, Tasma uses *Nuit noire* to provide a searing and unsettling account of those events as they unfolded at the time. We might say that Tasma's version presents a kind of graphic illustration of Georges's very elliptical account as told to his wife (above). In this other version, we learn the context of the FLN (the National Liberation Front of Algeria) terrorism in Paris. According to Tasma, North Africans were being routinely arrested and brutalized by the Parisian *forces de l'ordre* throughout the late summer and early fall of 1961. In September, the FLN staged several attacks on the police that the Algerians deemed to be retaliations for these many brutalities. The demonstration of October 17, however, was never intended to be a form of terror. In *Nuit noire*, the organizers of the protest issued a strict order that no weapons of any kind were to be carried, and carefully instructed every participant that the demonstration was to be above all a peaceful one. The film portrays a police action carefully orchestrated by the Police Commissioner Maurice Papon, in which some 7,500 persons resembling North Africans were swept up in police vans before they could reach the center of Paris.

Meanwhile, those who did march were met by brigades of CRS forces wielding night sticks and automatic weapons. The situation in *Nuit noire* reaches a climax when the police confront the demonstrating Algerians on the Pont de Neuilly in Paris, shoot and/or brutally beat them and throw their bodies, whether dead or still alive, into the Seine. (The horror of this scene is no doubt magnified by uncanny resemblance to another infamous massacre that took place on Saint Bartholomew's Day, August 24, 1572, when French Catholics murdered thousands of Protestants and threw so many of their bodies into the Seine that the river was dammed up by the sheer mass of their floating corpses.) In the aftermath of this police action, Papon was able to convince the great majority of the French press corps that the Algerians had fired on the police and that the number of deaths and arrests of the marchers was entirely justified. Tasma's purpose is quite clearly to paint a devastating picture of the racism, fear, and overreactions of the French *forces de l'ordre* in dealing with this Algerian "threat." According to *Nuit noire*, the French police staged an unprovoked massacre and then succeeded in covering it up. This contextualization of Georges's all-too-brief description will have important resonances for our understanding of his motivations later in the film.

But Tasma's film is important to our present discussion for two other reasons. First, the film depends heavily (as does Haneke's film) on images that are "borrowed" from Gillo Pontecorvo's famous docu-drama of the popular uprising in Algiers in 1962 that led to the ouster of the French from Algeria. Tasma repeatedly films events, both the bombs exploded by the Algerians at Paris police stations and the violence with which the police put down the FLN's demonstrations, in ways that are directly reminiscent of *The Battle of Algiers* (1966). The reasons for this homage to Pontecorvo will be extremely important for understanding both *Nuit noire* and, as we shall see, *Caché*.

The second connection between Tasma's and Haneke's films is the question of the control of the visual media. In *Nuit noire*, a member of the French press is able to capture on film some footage that directly contradicts Papon's "official" version of the night's events. When she attempts to show this film, however, it is impounded and destroyed by the police. One might say, then, that the real conflict in *Nuit noire* involves competing *images* of the night's events. In the end, Tasma suggests, whoever controls the media, controls the situation. This too will take on an important dimension in our discussion of *Caché*.

In Haneke's film, the content and authenticity of another set of films, in this case the "terrorist" videos, becomes the focal point of the narrative. When Georges finally shares with Anne the scene in Majid's apartment and denounces his childhood friend's involvement in the "terrorist tapes," Anne counters, "I don't think he's lying," certainly echoing what the viewer has likely felt after seeing the video of Georges's first visit to Majid's apartment, which corroborates the film's initial representation of the visit, but supplements it by showing Majid's tears after Georges has left. Majid comes across as a gentle, peaceable person, genuinely surprised and upset by Georges's accusations.

When, subsequently, Pierrot, the Laurents' eleven-year-old son, fails to come home one night, Georges and Anne go to the police and, without producing a shred of credible evidence, Georges has Majid and his son arrested and carted off to spend a night in jail. A short while after that Georges responds to Majid's request to visit, re-enters Majid's apartment and watches horrified as his Arab friend calmly takes a razor blade from his pocket and slits his own throat, an act so graphic that he seems more to drown in his own blood than to die of his wound.

What is particularly unsettling about Haneke's film is our absolute inability to guess how or by whom any of the videos that are produced and sent to Georges, his wife, and his boss could have been shot. Each successive video has a quiet authenticity to it that we do not question. And *Caché*

Plate 8.2   Majid slits his throat

strongly suggests to us that each is taken from a point that should have been – no, that *had to be* – visible to those being filmed. This is true not only of the tape of the Laurents' house since Georges walks directly by the exact location in which the camera had to have been placed, but is also true of the film in which he threatens Majid. At the film's end we are offered no solutions to this puzzle and must simply accept our inability to solve this mystery. It is indeed rare to leave a theater unable to account for the major mystery presented by the film we have been watching! In a short five years in France, we conclude, this Austrian director has become authentically "French," so able is he to present us with such an insoluble paradox!

Although we can never know who made these videos, what we *do* know is that Georges immediately becomes convinced, first, that these videos constitute an act of *terrorism* against himself and his family, and second, that they *must* originate at the hands of an Algerian man who once lived in his family's house. They very quickly offer him a reason to visit Majid, to threaten him and to have him arrested, all of which will push the Algerian to his death.

When we think of the film's events in the larger context of the French–Algerian conflict and the question of the authenticity and credibility of the media, we begin to feel that this story is not new, that it has its origins in other stories. Let us turn to what is perhaps the most celebrated version of this story.

In the most crucial scene of what is arguably the most famous French novel of the twentieth century, Albert Camus's absurdist hero, Meursault, walks along an Algerian beach in search of an unnamed Algerian, subsequently known only as "The Arab" in the novel. Meursault carries a gun, for reasons even he cannot name, and his purpose in pursuing this particular Arab is hazy at best. Raymond, the friend who invited Meursault to the beach and then provided him with a gun, has already demonstrated his hateful tendency to sexually exploit Algerian women and has artfully drawn Meursault into a nasty dust-up with a trio of Arabs encountered earlier on this same beach. Raymond's pattern is to provoke the Arabs through violence to their women, and then to blame and punish them if they react. Raymond is able to convince Meursault that their friendship obliges Meursault to join him in the unpleasant and violent business of teaching these Arabs a lesson about interfering in the "business interests" of the French. In other words, Meursault has no personal stake in this fight, yet participates in it out of some vague cultural duty to his fellow Europeans. As Meursault approaches his "man," Camus, who has until this passage of the novel written almost without any metaphoric language whatsoever, overwhelms the reader with a burst of violent images. As he walks along the beach toward his eventual victim, Meursault is assailed by "épées de lumière" [swords of light]" from the early afternoon sun, and, in the "halo" of light on the far rocks, he perceives the Arab boy's image as "dancing in the enflamed air" as if this boy were an incarnation of everything diabolical. As the Arab draws a knife, Camus's language transforms this pitiful weapon into "une longue lame étincellante qui m'atteignait au front [a long *blade* which shot upward and transfixed my forehead]" and then as "a keen *blade* of light flashing up from the knife ... gouging my eyeballs."[1] In other words, the actual weapons are transformed metaphorically into a kind of epic sword battle, rendered all the more curious by the phrase, "Il y avait déjà deux heures que la journée n'avançait plus, deux heures qu'elle avait jeté l'ancre dans un ocean de metal bouillant (p. 93) [For two hours the sun had stood still in the sky, two hours that it had been anchored in an ocean of molten steel" (p. 74)].

As if obeying some urgency that comes from without, Meursault fires once, and then after realizing he has upset "the equilibrium of the day," he fires four more bullets into the inert body of the defenseless Arab boy now lying in the pool of his blood flowing into the spring water before him. The rhetorical intensity of this passage is all the more inexplicable since the

Arab in question will be virtually forgotten for the rest of the novel. What's more, as readers of this work can attest, Meursault will be condemned to the guillotine not because he has shot a defenseless North African boy, but because he failed to shed a tear at his mother's funeral the previous day. What Camus does so skillfully is to gradually efface this horrific murder and "hide" it behind the public outrage that greets Meursault's apparent indifference to his mother.

Those with a knowledge of French literature and history remain troubled, however, by Camus's rhetorical flourish here, for the insistent language of swords flashing, leading to the phrase "for two hours the sun stood still in the sky" evoke without doubt the most celebrated of all French texts, *The Song of Roland*. In that famous twelfth century epic, we encounter another Frenchman in pursuit of an Arab foe: Charlemagne has just learned that his beloved Roland has fallen prey to a heinous ambush and, in his bereaved fury, he sets out after the Saracen Caliph, begging God to allow the sun to remain in the sky long enough for him to reach his enemy and kill him. God grants his wish and the Saracens are all massacred *and, significantly, thrown in the river to drown*.[2] Charlemagne's Christian God appears to endorse and even to abet this bloody massacre and drowning.

And so it is that pursuing Arabs and killing them by sword and by water belongs to a long and "noble" tradition in French culture – a history which subtly infiltrates Camus's absurdist novel, *The Stranger*, a work generally considered to be quite devoid of any concern with Franco–Arab relations. I would like to suggest that in this respect, *The Stranger* and, by extension, *The Song of Roland* constitute powerful sources for Haneke's remarkably *French* film, *Caché*.

We might say that one of the things that is hidden in *Caché* is a system of allusions to a set of books and films (*The Battle of Algiers* being principal among them) – thinly veiled references that spur us to meditate on the age-old history of Franco–Arab relations, and to reflect on the way our own interpretation of the images of the Franco–Arab conflict in this film may be manipulated and disseminated by powerful forces that we cannot see.

Or can we see them without really being aware of it?

Twice during the film, and at the height of their anxiety over the "terrorism" which afflicts them, Georges and Anne carry on a discussion sitting on their living-room couch in such a way as to frame the large television in front of them. In the first instance, there is a newscast on an outbreak of an epidemic in China. Although this reportage at first seems entirely divorced from the Laurents' problems, the word *caché*, emanating from the newscast, suddenly bleeds through their conversation and becomes audible to the film's spectator. Alerted by hearing the film's title

Plate 8.3   Mideast violence on the TV

in the background, our attention is drawn to the newscast. We see men in germ-proof suits carrying a body on a stretcher into an ambulance.

What could be going on here? One way to think of this "invasion" of the word and the images of an *epidemic* is that Haneke has subtly but insistently included an apparently "innocuous" image stream that may provide a significant commentary on the so-called "terrorist" tapes mysteriously sent to the Laurent household. What would news of an epidemic have to do with the violence Georges is experiencing? Could there be a connection between violence and contagion?

Yes, certainly, argues René Girard, one of France's most influential cultural anthropologists. We remember from our discussion of Renoir's *Rules of the Game* (see pp. 49–53) that, in *Violence and the Sacred* (1977), Girard looked at the way the earliest ("primitive") societies coped with violence. By studying the myths of cultures the world over, Girard hypothesized that when violence broke out in primitive societies, there seemed to be no way to stop its spread. Once a member of one family had been slain by a member of another tribe, a *reciprocal* act was required, which itself called for a reprisal. In this way, members of the community knew that reciprocal violence had a way of spreading that no one seemed to be able to control.

(The Hatfield-McCoy feuds during the last century in the United States and the feuds of the Kerrs and Scots in sixteenth-century Scotland are latter-day examples of such unstoppable violence.) For these reasons, Girard regards violence "as something eminently communicable ... a contaminating process ... There is something infectious about the spectacle of violence.... The more men strive to curb their violent impulses, the more these impulses seem to prosper." Ultimately, Girard argues, communities suffering from this "plague" of violence discover that the only solution involves what he calls "violent unanimity": an act in which all of the members of a community together discover a victim who is in some way marginal – that is to say, does not evoke a reciprocal act of revenge – and collectively murder that person. In this way, the community discovers the purifying value of sacrifice. This scapegoat, victim of a collective act, is instinctively recognized as the savior of the community and becomes revered as an emissary of their collective health. And so, the ritual of sacrifice (first of humans, later of animals) becomes institutionalized and repeated to ward off the "germs" of reciprocal violence. Sadly, however, the more communities evolve away from rituals of sacrifice, the more they are prone to what Girard calls "a sacrificial crisis" in which violence can reappear and rage seemingly without any form of "anti-virus." And the mythical evidence of this "sacrificial crisis" brings us eerily close to the central conflict in *Caché*. Citing the examples of Cain and Abel, Jacob and Esau, Eteocles and Polynices, Romulus and Remus, Richard the Lionheart and John Lackland, Girard notes that "The proliferation of enemy brothers in myth and in dramatic adaptations of myth implies the continual presence of a 'sacrificial crisis' ... rooted in the distinctive traits of fraternal strife."[3] The central *agon* of Haneke's film involves two boys forced to live as brothers, but whose relationship rapidly devolves into images of violence. This first TV allusion to contagion takes on even more significance when it is subsequently juxtaposed to a second intrusion of the Laurents' television into their own interaction.

Haneke repeats this "tele-intrusion" (at the seventieth minute of the film) when Anne arrives home late from work (and/or her adulterous affair) and finds Georges at his desk in the living room. Together they position themselves in such a way as to pointedly frame the television screen so that it occupies the focal point of the image, at the direct center of the screen. Even when Anne moves, she takes up a position across from Georges that reframes the TV. Interposed with their angry dialogue about her lateness, we see a series of stories on *Euronews*: first of the Barbara Contini affair in which the Italian journalist was fired on by US troops in Iraq, an affront which led her to call for a unified set of "rules of engagement" for all the "occupying forces" in Iraq. This is followed by a long take of an American soldier next to an American flag; and finally, under the heading "Mid-East," a view of Palestinians rioting in the streets, protesting the death and injury of some of their countrymen. In this last story, we see several bloodied bodies of Palestinians being carried past the camera.

These images provide a significant contemporary commentary on Georges's violent reactions and, as they roll, we learn, in the foreground of the shot, that the Laurents' son, Pierrot, has gone missing.

The unexplained absence of Pierrot will lead Georges directly to the *gendarmerie*, and with a contingent of armed police, to Majid's apartment in Roumainville. The images of Majid and his son being roughly hauled out of their apartment by the police only add to a store of images that have an increasingly familiar feel to them. The television footage (almost occulted by the conversation between Georges and Anne) is crucial in the lead up to Majid's arrest.

The combined set of images here, including first the rioting Palestinians, next the invasion of Majid's apartment and brutal arrest of the two Algerians, and finally the bloodied body of Majid's suicided body, are not "innocently" produced and they certainly do not belong solely to the private war between Georges Laurent and his boyhood rival, Majid. It turns out that, like many images of Tasma's *Nuit noire*, they all have a common origin in another docu-fiction film: Pontecorvo's celebrated *Battle of Algiers* (1966). That earlier film opens with a raid on the Arab quarter in Algiers. As the film's credits flow across the screen, jackbooted French paratroopers storm an unarmed housing complex, bang on apartment doors, rush the inhabitants of each unit onto the open-air landings and herd them brutally toward the waiting paddy wagons. No explanation is provided (or needed) for this invasion, and it visually mirrors Georges's use of the police to conduct a similar operation on the unarmed and unprepared Algerians at Roumainville. The TV images of Palestinians rioting in the streets are also "borrowed" from Pontecorvo's film where Algerians protesting French brutality are attacked by French tanks. Finally, the images of Majid's bloodied body echoes a stark and haunting image of torture in *The Battle of Algiers*.

Yet in creating such a symbolic stream, Haneke not only seems to bring the film's fictional events into an interpretive arrangement with the history of the Franco–Arab conflict but also with the current dynamics of the war on terror. But how are we to understand the connections between this larger context and Georges's particular problems with "terrorism"?

Certainly at the level of contemporary political allegory, it is evident that, whatever their origin, Georges has used the appearance of the set of "terrorist" videos to get back at an enemy from his childhood, whose sole crime was to have encroached on Georges's personal sense of his home(land). As an adult, Georges now discovers the means to inflict a terrible retribution on an Algerian who has no reason to suspect he is the target of such a crusade. For, as we know from the history of another George, the decision to launch a "crusade" against "the forces of evil" brought untold suffering upon both his enemies and his own people.[4]

But Michael Haneke raises the stakes in this film. Perhaps we can appreciate this other level of interpretation if we turn back to the videos that arrive at the Laurent residence in Paris.

Many viewers of *Caché* have expressed their frustration at the film's ultimate ambiguity. We simply can never know who has produced the videos that Georges immediately labels a form of terrorism: Could it be Majid? This is quite unlikely given our (and Anne's) trust in his genuinely uncomprehending reception of Georges's first visit and given the absence of a video of the suicide which should have been included in the "terrorist," films were Majid trying to frame Georges.

Could it be that Georges's son is in concert with Majid's son, since we see them leaving the schoolyard together at the end of the film? This suggestion derives some plausibility from the poster of Eminem prominently displayed in Pierrot's room, allowing us to consider the possibility that, like Eminem, the son may be one of those who "cross over" to identify with a racial minority. So, perhaps the two sons are complicit, but even their complicity would not be sufficient to explain the existence of images of Georges's childhood family home, mingled with Georges's own nightmares of events that only he could remember having taken place there. There are simply too many elements in the third and fourth videos that are known only to Georges and Majid.

Could it be Georges himself? This hypothesis is worth exploring on several grounds. The most compelling argument for suspecting Georges is that he is the only character in this film able to control video images in a way that "mimics" the "terrorist" videos. This becomes clear when we are surprised that a scene purporting to be a broadcast of his talk show turns out (much like the terrorist tapes) to be a tape. Our experience of the talk show, thought to be in diegetic time but suddenly rewound, exactly replicates the viewer's uneasy experience of the "terrorist" videos. At no other point in the film, other than in those "terrorist" videos, are we, as spectators, subjected to this kind of uncertainty about the "real time" and origin of the images we are watching.

Certain aspects of Georges's behavior must also strike us as suspicious. Why does he hide from Anne his first visit to Majid's apartment? After all, she should be his primary ally in this struggle. Why does his repeated inability to rationalize his behavior lead to such a violent misunderstanding with his wife? Why does he claim not to know that Pierrot is absent from the apartment where he has been working for hours? Why doesn't Georges call the police immediately when Majid takes a knife to his own throat but instead *goes to the movies*? In general then, his behavior (feigning ignorance when he already has a suspect), his diffidence about involving the police until he can get an arrest on other grounds, and his general propensity to lie about his involvement with Majid would constitute solid grounds for suspicion.

But the fact is *we cannot know for sure*. And the reason we cannot know is crucial, it seems to me, for the most significant of Haneke's objectives in this film. For one thing, the "terrorist" images are absolutely indistinguishable from the "image maker's" presentation of the real time of *Caché*. The first "terrorist video", especially, carries imbedded in it the film's credits, legitimizing it as deriving directly from the film's image-maker (i.e. Haneke himself). Secondly, all of the "terrorist" submissions are together, unlike the specifically *video* images in the film deriving from the television in the Laurents' apartment. Rather the mailed images have the look of 35-mm film rather than the pixilated video quality we would expect. We end up, as a result, anxious about our ability to distinguish between (the film's) reality and the images that are represented as "produced by terrorists." If, indeed, these images can have been produced only by the official image-maker, then the question arises, who is producing terror? And is this not Haneke's intent after all? We *should* not be able to distinguish because, in "the war on terror," it is precisely in the interests of those in power to confuse reality with ideology. In this sense, Haneke's *Caché* can be read as part-allegory (the story of Georges and Majid repeats in its basic outlines that story of the massacre of Majid's parents, and *that* story eerily replicates in detail the "original" story of this conflict told in *La chanson de Roland*). The film is also (and therefore) a searing critique of the way images are produced (and or repressed as they are shown to be in Tasma's film) – and why. If the production (by those deemed to be the objective and authoritative sources) of "terrorist videos" allows Georges to pursue his crusade against this Arab – to arrest him and drive to suicide a North African against whom he harbors an age-old grudge – then these videos have achieved their purpose.

I do not need to remind you how the United States government used a carefully concocted Arab threat of nuclear terror to justify war against an Arab nation. Few thought to question or disprove these positions, because the United States government produced visual and discursive "evidence" of this Arab threat. If the production of images of an Arab threat in Iraq convinced many to believe in the justness of this war, then those images (like the "terrorist" videos in *Caché*) have also achieved their purpose. And, like the viewers of terrorist videos in *Caché*, the average Western viewer had no way to distinguish fictional from real images of Iraq's threats, nor any way to deviate from the interpretations given by the image-makers. However skeptical we might be of Georges's manipulation of events, we simply have no way to step outside the diegesis of the film to critique the veracity of the images produced. The film helps us understand how the control and dissemination of "documented" images has become a feature of governance and manipulation. That this control has been exercised against a particular "threat" (in both the France of 1961 and the United States of 2003) should not surprise us given the millennial rehearsal of this "crusade" from the twelfth century forward. Its presence in Haneke's film constitutes a subtle and unsettling reminder of the control exercised by the media that surround us and the fragility of our hold on the truth.

What Haneke has achieved here, then, is yet another optic on the question, "What is cinema?" In this new twist, we see (and perhaps wish it were not so) the nearly limitless power to present what Haneke himself calls "24 lies per second at the service of truth, or at the service of the attempt to find the truth."[5] Or, we sadly surmise, at the service of an attempt to hide the truth.

Suggested Further Reading

Grundman, R. (ed.) (2009), *Michael Haneke's Films*. Oxford: Wiley-Blackwell.
    Provides a variety of perspectives on Haneke's films.

Beautiful Fragments
Discontinuity and the French Cinema

"There are so many injurious or superfluous precepts mingled with the true, that it is difficult to effect a severance of the true from the false so that I was induced to seek some other method which would be exempt from defects. And as a multitude of laws often only hampers justice, whereas with few laws, these are rigidly administered; in like manner, I believed that the four following would prove perfectly sufficient for me, provided I took the firm and unwavering resolution never in a single instance to fail in observing them. The first was never to accept anything for true which I did not clearly know to be such ..." (René Descartes, *Discourse on Method*)

In his affectionately bemused portrait of his people, *The French*, Sanche de Gramont points out that Descartes is not so much revered by his compatriots for his conclusions, which are often considered to be erroneous, as he is for his quest: "The highest adventure of the mind, to conquer the universe without ever leaving his study."[1] He adds, "The French mind seems naturally to fall into Cartesian pattern in its respect for knowledge, its belief that good conduct depends on clear thinking, its fondness for the systematic, its attraction toward what is clearly and sharply defined, and its distaste for what is murky and unintelligible."[2] But there are drawbacks to Cartesianism, Gramont concedes, the first among them being, "the tautological strain" implied by Descartes's first principle: "It is true since I know it to be true." "This tautological strain in Cartesian thinking finds unexpected echoes in contemporary France. General de Gaulle's speaking style rested partly on the enunciation of self-evident propositions [such as] 'The national discussion must for us be summed up with this question: France must be France.' "[3]

Certainly Charles de Gaulle was not the first to lapse into such epic tautology. We remember that already in the 1920s Louis Delluc fired the first critical broadside against the Hollywood colonizers with the ultimate Cartesian double tautology: "Let the French cinema be French! Let the French cinema be cinematic!"[4] But since no one really knew exactly what it meant either to be French or to be cinematic, the French could not help but attempt to exemplify the former and to "clearly and sharply" define the latter. Neither category, however, yields easily to a clear definition.

Defining Frenchness becomes a remarkably slippery enterprise even – or especially when – applied to that paragon of Frenchness, Descartes. "Is Descartes French?" de Gramont asks. "By birth he was of course French.... But there was clearly something uncongenial to him about his own country. As soon as he came of age he went abroad [and] his first published work was written in Latin."[5] And yet, for every French person worth their salt, Descartes is assumed to be as French as … Cartesianism! His example is instructive, however, since it puts into play the difference between geography (simply living in, originating from, or even creating things in France doesn't guarantee "Frenchness") and culture (it is possible to engage in French Thinking even if you are not "authentically" French). Neither Krystof Kieslowski nor Michael Haneke, for example, is French, and yet this Pole and this Austrian have, as we have seen, authored films that are unmistakably French.

Indeed, France exercises strange powers of attraction and of absorption. The "French" writers Jean-Jacques Rousseau, Georges Simenon, Eugène Ionesco, and Samuel Beckett are Swiss, Belgian, Rumanian, and Irish respectively; the poets José-María Heredia and Guillaume Apollinaire Cuban- and Roman-born. The French Post-Impressionist, Vincent Van Gogh, and the "French" Cubist, Pablo Picasso, are Dutch and Spanish respectively and the "French" composers Lulli and Glück are of Italian and German origins. What seems to make their work unquestionably *French* is, in every case, an adherence to the dominant Parisian cultural imperative of the moment. There can be little doubt that both Kieslowski and Haneke came to France in order to make films that, unlike anything else they had previously undertaken, conform to the intellectualism, historicism, and theoretical tendencies of French cinema. To be "French," then, looks a lot like what it meant to be "a poem" in our opening exercise on poetry. It is less a matter of one's "shape" than of the set of attitudes one adopts toward specifically cultural events.

It would seem to follow, therefore, that it is only when we combine the questions "What is French?" and "What is cinema?" into a single query, "What is French cinema?" that we arrive at that very particular set of characteristics that become exclusively and recognizably *French*.

What makes the category of French cinema all the more perplexing is that French cinema may not even appeal to the majority of French moviegoers! The steady influx of American films into Paris from the 1930s on – and especially after the Blum-Byrnes Accords of 1946, *guaranteed* that Hollywood would dominate Paris movie-houses for the entire postwar period[6] – ended up forming popular taste and guaranteeing the Americans a dominant share of French movie-house receipts. That very popularity, of course, obligated the French to attempt to imitate the American formulas for success "à leurs risques et périls." And no doubt, a few French studios continue to produce relatively successful dramas, thrillers, and comedies that, to some extent, rival the success of their Hollywood counterparts, but for the most part such imitation has doomed the French studio system to economic failure. Ironically then, despite – or more likely because of – these failures, if one were to ask the average French filmgoer to nominate a pantheon of French directors, it is the avant-garde or "maudit" directors[7] such as Jean Vigo, Jean Renoir, Marcel Carné, Jean-Luc Godard, and François Truffaut who would certainly seize a place in the French canon. Each of these (and the other directors encountered in these pages) becomes cherished for that "essential something" that makes him unmistakably French.

Occasionally, however, even popular French whodunits can display that "essential something," sometimes to the delight and, occasionally, to the dismay of their Anglo-American audiences. Take, for example, Guillaume Canet's thriller, *Tell No One* (2006). Winner of several awards at the French *Césars* (the equivalent of the Oscars), the film was released in the United States in 2008. Based on an American novel of the same title by Harlan Coban (2001), the film tells the story of a successful pediatrician (François Cluzet) and his wife (Marie-Josée Croze) who have escaped to a secluded lake near their country house for an evening swim. Their tryst is brutally interrupted when the wife is seized, tortured, and apparently killed and the husband knocked unconscious. Eight years later, still grieving for his wife, the doctor begins receiving emails that seem to indicate his wife is still alive. In his attempt to find her, he happens on a plot that had been hatched by a high-ranking officer of the Paris police. As events rapidly unfold, and the doctor learns that he is being re-investigated for the murder of his wife, he also discovers that he is being protected from the over-aggressive police by the leading drug lord of Paris, whose son he had saved from internal bleeding. Events quickly spiral out of control but gradually, thanks to the intervention of another detective who doubts the evidence produced in the original murder investigation, the dastardly plot is uncovered and the pediatrician and his wife are reunited. What turns out to be difficult about this film is not the complexity of its plot (which, after all, is based on an American novel), but the way the film is edited.

One could argue that the *Bourne* films are not so different from Canet's thriller, and pushed the Hollywood envelope as far as it could go with their nervous jumpiness, a style that seemed almost a homage to the French New Wave and, in particular to Jean-Luc Godard's radical editing.[8] But *The Bourne Identity* and its sequels are models of continuity when compared to Guillaume Canet's editing of *Tell No One*. Canet's film is composed of a series of fragments, cut in such short segments and linked, in most cases, by so little continuity of character, place or time that for the first two hours, the film feels more like a kaleidoscope of shifting, unrelated pieces than a coherent picture.[9] It is well-nigh impossible at a first viewing to get one's bearings, to know who is doing what and/or to whom. Viewers must simply abandon themselves to Canet's chaotic montage and wait for illumination. The American critic, Roger Ebert, wrote, "There will be times you think it's too perplexing, when you're sure you're witnessing loose ends ... it's baffling."[10] Chris Barsanti advises his readers that "Guillaume Canet brings a distancing Gallic fracturedness" to his story,[11] and Owen Gleiberman adds *Tell No One* "has a strategy of narrative murk ... a mesmerizing labyrinth – a movie in which confusion, and the promise that it will all become clear, wires you to the screen."[12] What Guillaume Canet has managed, in other words, is to inject a very French degree of *radical discontinuity* into his film – a trait that comes near to derailing his project for American critics, and one that has some of his critics wondering how quickly Hollywood can pull together the American remake. It is important, however, to understand that Canet's fractured style serves an extremely important function in the film: the concatenation of seemingly unconnected events that assault the viewers and leave us desperate for some connecting thread is intended to produce in us the same disorientation and panic that it produces in the character of the doctor. His experience of discovering that someone he has mourned for eight years may still be alive, his confusion at finding himself a suspect in the murder of someone he loved, the bewildering series of murders and accusations that begin to accumulate around him quite naturally leave all of us in the same rudderless boat. Canet's purpose here is to describe a world that suddenly has no map, in which events occur in such disjointed ways that they feel like a dream, and in which all our certainties disappear and need to be re-examined. We must realize, finally, that the film has to be read several times, backwards and forwards, in order to pick up all the clues necessary to solving this "crime." In this sense, the film requires to be read as a poem, yet feels as hauntingly real as our worst nightmare.

You will remember that we began this journey by pointing out that, whereas Hollywood worked with "storyboards" to ensure continuity editing, the French filmed from a "decoupage" – a difference in terminology which we took to be emblematic of the differences between classical Hollywood style and French cinematic practice. Here, in this twenty-first century popular thriller, we can see this critical difference embedded in Canet's film – so embedded that it "begs" for an American version which will "correct" it (as Jim McBride's *Breathless* "corrected" Jean-Luc Godard's "mistakes" in his remake of *A bout de souffle*).

In other words, quite eerily, Canet has introduced into his "thriller" in one way or another many of the characteristics that we have uncovered in our journey through the French cinema: a radical discontinuity which breaks the rules of classical Hollywood film, a deep sense of mourning, the need to re-see and re-read the entire work in order to discover a map that will enable us to get our bearings, and, uncomfortably, the sense that we are powerless to evaluate the truth of the images that assault us. It is worth adding, as well, that Canet (like Carné, Bresson, and Godard before him) puts himself in the role of the villain of the film and leaves us (as did his predecessors) with the sense that he is in some dark way assaulting our traditional expectations of the "thriller" genre every bit as much as he has assaulted the heroine of the film. We are likely to feel, at times, just as culturally bruised as she is physically represented to be in photographs taken after his attack on her.[13] All in all, then, this remarkably "popular" whodunit thriller turns out, at its deepest level, to be unmistakably French.

An "unmistakably French" film, then, originates from a culture that unabashedly prides itself on its intellectualism, a tendency that both springs from the French educational system and flees it. If Parisian filmmakers find themselves unconsciously conforming to their intellectual caste, they simultaneously flee it through conscious revolt against the very traditions that spawned them. Truffaut's concept of the film *auteur* was articulated as a rejection of the *cinéma de qualité* he had watched as a truant from school. To be an *auteur* meant first of all financial and intellectual *autonomy* from public taste. Pierre Bourdieu has argued that it is a rule of the French artist that "the more his intellectual field gains in autonomy, the more he lays claim to that autonomy by proclaiming his indifference to his public."[14] What motivates the "true French artist", then, is less the public's appreciation for the work produced than the pleasure of the debate that awaits whatever the work produced, and the inevitable dust-up over definitions.

As a microcosm of this entire process, we might take a look back at the "debate" that animated film practitioners, critics, and theorists in the late 1940s and 1950s.

By 1959, André Bazin had published in various journals a set of seminal essays that would be collected in a volume entitled *What Is Cinema?* As we saw in the chapter on Renoir's *Rules of the Game*, these essays collectively offered a definition of cinema based on Bazin's claim that the ontology of the cinema was the photographic image, and therefore that cinematic ontology was based in "true realism, the need, that is, to give significant expression to the world both concretely and in its essence."[15] Bazin's mantra from beginning to end lies in the confluence of photography and the cinema, "for these are discoveries that satisfy once and for *all in its very essence* our obsession with realism."[16] "Because of the *essentially* objective character of photography ... photography affects us like a phenomenon in nature [and] the objective nature of photography confers on it a quality of credibility [such that] we are forced to accept as *real* the existence of the object reproduced."[17] It seems to follow, then, for Bazin that because "the photographic image *is* the object itself, the object freed from the conditions of time and space ... it *is* the model of which it is the reproduction."[18]

We should note the number of times Bazin uses the word "essential" or "essence" here (and elsewhere in his writings). This essentialism should come as no surprise, for Bazin would have internalized this ideal from his early involvement with Marcel Legaut's militant Action Catholique, Jacques Maritain's notion of "the secret substance of visible reality" and Emmanuel Mounier's "personalist" notions of "the mysterious otherness" of external reality.[19] Dudley Andrew explains that "beneath Bazin's concepts such as the limitation of perception and the integrity of space lies a belief in the signifying power of nature ... its *preexisting* relations [and] ... a sudden dazzling revelation of their meaning."[20] Such a position will lead Bazin to such statements as, "The cinema has always been interested in God.... And the cinema is in itself already a kind of miracle."[21] In his book on Renoir, Bazin wrote, "The point of view of the camera is ... a way of seeing which, while free of all contingency, is at the same time limited by the concrete qualities of vision: its continuity in time and its vanishing point in space. *It is like the eye of God in the proper sense of the word*" (my italics).[22] Not content with such an apotheosis of the cinematic, he adds, "Depth of field ... confirms the unity [and] total interdependence of everything real ... [and] opens to a universe of analogies, of metaphors, or to use Baudelaire's word ... of correspondences."[23] It is clear, then, that much of Bazin's thinking comes out of a Christian Existentialism position, and owed some of its popularity to its resonance with the predominantly Catholic culture of France.

An alternative view of "the real," however, was being advanced at the very moment that Bazin was proposing his essentialist views – a view that, though it received little significant press at the time, takes up this passionate debate about the "whatness" of cinema. In his 1947 work *Le Cinéma du diable*, Jean, a "retired" director of poetic films of the twenties, chose to focus not on the photography that fixes the cinematic image, but rather on the projection that animates them. Epstein used his approach to take aim at traditional and unquestioned notions of cinematic time and space and to "deconstruct" them. In diametric opposition to Bazin's notion that the cinema has always been interested in God, Epstein saw the cinema as "much more a work of the devil."

In *Le Cinéma du diable*, Epstein articulates a vision of the seventh art that is not only radically anti-classical (and rigorously anti-essentialist), but insists that the apparatus of the cinema produces, by its very ontology, a challenge to the entire classical belief in the *real*.[24] Epstein proposes that we regard the cinema as producing not a sense of the unity of nature, as Bazin was claiming, but instead the revelation that "ultimately life is disequilibrium and perpetual change ... Every form is merely a moment of equilibrium in the play of rhythms whose *movement* is the sole constitution of all forms, all life" (CD 55). "Everything," Epstein concludes "is composed of quantified *movement*, that is to say, *movement* conceived in space and time" (CD 58). Man's need to analyze, to classify, to interrupt the continuity of nature by dividing it into identifiable pieces is born of a classical (theological) misconception, a mistaken belief in the unchanging nature of things and thus classical analysis "accepted Nature only on condition that it be *de*-natured" (CD 12). Reality is not, Epstein contends, sounding like a cross between de Saussure and Einstein, "an absolute value, but merely a function of relations – a general system of relativity"(CD 52). In the face of nature, Epstein concludes, "intelligence must give way to instinct."

Epstein then goes on the theological offensive. He argues that, because of the Judeo-Christian need to posit a God who "condemns and punishes in the name of ... inertia, of static mass, of the comfortable equilibrium of a fixed universe" (CD 10), we are left to inhabit a world "not even dead but already null and stillborn" (CD 14). And because, this necessarily unchanging God has created a static world, " It is the devil" who inspires "all research, all curiosity ... and he thus appears as the great inventor, master of discovery, the prince of science, the tool maker of civilization, the animator of every thing considered to be progress" (CD 11, 10, 6). All change, all invention, all knowledge of the world thus becomes viewed as diabolical and particularly so since the word "diabol" has the sense of a breaking apart – the opposite of symbol.[25] The cinema is, thus, *diabolical* (anti-Bazinian) *both* because it seeks through its inventiveness to go beyond the static nature of photography *and* because, as we shall see, it proposes an entirely different idea of the *real* itself!

The specifically revolutionary qualities that Epstein now attributes to the cinema as a form and an apparatus he groups as considerations of time, space, psychology, and the logic of the image. As for time, rather than being elements of a poetics of cinema, "Fast-motion and slow-motion shots," Epstein writes, "reveal the fragmentary nature of the universe, seen through a variety of forms and different moments ... and so the evidence gathered from these displays of cinematic time proves that time has no absolute scale but is rather scaled to variable dimensions that produce variations of the experience of time within a specific period of time" (CD 40). Moreover, by running the film backwards, Epstein argues, cinema not only recalls the way memory and dream work, but that such reversals teach us that "film time can vary quantitatively, i.e. that it can embrace an infinite gamut of different rhythms some slower, some more rapid.... Cinematographic time allows us to see the fundamental plurality in the very idea of time itself" (CD 50–1). By so inflecting not only the constancy of flow of time but its potential reversibility, the cinema teaches us that classical notions of inflexible chronometry are but attempts to reassure ourselves of the illusion of order. This is a "revolutionary revelation whose importance seems to have gone unnoticed by most film spectators" (CD 43).

Just as the classical notion of the irreversibility of time is undermined by the cinema, so to, according to Jean Epstein, is the classical notion of space. Montage alone undoes our faith in the fixity of geography since "the transformation of appearances in the cinema's variability of space–time relations ... suddenly reveals a stupefying complexity and an inexplicable obscurity" (CD 60). The cinema is obliged to take on the role of teaching us the "real" reality: "This mix of an infinite multiplicity of dimensional scales and angles constitutes the best preparation for a critique and revisitation of all those old notions that were thought to be absolutes, and for the formation of a new relativism which today is penetrating every domain of knowledge" (CD 36).

Finally, since the cinematic space–time can unfold on its own terms, as we have seen, terms entirely different from the space–time attributed to external life, the cinema, according to Epstein, becomes "the appropriate instrument for the description of our deepest mental life, in which the memory of dreams, however imperfect it may be, provides an excellent example" (CD 26). Elsewhere Epstein adds, "Whether for good or ill, the cinema, in its recording and reproduction of a subject, transforms the latter, and refashions it into a second personality, whose aspect can so trouble our consciousness as to lead it to ask, 'Who am I?' ".[26] As the self is deconstructed as a fixed notion, all logic and ethics seem to dissolve as well: "Man experiences vertigo in sounding his own depths.... This is an exercise reputed to be dangerous to our morality and our reason since it is drawn from the study of an affective, irrational ego, whose movements are anterior to any logical or ethical operation" (CD 27). The ego ends up being merely a variable, whose configurations merely evoke the innumerable possibilities of existence (CD 65).

In a summation of this thinking about diabolical cinema, Epstein concludes:

> The most significant value of the invention of the cinema is to have brought us the possibility of experiences which communicate the relativism as characteristic of our time as humanism and encyclopedism were to the Renaissance and the Revolution ... and whose force is pushing back and supplanting the Cartesian and Kantian traditions. This anticyclone is propagated by means of the silver screen where subtly we can see a revolutionary philosophy at work, the enemy of all stability, destructive of all stable order, a philosophy assuredly diabolical. (CD 49)

It is thus that Epstein's metaphysics of the cinema reach their most revolutionary point. Cinema becomes "the new art in service of the forces of transgression and revolt" (CD 17), "a law outside the law" (CD 77). Bazin's unity of nature has been exploded in Epstein's response into a Humpty Dumpty of a concept that "couldn't be put back together again."

It is not clear, given the emerging predominance of existentialism, Lacanian psychoanalysis and structuralism in the late 1940s, why it was Bazin's ideas that were "selected," in the Darwinian sense, for survival and dissemination. No doubt it had much to do with Bazin's savvy move to command the major film journal of his time, *Les Cahiers du cinéma*, rather than consign his ideas to monographs that might have ended up in relative oblivion. What is abundantly clear, however, is the delight and passion of such a debate. The Bazin–Epstein opposition crystallizes all that we have attempted to categorize as "thinking French." On the one hand, we understand the necessity for seeing the cinema as a "faithful" representation of the visible reality before our eyes. On the other, we comprehend the need to bring the cinema in line with prevailing French philosophies of existentialism and deconstruction. Epstein's view, however, "enables" a cinema in which the filmmaker sees himself as a criminal, working against tradition, creating new extra-geographical maps, and theorizing the cinema as alternatively a form of dream, hypnosis or terror.

Indeed, Epstein represents a worldview that has vexed and challenged Anglo-Saxon thinking throughout the "Age of Cinema," for that "era" corresponds exactly to the birth of an epistemology in France that has consistently rejected Anglo-American pragmatism. Throughout the twentieth century, French thought in virtually every domain has been inflected by this sense of discontinuity. From the very dawn of the twentieth century, France confronted a new way of thinking, one that seemed to stem from (at least) three principal sources, all generated during the last decade of the nineteenth century and the first decade of the twentieth. Of course we must begin by recognizing that the work of Albert Einstein and his theories of relativity, published in 1907 and 1915 respectively, helped propel the new century into an extended engagement with relativism in all fields.

In linguistics, Ferdinand de Saussure (whose work you will recall from our discussion of Bresson's theory of the image) introduced the notion that the building blocks of language have no positive value but only an arbitrary and relative one. In proposing that phonemes no longer designated things themselves, but functioned only by their difference from the other elements in an arbitrary system, de Saussure effected a *radical break* between language and the reality it was meant to represent, and opened a space for the ensuing debates about whether language could be adequate to represent reality. (These debates would culminate in the work of Jacques Derrida, whose work has become nearly synonymous with the word "deconstruction." In its starkest terms, Derrida's philosophy begins where de Saussure left off: if language is metaphorical and can therefore give rise only to endless streams of analogies, then we can never really reach reality through language. Derrida thus saw man's attempts to comprehend the world as lost in a "free fall" in which no grounding could ever be reached.)

In a different but related domain, Henri Bergson published two works that bridge the nineteenth and twentieth centuries, each of which further undermines our faith in the reliability of rational analysis. In *Matière et mémoire [Matter and Memory]* (1896) and *L'Evolution créatrice [Creative Evolution]* (1907), Bergson proposed that both time and matter were composed of such absolute continuity that neither could ever be adequately understood by the human mind. "We change constantly so that we might say that our very 'state' is change and yet this change is so gradual that we cannot measure it." Any attempt to do so necessarily involves focusing our attention "by a series of *discontinuous* acts" that cannot ever stop or fix the "moving zone whose very movement, in reality, constitutes our state."[27]

Thus, any attempt to cut up time into representable pieces (seconds, minutes, hours, days) destroys what is most essential about time: its continual flow. Interestingly, it was by analogy to the cinema that Bergson made his most radical critique of Cartesianism:

> Suppose we wanted to reproduce on a screen an animated scene, a military parade, for example.... One way of proceeding would be to take a series of snapshots and project them onto the screen so that each would quickly replace the previous one. This is what the cinematograph does. It reconstitutes the mobility of the regiment going by. But, since we are dealing with individual photographs, we can look at them all we want and they'll never come to life: no matter how much we juxtapose them, a series of immobile frames will never get them to move. The movement is in the apparatus, not the photographs.... Such is the artifice of the cinematographer. And such is the artificiality of our knowledge.... What is not representable is "general becoming". I can make only a verbal approximation of it. What an absurd proposition it is to say that movement is made of immobilities. (CE 304–07)

Bergson goes on to argue that what is true of time is also true of the physical universe. Any categorization we make of nature is an arbitrary cut into something that itself knows no classifications, no set boundaries. The distinctions, masculine/feminine or animal/plant, are bound to fail at those incidences where the differences between these categories are so blurred as to be unmeasurable.[28] Bergson further hypothesizes that in the evolution of the human mind, we passed from an older, more instinctual brain to a newer, more analytical one. It is this later brain that seeks knowledge through making what is continuous into discontinuous units and thus finds itself incapable of understanding what is most essential about nature. Our (older) instinct alone has the capacity to capture the *organic* nature of the world around us. On the other hand, "what is most essential in the instinct cannot be expressed in intellectual terms and cannot therefore be analyzed" (EC 169). Since "science can only explain what is inert [whereas] instinct alone can explain life," we must resign ourselves to the inadequacy of reason and intellect to get at what is essential – what Bergson calls "l'élan vital" (EC 254).

Bergson's attack on the efficacy of reason contained some thoughts as well on the role of our memory of the past. He believed, for example that the past resided almost entirely in the unconscious part of our minds, and that it only (re)surfaced when it was momentarily useful. In this sense, Bergson's work can be considered to have paralleled that of the father of psychoanalysis.

Sigmund Freud (much of whose early work would be influenced by the Frenchman Charcot and who was introduced to the French by Marie Bonaparte) was to propose a theory of the unconscious that stressed the mind's difficulty in distinguishing between the real and its distortions of the real. If, as Freud proposed, our unconscious mind contained dynamic forces that constantly sought expression, and if the only expression they could find was through projection, displacement, condensation, dream, and Freudian slips (or more drastically through psychosis), then our reason could apprehend reality only through a constant smokescreen of unconscious interference. Of course we have already observed this activity at work in *Adele H.*, but it bears repeating here that, already in the first decades of the twentieth century, the Viennese analyst was exercising an enormous influence on the thought of his contemporaries. In the later Lacanian revisions of Freudian theory – a body of thought that Jeffrey Mehlman has termed "the French Freud" – we see an accentuation of the notion of discontinuity.[29] Where Freud believed in the potential integrity of the ego, Lacan hypothesized that the ego was always already fractured by its perception of itself as an unassimilable otherness in the mirror-stage of development. Mehlman would contrast the Freudian and Lacanian systems as "a *discontinuity* then between a metaphorics of continuity [Freud] and one of discontinuity [Lacan]."

The final blow to the old faith in empiricism was struck by Jean-Paul Sartre beginning in the mid-thirties with his essay, *L'Imagination* (1936). Sartre's contribution to the end of Cartesian certainty reached its apogee in 1943 with the publication of *L'Etre et le néant [Being and Nothingness]*. To French twentieth-century thought, Sartre brought the depressing announcement that, in a world without God, man was condemned to being merely contingent, i.e. without a trace of justification for his existence and thus condemned to living in a world without meaning. "Every existent is born without reason, prolongs itself only through weakness and dies by chance," Sartre wrote in *La Nausée [Nausea]* (1938),[30] and so in Sartrean existentialism, we end up being alienated from God, from the world and from others. The death knell of traditional belief in man's ability to trust his powers of observation came in *Being and Nothingness* where Sartre argued that "consciousness is born supported by a being which is not itself" (B&N 23). Sartre's adherence to phenomenology led him to the conclusion that objects would be revealed by a succession of perceptions none of which could be complete since no object can be exhausted by its appearances, which are potentially infinite. Sartre condemns human consciousness to what he calls "a nonsubstantial absolute" – absolute only in the sense that it is nonsubstantial. All consciousness is necessarily consciousness *of* something, but that something can never be fully apprehended.[31] And, just as the world outside consciousness never stopped unfolding, so too was the self a ceaselessly unfolding entity. In a world without God, there could be no essences and therefore no "human nature."

> If Man, as conceived by existentialism, remains indefinable, it's because, at the outset, he is nothing. He will become something only subsequently and he will be nothing more than the sum of his acts ... he is at first only a project yet is entirely responsible for what he becomes.... He is *condemned* to be free.... His definition remains always open."[32]

In relation to the certainties of the Classical age, and even to the confident empiricism of the comparatively reasonable nineteenth century, modern French thought, with its confirmation of Nietzsche's proclamation that God is dead, must ultimately be understood as perfectly diabolical. It should come as little surprise, then, that this Gallic epistemology would have a huge impact on both the theory and practice of the cinema.

Perhaps now we can better appreciate how thoroughly *intellectualism* and *discontinuity* can be considered the *alpha* and *omega* of the Gallic style. In unraveling the French cinema we have not found a long narrative thread, but rather a collection of silver slivers – fragments that endlessly point to the fundamental ontology of film: its paradox of an apparent continuity created by pasting together discontinuous elements (frames, scenes, sounds and images). Hollywood's dream machine has always managed to cover over this disturbing fact through a rigorous film grammar that convinces us of the connections – spatial, temporal, narrative, psychological, and political – between every element that appears on the screen. France's cinematic "nightmare," by contrast, is to make us painfully aware of the fragmentary nature of what we're watching and doing. Indeed, we can see the shadow of discontinuity in virtually every one of the "definitions" of film we encountered in this journey. To promote the idea that film is a form of poetry, Jean Vigo used combinations of fragmentary editing and surreal connections between objects and people to make us "wake" up from his rather mundane narrative and ask, "What's going on here?" Even Renoir's realism relied on his insistent use of depth of focus – a style explicitly intended to cause the spectator to confront the *ambiguities* rather than the comfortable certainty of his characters' lives.

All of these experiments against continuity culminate in the radical disjuncture of the late 1940s and 1950s when Carné and Bresson upend all of our assumptions about the dramatic nature of film, and Godard's *Breathless* unsystematically explodes every comfortable trick of Hollywood continuity editing. With all of these traditional signposts uprooted, no limits, nor recognizable geography, appear to remain. (In French the word for road marker, *borne*, also has the meaning of limit or frontier!) What seems needed, then, is a "remapping" of the cinema according to a new set of geographical terms – a cartography that operates through affective, associative, or purely visual ways rather than within the comfortable traditions of spatial continuity. In other words, the French have repeatedly dared to strike out from everything that is familiar in order to imagine a new way, one that more fully corresponds to the world they inhabit, rather than to an escapist flight to one they can only dream of.

Truffaut employed every discontinuity at his disposal to convince us that, in order to participate authentically in Adele's experience, we had to follow her through a series of highly idiosyncratic and disjunctive associations. Benoît Jacquot's presentation of hypnosis forced us, in turn, to imagine someone to be present that was not really there. Mathilde's encounters with her doctor kept us jumping from one reality to another, eerily alerted to this other reality by two notes from a disembodied flute. Anne Fontaine found herself replicating this same kind of fracture when it came to exploring the connections between mourning and film. Jean-Luc's father cannot ultimately be assimilated into the "reality" of his world, a discomfiting realization that upends all our assumptions about how that world can, in fact be "explained."

From Vigo's poetics to Haneke's terror, we can now understand that the fragmented shadows of French modernism have been intermittently cast in ways as various and wonderful as any single film could ever produce. Our particular voyage must come to an end here, but I invite you to continue this journey by re-engaging with the particular optics of the Gallic silver screen. I encourage you to create a film club (like the book clubs that so many of us have joined) to pursue and enhance your enjoyment of French film – forewarned with the sober knowledge that the medium *needs unraveling* but now armed, hopefully, with some of the tools necessary to that work.

Notes

Introduction

1 Lagarde, C. (2007), quoted in *The Boston Globe*, July 22, A14.
2 Cited in Sadoul, G. (1948), *Histoire générale du cinéma I*. Paris: Denoel, p. 210.
3 Foucault, M. (1966), *Les mots et les choses*. Paris: Gallimard, pp. 229–313.
4 Williams, A. (1992), *Republic of Images*. Cambridge, MA: Harvard University Press, pp. 9–19.
5 Cited in Burch, N. (1990), *Life to those Shadows*, trans. B. Brewster. Berkeley, CA: University of California Press, pp. 18–19.
6 Burch (1990), pp. 17–19.
7 Abel, R. (1984), *French Cinema: The First Wave, 1915–1929*. Princeton, NJ: Princeton University Press, p. 12.
8 Bordwell, D., Staiger, J., and Thompson, K. (1985), *The Classical Hollywood Cinema*. New York: Columbia University Press, p. 3.
9 Cited in Burch, N. (1980), *French Impressionist Cinema*. New York: Arno Press, p. 58, trans. mine.
10 Delluc, L. (1918), "Notes to Myself." In *La Dixième Symphonie*," *Le Film* 99 (4 February): 3–4. Cited in Abel R. (1988), *French Film Theory and Criticism: 1907–1939*, Vol. I, Princeton, NJ: Princeton University Press, p. 144.
11 Clair, R. (1924), "Les Films du mois." *Coeur fidèle* in *Théâtre et Comoedia illustré*, February 1. Reprinted in Abel (1988), Vol. I, p. 305.
12 Porte, P. (1926), "Le cinéma pur." *Cinéa-ciné-pour-tous* 52 (January 1): 12–13. Reprinted in Abel (1988) Vol. I, p. 385.

13   Faure, E. (1922), "De la cinéplastique." In *L'Arbre d'Eden.* Paris: G. Crès, pp. 277–304. Reprinted in Abel (1988), p. 263.

14   Bazin, A. (1958), *Qu'est-ce que le cinéma?* Paris: Editions de cerf, trans. H. Gray (1967), as *What Is Cinema?* Berkeley, CA: University of California Press.

15   See Bowser, E. (1990), *The Transformation of Cinema, 1907–1918.* Berkeley, CA: University of California Press; and Richard Koszarski (1990), *An Evening's Entertainment: The Age of the Silent Feature Picture, 1915–1928.* Berkeley: University of California Press.

16   Canudo, R. (1926), "Naissance d'un sixième art." In *L'Usine aux images.* Paris: Chiron, pp. 13–26. Reprinted in Abel (1988), p. 59.

17   Delluc, L. (1920), *Photogénie.* Paris: De Brunhoff, pp. 11–12.

18   Epstein, J. (1921), "Le Cinéma et les lettres modernes." In *La Poésie d'aujourd'hui: un nouvel état d'intelligence.* Paris: Editions de la Sirène, p. 177.

19   Vuillermoz, E. Cited in Abel (1988), Vol. I, p. 206.

20   Epstein, J. (1924), "L"Elément photogénique." *Cinéa-ciné-pour-tous* 12 (May 1): 7.

21   Gance, A. (1930), "Images d'hier et voix de demain." *Cinéopse* 125 (January): 26.

22   Clair, R. "Les Films du mois," p. 305.

23   Pierre Porte (1926), "Le Cinéma pur," p. 387.

24   Robert, L. Cited in Sadoul, G., *Histoire générale du cinéma I*, p. 414, trans. mine.

25   Dulac, D. (1924), "Le Procédés expressifs du cinématographe." *Ciné magazine* 4 (July 4): 15–18. Cited in Abel (1988), Vol. I, p. 308.

26   Fescourt, H. and Bouquet, J.-L. (1926), *L'Idée et l'écran.* Paris: Haberschill and Sergent, pp. 9–11, 32–3. Reprinted in Abel (1988), Vol. I, p. 384.

27   Moussinac, L. (1921), "Cinématographie." *Mercure de France* (November 1): 784 –91. Reprinted in Abel (1988), Vol. I, p. 250.

28   Vuillermoz, E. (1920), "Devant l'écran: Esthétique." *Le Temps* (March 27): 3. Reprinted in Abel (1988), Vol. I, pp. 226–7.

29   Garrell, P. Cited in Jill Forbes. (1992), *The Cinema in France after the New Wave.* London: British Film Institute, pp. 127–8.

30   Delluc, L. (1923), "Prologue." In *Drames du cinéma.* Paris: Editions du monde nouveau, pp. i–xiv. Reprinted in Abel (1988), Vol. I, p. 285.

31   Epstein, J. (1921), "Grossissement." In *Bonjour cinéma.* Paris: Editions de la sirène, pp. 107–8.

32   Altman, G. (1931), "Esprit du film." *La Revue des vivants,* 5 (October): 529–38. Reprinted in Abel (1988), Vol. II, p. 82.

33   Delluc (1923), p. 285.

34   Crisp C. (2004), cited in Temple M. and Witt, L. (eds.), *The French Cinema Book.* London: The British Film Institute, p. 119. Ginette Vincendeau notes that in the early 1930s more than half of the films came out of small production companies and during the second half of the decade over 100 independents were in operation. Vincendeau, G., *French Cinema in the 1930s: Social Texts and Contexts.* Unpublished PhD thesis, University of East Anglia, pp. 48–50.

35 Altman (1931), p. 82.
36 Collet, J., Delhaye, M., Fieschi, J. A., Labarthe A. and Tavernier, B. (1962), "François Truffaut." *Cahiers du cinéma* 138 (December): 55.
37 Vuillermoz, E. (1938), "Cas de conscience." *La Cinématographie française,* 1032 (August 12): 47–8. Reprinted in Abel (1988), Vol. II, p. 250.
38 Williams, A. (1992), *The Republic of Images.* Cambridge, MA: Harvard University Press; Hayward, S. (1993), *French National Cinema,* New York: Routledge; and Powrie, P. and Reader, K. (2002), *French Cinema: A Student's Guide.* London: Arnold Press.
39 L'Herbier, M. (1919), "*Rose-France.*" *Comoedia illustré* (December 5). Cited in Abel, R. (1984), *French Cinema: The First Wave, 1915–1929.* Princeton, NJ: Princeton University Press, p. 302.
40 Epstein, J. (1928), "Les images du ciel." *Cinéa-ciné-pour-tous* 107 (April 15): 11–12. Cited in Abel (1984), p. 464.
41 Baudry, J.-L. (1975), "Le Dispositif; approaches métapsychologiques de l'impression de réalité," *Psychanalyse et cinéma Communications* 23 (February): 56–72.

Chapter 1   Cinema and/as Poetry: *L'Atalante*'s Apples as Poems

1 Bordwell, D. (1985), "The Classical Hollywood Style, 1917–60." In Bordwell, D., Staiger J., and Thompson, K. (1985), *The Classical Hollywood Cinema: Film Style and Mode of Production to 1960.* New York: Columbia University Press. Noel Burch calls this the Institutional Mode of Representation (1990), *Life to Those Shadows.* Berkeley, CA: University of California Press, p. 33.
2 Canudo, R. (1926), L'Esthétique du septième art," in *L'Usine aux images.* Paris: Etienne Chiron, pp. 13–26. Reprinted as "The Birth of the Sixth Art," in Richard Abel (1988), *French Film Theory and Criticism: 1907–1929,* Vol. I. Princeton, NJ: Princeton University Press, p. 59.
3 Epstein, J. (1921), "Le cinéma et les lettres modernes." In *La Poésie d'aujourd'hui: Un nouvel état d'intelligence.* Paris: Editions de la sirène, p. 171. Reprinted in Abel (1988), Vol. I, p. 213.
4 Vuillermoz, E. (1920), "Devant l'écran: Esthétique." *Le Temps* (March 27), p. 3. Reprinted in Abel (1988), Vol. I, p. 227.
5 Epstein, J. (1923), "L'Elément photogénique." *Cinéa-ciné-pour-tous* 12 (May 1), p. 7. Cited in Abel (1988), Vol. I, p. 207.
6 Gance, A. (1930), "Images d'hier et voix de demain," *Cinéopse* 125 (January): 25–6. Reprinted in Abel (1988), Vol. II, p. 41.
7 Vuillermoz, E., "Devant l'écran: Esthétique," p. 3. Reprinted in Abel (1988), Vol. I, p. 225.
8 Consider the following as exemplars: Lacenaire, the dramatist of Carné's *Les enfants du paradis;* Antoine Doinel, the bad boy of Truffaut's *Les 400 coups;*

Michel Poiccard, the invent-as-you-go hero of Godard's *A bout de souffle*; and Michel the pickpocket of Bresson's *Pickpocket* to mention but a few.

9   I am indebted to Jonathan Culler (1975) for introducing this approach in *Structuralist Poetics*, Ithaca, NY: Cornell University Press, pp. 161–2.

10 I am referring, of course, to the rebellious computer in *2001: A Space Odyssey*.

11 Shakespeare, W., *Macbeth*, V, v.

12 I am indebted for some aspects of this approach to Professor Rick Renschel of Harvard University.

13 Vigo, J. (1983), *The Complete Jean Vigo* (Pierre L'herminier, ed.). Paris: Lorrimer, p. 43.

14 Surrealism was defined by André Breton as a:

> Psychic automatism in its pure state, by which one proposes to express – verbally, by means of the written word, or in any other manner, the actual functioning of thought. Dictated by thought, in the absence of any control exercised by reason, exempt from any esthetic or moral concern ... Surrealism is based on a belief in the superior reality of certain forms of previously neglected associations; in the omnipotence of dream, in the disinterested play of thought.

> Elsewhere in his First Manifesto (1924), Breton had written,

> Freud very rightly brought his critical faculties to bear upon the dream. It is, in fact, inadmissible that this considerable portion of psychic activity (since, at least from man's birth until his death, thought offers no solution of continuity, the sum of the moments of dream, from the point of view of time, and taking into consideration only the time of pure dreaming, that is the dreams of sleep, is not inferior to the sum of the moments of reality, or, to be more precisely limiting, the moments of waking) has still today been so grossly neglected.... This curious state of affairs seems to me to call for certain reflections: (1) within the limits where they operate ... dreams give every evidence of being continuous and show signs of organization.... Why should I not grant to dreams what I occasionally refuse reality, that is, this value of certainty in itself which, in its own time, is not open to my repudiation? Why should I not expect from the sign of the dream more than I expect from a degree of consciousness which is daily more acute? Can't the dream also be used in solving the fundamental questions of life? (2) I have no choice but to consider the waking state ... a phenomenon of interference; (3) The mind of the man who dreams is fully satisfied by what happens to him. The agonizing question of possibility is no longer pertinent; (4) I believe in the future resolution of these two states, dream and reality, which are seemingly so contradictory, into a kind of absolute reality, a surreality, if one may so speak. (Breton, A. (1924), *Manifestes du surrealism*. Paris: Pauvert, pp. 37, 20–4 passim. Trans. mine)

15 *The Complete Jean Vigo*, p.14.

16 In this respect it is worth noting that even the music was composed "surreally." Maurice Jaubert (1936), who scored the film, wrote, "We have even employed the running of sound in reverse ... to obtain a truly 'unheard of' tone. We transcribed the score backwards, the last bar becoming the first, and within each bar, the last note becoming the first.... By 'turning around' this soundtrack in the film, the music took on all its mystery." "Le Cinéma: La musique," *Esprit* 43 (April): 114–19.

17 The box cover of the New York Films edition of the DVD is adorned with a quote from Georgia Brown of *The Village Voice* to the effect that this film "may be the greatest film ever made."

18 Her face, suddenly death-like and waxen, makes us think more of a statue than a lively newlywed. Is she to be Pygmalion's statue?

19 This destination at the river bank recalls the French popular song, "Qui me passera sur l'autre rive?" – a dirge-like meditation on our journey into death.

20 Baudelaire, C., "Les Chats," trans. W. Aggeler (1954) as "Cats" in *The Flowers of Evil*. Fresno, CA: Academy Library Guild, p. 36.

21 I use the term in the sense that Mikhail Bakhtin (1973) employs it: In Carnival, "the laws, prohibitions and restrictions which determine the system and order of normal life are suspended, above all the hierarchical system and all the connected forms of fear, awe, piety, etiquette etc. are suspended ... and the latent sides of human nature are revealed and developed in a concretely sensuous form." *Problems of Dostoevsky's Poetics*, trans. R. W. Rotsel. New York: Ardis, pp. 87, 100–1.

22 We shall re-encounter this symbolic landscape, specifically named a "Christian Hades," in our discussion of Benoît Jacquot's film, *Seventh Heaven*. See below, p. 136.

23 Freud, S. (1910), *Five Lectures on Psychoanalysis*, S. E. XI, p. 51.

24 Breton, *Manifestes*, pp. 76–7.

25 Remembering that Vigo had referenced Buñuel's *Chien Andalou* when showing his own film *Zero for Conduct*, it is worth noting that this cut recalls the razor blade slicing open a woman's eyeball in that earlier film.

26 We will have much to say about film, crime and, specifically the symbolism of *pickpocketing*. See below pp. 64–75.

27 François Truffaut will copy this scene shot for shot in the final moments of his *400 Blows* (1958). The affinities between Vigo and Truffaut could not be more marked.

28 Breton, *Manifestes*, p. 23.

29 See Freud, S. (1900), *The Interpretation of Dreams: The Standard Edition of the Complete Psychological Works of Sigmund Freud*, Vols IV, V. London: Hogarth Press.

30 Freud, S. (1905), *Jokes and Their Relation to the Unconscious*. S. E. VIII, p. 174.

31 Breton, *Manifestes*, p. 11.

32 Atalanta, a princess, was urged by her father to marry, but she had been warned by the Oracle against matrimony. Atalanta, certain of her own surpassing swiftness, announced that whoever beat her in the foot race could marry her, but if she won, her competitor would die. Hippomenes, having fallen in love with the princess and desiring to marry her, knew he could never best her in a foot race, so he called on Aphrodite for assistance. The goddess provided Hippomenes with three golden apples with which to entice Atalanta. During the race, whenever Atalanta would get ahead of Hippomenes, he would throw one of the golden apples in her path, enticing Atalanta to stop to gather up the fruit. His trick allowed Hippomenes to win the race and, consequently, the princess's hand in marriage.

Chapter 2   Cinema and the Real: Renoir's *Rules*

1 Bertolucci, B. Cited in Bragin, J. (1966), "A Conversation with Bernardo Bertolucci," *Film Quarterly* 20(1) (Fall): 42, 44.
2 Bazin, A. (1967), *What Is Cinema?* Vol. I. Berkeley, CA: University of California Press, trans. Hugh Gray.
3 Bazin (1967), Vol. I, p. 12.
4 Bazin (1967), Vol. I, pp. 13–14.
5 Renoir, J. (1970), *The Rules of the Game*, trans. J. McGrath and M. Teitelbaum. London: Lorrimer, p. 74.
6 Renoir, cited in Bazin (1967), Vol. I, p. 35.
7 Sartre, J. P. (1943), "The Existence of Others," *Being and Nothingness*. New York: Citadel Press (Orig. Paris: Gallimard, 1943), pp. 197–278.
8 Bazin. A. (1967), "The Evolution of the Language of Cinema," *What Is Cinema?* Vol. I, p. 35.
9 Bazin, A. (1967), "The Evolution of the Language of Cinema," *What Is Cinema?* Vol. I, pp. 35–6.
10 Bazin. A., "The Evolution of the Language of Cinema," pp. 35–8 passim. Italics mine.
11 Renoir, J. (1979), *Entretiens et propos*. Paris: Ramsay, pp. 18–19, trans. mine.
12 We shall be taking up the question of the relationship between the theater and the cinema again in our discussion of Carné's *Children of Paradise* and Bresson's *Pickpocket*. See below pp. 55–75.
13 Those familiar with Resnais's *Last Year at Marienbad* might see an uncanny connection between the entrapment of Renoir's characters here and the robotic inauthenticity of Resnais's creations.
14 Renoir, *Entretiens et propos*, p. 125, trans. mine.
15 You will no doubt have begun to appreciate how much Renoir's realism also requires a "poetic" reading of the film, not unlike our reading of Vigo. At this point we can appreciate the necessary intersection of realism and poetry in any "prose" work of art.

16 François Vinneul (1939) wrote scathingly of Renoir's choice of a Jew for this role in *Action Française* (July 7). Reprinted in Richard Abel (1988), Vol. II, p. 273.

17 Renoir, *Entretiens et propos*, p. 125, trans. mine.

18 Girard, R. (1977), *Violence and the Sacred*. Baltimore, MD: The Johns Hopkins Press, pp. 14–15. We shall have occasion to revisit Girard's theories in our discussion of Haneke's *Caché*. See below pp. 173–4.

19 Girard (1977), p. 31.

20 Girard (1977), pp. 81–2.

21 Renoir, *Entretiens et propos*, pp. 119–20, trans. mine.

22 Cited in Sessonske, A. (1980), *Jean Renoir: The French Films 1924–1939*. Cambridge, MA: Harvard University Press, p. 381.

23 Cited in Sessonske (1980), p. 384.

Chapter 3 Cinema and/as Crime: Breaking the Law in *The Children of Paradise, Pickpocket*, and *Breathless*

1 In *The Myth of Sisyphus*, Camus wrote, "La révolte, voici la manière de vivre l'absurde. La révolte c'est connaître notre destin fatal et néanmoins l'affronter, c'est l'intelligence aux prises avec le silence déraisonnable du monde, c'est le condamné à mort qui refuse le suicide.... L'une des seules positions philosophiques cohérentes, c'est ainsi la révolte."

2 Bazin, "Theater and Cinema," in *What Is Cinema?*, Vol. I, p. 107.

3 Braudy, L. (1976), *The World in a Frame*. New York: Doubleday.

4 And it nearly ended there! A huge fire caused by the lanterns needed for illumination destroyed a fairground tent filled with over one hundred spectators. The tragedy caused the cinema briefly to be outlawed in such venues.

5 This scene invites comparison with the exercise on poetry in which we took a sentence from a newspaper and turned it into a poem without changing a single word.

6 Cobban, A. (1965), *A History of Modern France*, III, New York: Braziller. As for the question of the Nazi's pursuit of homosexuals in the film industry, I invite you to view *Le Plus beau pays du monde* (1999), directed by Marcel Bluwal. It presents the story of Robert Hugues Lambert who was arrested during the filming of *Mermoz* in 1939 and imprisoned at Drangy.

7 Baudelaire, C. (1956[1863]), "The Dandy," trans. N. Cameron. In Quennell, P. (ed.), *The Essence of Laughter and Other Essays*. New York: Meridian Books, p. 46 ff.

8 In addition to the other traits he shares with Lacenaire, Carné shared Lacenaire's sexual orientation.

9 Bresson, R. (1975), *Notes sur le cinématographe*. Paris: Gallimard. Trans. J. Griffin, as *Notes on Cinematography*. New York: Urizen Books, pp. 3/13. Hereafter NC in the body of the text with French/English pagination.

10   Gebaston, P. (1990), "Conversation with Marika Green." In *Pickpocket de Robert Bresson*. Paris: Editions Yellow Now, trans. mine, p. 19.

11   Gebaston (1990), p. 20.

12   In Nogueira, R. (1976–7), "Burel and Bresson." *Sight and Sound* 46(1): 21.

13   Bresson (1975), pp. 3/4, 13/14, 5/16.

14   Bordwell, D. (1985), pp. 12–23 passim.

15   Michel will write: "I spent several years in London where I lost large sums of money on women and gambling," a patently ludicrous statement given the presentation of this particular character.

16   We will discover this effect again, and quite unexpectedly, in a popular thriller. See below pp. 181–3

17   Bordwell (1985), pp. 12–13.

18   Truffaut, F. (1975[1954]), "Robert Bresson." In *Les Films de ma vie*. Paris: Flammarion, p. 209, trans. mine. See also Truffaut, F. (1987)"Une certaine tendance du cinéma" *Le Plaisir des Jeux*. Paris: Seuil.

19   De Saussure, F. (1966), *Course in General Linguistics*, trans. Wade Baskin. New York: McGraw Hill, pp. 114–16.

20   See Sontag, S. (1973), *On Photography*. New York: Dell, pp. 4–7, 111–12; and Barthes, R. (1981), *Camera Lucida*, trans. Richard Howard. New York: Hill and Wang.

21   Dostoevsky, F. (n.d.), *Crime and Punishment*, trans. C. Garnet. New York: Modern Library, pp. 254–5.

22   The quotation occurs when the inspector accuses Michel of a crime, using exactly the same language used by Dostoyevsky's Porphiry in accusing Raskolnikov of killing the old pawnbroker and her sister.

23   Doniol-Valcroze, J. and Godard, J.-L. (1960), "Entretien avec Robert Bresson." *Cahiers du cinéma* 104 (February): 6, 7.

24   In Pinel, V. (1962), "Le Paradoxe du non-comédien," *Etudes cinématographiques* 14–15: 81–2, trans. mine.

25   Lambert, R. S. (1930), *The Prince of Pickpockets: A Study of George Barrington Who Left his Country for his Country's Good*. London: Faber and Faber, pp. 245–6.

26   Pinel, V. (1962), "Le Paradoxe du non-comédien." *Etudes cinématographiques* 14–15: 81.

27   In Touratier, J.-M., and Busto, D. (1979), *Jean-Luc Godard: télévision/écritures*. Paris: Galilée, pp. 32–3.

28   Cited in Collet, J. (1962), "Entretien avec Jean-Luc Godard." *Cahiers du cinéma* 138 (December): 24.

29   And Camus. His shooting of the sun earlier in the film looks to be a "quotation" from the scene on the beach in Camus's *The Stranger* in which Meursault, desperate to escape the sword blades of sun blinding him, shoots, but hits an Arab boy nearby, an act that leads to his discovery of the Absurd.

30   There is a footnote to Godard's attack on Hollywood style which bears mentioning in this respect. I invite you to watch Jim McBride's 1983 remake

of Godard's film in which the American director is at pains to *erase* every single one of Godard's "mistakes" of editing, camera work, perspective and sound. McBride's recuperation of this film into a perfectly rationalized Hollywood style is perhaps, if ironically so, the greatest tribute to Godard's success as a "criminal" French director.

31 Charles Biro launched the American crime comic genre with *Crime Does Not Pay*, a series published between 1942 and 1955.

Chapter 4   Cinema and/as Mapping: Reorienting Ourselves Through Film

1 Conley, T. (2007), *Cartographic Cinema*, Minneapolis, MN: University of Minnesota Press. While Conley's excellent study ranges over the whole corpus of film (including some of the films I will discuss here), his purposes are somewhat broader than mine. What I will focus on here is the way French cinema brings the map to our attention in an insistently graphic way, forcing us to step outside of the "geography" of the film to consider the relation of the film we are watching to the map we have seen within it.

2 Louis Malle was warned by his producer to eliminate this scene, but insisted that it was crucial to his film.

3 Malle, L. (1978). In *Louis Malle par Louis Malle*, Mallecot, J. and Kant, S. (eds.), Paris: Athanor, p. 14; and Cott, J. (1977), "Fires Within: The Chaste Sensuality of Director Louis Malle," *Rolling Stone* 6 (April): 43–4.

4 De Jean, J. (1989), "The Salons, 'Preciosity,' and the Sphere of Women's Influence." In Hollier, D. (ed.), *A New History of French Literature*. Cambridge, MA: Harvard University Press, pp. 297–303.

5 Most of the films starring Humphrey Bogart in his engagement with the Free French Forces during the Second World War open with such a masculine narrative voice. Look for example at *Passage to Marseille, To Have and to Have Not*, and *Action in the North Atlantic*.

6 Silverman, K. (1988), *The Acoustic Mirror: The Feminine Voice in Psychoanalysis and Cinema*. Bloomington, IN: Indiana University Press.

7 Filteau, C. (1979), "Le Pays de Tendre: l'enjeu d'une carte." *Littérature* 36 (December): 52, 60, trans. mine.

8 Filteau (1979): 40–3.

9 Malle, L. (1978), p. 67.

10 The phrase "*l'heure dangereuse du matin*" is borrowed from Colette's novel *La Vagabonde* (1912) in which another woman contemplates a life of servitude with a prospective husband and chooses instead a life of *vagabondage* and creativity.

11 Malle, L. (1978), p. 70.

12 Hart, J. (1991), *Damage*. New York: Ivy Books, p. 1. All further quotations from this work will be indicated by parentheses and page numbers in the body of the essay.

13   Louis Marin reminds us that, just as Utopia was specifically unlocatable on a map of the earth, its discursive status was intended to be ambiguous as well, sitting "somewhere between yes and no, false and true, but as the double of figure, the ambiguous representation, the equivocal image of possible synthesis and productive differentiation." Marin, L. (1984), *Utopics: Spatial Play*, trans. Robert A. Vollrath. Atlantic Highlands, NJ: Humanities Press, p. 9.

14   In *Le Roi des aulnes*, Michel Tournier notes that the word "diabol" is the opposite of "symbol" – i.e. it means a throwing apart of objects formerly held together.

15   Freud, S. (1920), *S. E.* XVIII, pp. 36, 38.

16   Kline, T. J. (1987), "Last Tango in Paris." In *Bertolucci's Dream Loom*. Amherst, MA: University of Massachusetts Press, pp. 106–26.

17   Malle, L. (1993), "Damage." In Philip French (ed.), *Malle on Malle*, London: Faber and Faber, pp. 200–2.

18   Kline, T. J. (2006), "*Last Year at Marienbad*: High Modern and Postmodern." In Perry, T. (ed.), *Masterpieces of Modernist Cinema*. Bloomington, IN: Indiana University Press, pp. 208–35.

19   *Adele* is of course another version of this scenario.

20   In his films shot in America, *Pretty Baby, Atlantic City*, and *Vanya on 42nd Street*.

21   Remember Victor Hugo's drawing of the wave, entitled "La destinée"?

22   "*Le monde à l'envers* [the world upside down]" is the term used famously by Mikhail Bakhtin in his discussion of the carnivalesque world. This suggests a link to several other films discussed in the chapter on film as crime. See Bakhtin, M. (1973), *Problems of Dostoevsky's Poetics*, trans. R. W. Rotsel, New York: Ardis, pp. 87, 100–1.

23   This is not unlike the eerie sound of the flute in *Seventh Heaven* that always announces the mysterious doctor.

24   Deleuze, G. (1986), *The Movement Image*. Minneapolis, MN: University of Minnesota Press, p. 118.

25   Deleuze, G. (1986), p. 120.

26   Stok, D. (ed.) (1993), *Kieslowski on Kieslowski*. London: Faber & Faber, pp. 218, 220.

27   Stok (1993), p. 149.

28   Stok (1993), p. 218. The director adds, "*Red* is really about whether people aren't by chance sometimes born at the wrong time."

29   This is, by the way, the second instance of an uncanny wind. When, earlier, she is standing outside his house, we catch sight of her from a position in the road. As she calls, "Are you still breathing?" a sudden wind arises which causes the withered leaves of the tree in the foreground to rustle loudly as if in answer.

30   J. M. Frodon, reviewing the film for *Le Monde*, angrily condemned this "incarnation of a guardian angel" and argued that "to save his own characters, Kieslowski doesn't hesitate to condemn fifteen hundred victims who will not survive the shipwreck any more than if they were all evil." Frodon, J. M. (1994), "Trois Couleurs Rouge de Kryzsztof Kieslowski," *Le Monde* (May 18).

31 Stok (1993), pp. 134–5. I ask you to keep this quotation in mind for the chapter on Anne Fontaine's *How I Killed My Father*.

32 Stok (1993), pp. 149–50.

Chapter 5   Cinema and/as Dream: Truffaut's "Royal Road" to *Adele H.*

1 Cited in Aprà, A., Ponzi, M. and Spila, P., "Bernardo Bertolucci: *Partner*." In Gerard, F., Kline, T. J., and Sklarew, B. (1999), *Bernardo Bertolucci Interviews*. Jackson, MS: University Press of Mississippi, p. 49.

2 In *The Acoustic Mirror*, Kaja Silverman argues that cinema has, from its inception, presented as its discursive origin a disembodied male voice. She will argue for a new consciousness of the possibilities of a feminine voice in the cinema that co-opts this male position. In another context, I have discussed the way Louis Malle and Louise de Vilmorin attempt to place a feminine voice at the discursive origin of *The Lovers* (1958). See Silverman, K. (1988), *The Acoustic Mirror*. Bloomington, IN: Indiana University Press. See also Kline, T. J. (1992), "Remapping Tenderness" in *Screening the Text: Intertextuality in New Wave French Cinema*. Baltimore, MD: Johns Hopkins University Press.

3 Collet, J., Delhaye, M., Fieschi, J.-A., Labarthe, A., and Tavernier, B. (1962), "François Truffaut," *Cahiers du cinéma* 138 (December): 55.

4 Freud, S. (1900), p. 219. Pontalis, J.-B. (1977) defined the dreamwork as "An ensemble of operations which transform very diverse material – provided by the body, by thought, by the 'remains' of the day – in order to work it into a product: a sequence of images which tends toward the form of a narrative and in which there intersect at nodal points almost indefinite chains of representations." *Entre le rêve et la douleur*. Paris: Gallimard, p. 241.

5 Truffaut, F. (1988), *Correspondance*. Paris: Hatier, p. 54.

6 Freud, S. (1952[1924]), *A General Introduction to Psychoanalysis*. New York: Washington Square Press, p. 126.

7 By 1975, this was, in fact, a subject that had received a great deal of attention from French film critics and theoreticians. In particular, Jean-Louis Baudry had suggested that it was Plato who first "theorized" the cinematographic apparatus and its representation of the real. In the famous passage on the Cave (*The Republic*, Chapter 10), Plato had us imagine a group of men chained in a "dim" cave, forced to sit immobilized before a large wall. Behind them, a huge fire burned "at some distance higher up," in front of which were passed a series of puppets whose shadows were cast on the wall in front of these prisoners. To add to the illusion of reality, the players behind them spoke in real voices which, according to Plato, echoed off the wall in front of them, producing the illusion that it was the shadows who were speaking. Of course, all of this "apparatus" is imagined by a philosopher who believes that all of us unwittingly in our ignorance of the higher reality confuse our

perception of the simulacrum of the world around us for that higher reality. So powerful is this experience – and so necessary – that when Plato's figure of the (Platonic) realist tells the cave viewers that they are but victims of illusion, they are so little interested in the "real" world and so infuriated that their illusions risk being taken away that they put this bearer of "bad" tidings to death. For Baudry, then, Plato's vision of these prisioners chained since childhood, eyes forced to contemplate this shadow play, corresponds first to Freud's notion of the "enforced immobility of the child at birth, deprived of the resources of mobility," second, to "that of the dreamer, also necessarily immobile", and, third, to that of the moviegoer riveted to his seat and eyes glued to the screen. Baudry notes that only in these three states do we experience *representation as if it were actual perception.* (Baudry, "The Apparatus: Metapsychological Approaches to the Impression of Reality in Cinema," in Gerald Mast, Marshall Cohen, and Leo Braudy (1992), *Film Theory and Criticism: Introductory Readings.* New York: Oxford University Press, p. 59). The success of the cinema would then be explained by this primary state.

8   Cavell, S. (1979), *The World Viewed.* Cambridge, MA: Harvard University Press, p. 41.

9   Sergei Eisenstein has, most forcefully, articulated the centrality of montage in the creation of art film. He argues that cinema's images are like hieroglyphs and that

> the combination of two [images] is to be regarded not as their sum, but as their product, i.e. as a value of another dimension, another degree; each separately corresponds to an *object*, to a fact, but their combination corresponds to a *concept*.... By the combination of two "depictables" is achieved the representation of something that is graphically undepictable. (Eisenstein (1949), *The Film Form.* New York: Harcourt, Brace and World, p. 109).

Here Eisenstein sounds like no one so much as Freud articulating the theory of condensation!

10 Inasmuch, then, as dreams constitute an imaginary space in which all kinds of fantasies may be explored, film and dreaming can both be understood to allow the functioning of a "transitional space" in which illusion is not simply a form of withdrawal (as in the daydream) but signals the possibility of growth and development through a balance between internal and external demands: a medium of potential creativity. In "Mirror Role of Mother and Family in Child Development," D. W. Winnicott (1967) termed a "transitional space" a space in which, on the one hand, primary drives may be completely satisfied yet, on the other, the primary object is totally unattainable. (*The Predicament of the Family* (ed. P. Lomas). London: Hogarth Press)

11 Chevreul (1854), *De la baguette divinatoire, du pendule dit explorateur et des tables tournantes, au point de vue de l'histoire, de la critique et de la méthode expérimentale* Paris: Mallet-Bachelier.

12 Truffaut, F. (1983), *Hitchcock*. New York: Simon & Schuster, p. 213.

13 Truffaut, F. (1978), *The Films of My Life*, trans. Leonare Mayhew. New York: Simon & Schuster, pp. 78–9.

14 Becca Krasner, one of my undergraduate film students, took the image of drowning and read it as a metaphor for the entire film. She noted that a person drowning goes through five stages: first, fear and shock cause the body to become rigid, cutting off movement of the legs; second, the body submerges for lack of propulsion; third, the difficulty of breathing prevents shouting for help; fourth, the esophagus closes and further cuts off breathing; fifth, without oxygen, the person faints and, emptied of air, the body loses buoyancy and sinks. What is most interesting about the entire phenomenon is that it is not water that kills, but the body that extinguishes itself by initiating reflexes that prevent survival. The implications for Adele are both obvious and very far-reaching. Drowning is but one of the ways she uses to inflict (pleasurable) pain on herself (unpublished paper).

15 In *Beyond the Pleasure Principle* (1920), Freud argued that the repetition compulsion represents a psychological paradox in as much as the subject discovers *pleasure* in repeating what is *unpleasurable*. "It seems," Freud wrote, "that an instinct is an urge to restore an earlier state of things ... i.e. the expression of the inertia inherent in organic life" (p. 36). This in turn convinced him that we have two opposing instincts in us, one (the erotic) toward life and the other (the thanatopic) toward death. This latter instinct leads him to "be compelled to say that 'the aim of all life is death.'" (*S. E.* XVIII, pp. 36, 38)

16 You will remember that François Truffaut was a great admirer of Jean Vigo and "quoted" Vigo's work frequently. Here we might see homage to the doubling of Juliette, Jules and the *camelot* in *L'Atalante*.

Chapter 6   Cinema and/as Hypnosis: Jacquot's *Seventh Heaven*

1 Remember that we have entered this "landscape" before, in our discussion of Vigo's *Atalante*. See above p. 27.

2 Compare the discussion of maps and mapping. See pp. 83–108.

3 The film's title, *Seventh Heaven*, may constitute an allusion to the orbit of Saturn. See Klibansky, R., Panofsky, E. and Saxl, F. (1964[1905]), *Saturn and Melancholy: Studies in the History of Natural Philosophy, Religion and Art*. London: Nelson. The authors indicate that, like the melancholy from which Mathilde seems to suffer, Saturn "menaced those in his power ... with depression or even madness" (p. 159). But for the renaissance mind, melancholia and sterility gradually evolve into their opposites: stillness of

contemplation and fruitful meditation. What is uncannily pertinent for our present inquiry is that these diametrically opposed views of Saturn may be held simultaneously, "either/or was softened to both/and" (p. 158). Saturn is seen to have a dual nature – dualities which themselves communicate the "essential unity of man and universe" (p. 157). Thus medieval cosmography has provided a kind of map of this seventh heaven –virtually congruent (as we shall see) with Roustang's "map" of the unconscious.

4   See Kline, T. J. (1992), *Screening the Text: Intertexuality in New Wave French Cinema*. Baltimore, MD: Johns Hopkins University Press, for an extended discussion of the tendency in French cinema to foreground literary texts as invitations to meta-cinematic interpretations.

5   The most notable exception, perhaps, being *Apocalypse Now* in which we catch sight of Jessie Weston's study *From Ritual to Romance* on the shelf of books in Marlon Brando's cave. Weston's book turns out to help us understand the mythology that Brando's character has attempted to re-create in his mountain retreat. Another rare allusion to literature occurs in *The Petrified Forest*, where the lovers use a copy of François Villon's poetry to convey their love to each other.

6   Lagerlöf, S. (1995[1906]), *The Wonderful Adventures of Nils*, translated by V. S. Howard. New York: Dover, p. 3. All further references to this book will be indicated in the body of the text by WAN and page numbers.

7   Howard, V. S. (1995), "Introduction," *The Wonderful Adventures of Nils*. New York: Dover, p. viii.

8   The world *nihil* in Latin means "nothing."

9   Roustang, F. (1994), *Qu'est-ce que l'hypnose?* Paris: Editions de Minuit. All references to this book in the text will be indicated in parentheses after the quote with the letter "R" and page numbers. Translations are mine.

10   I invite you to think about the scene in Jules's cabin in *L'Atalante* as you ponder this.

11   This is a position actually anticipated by François Truffaut in *Adele H* since on the one hand he debunks the theatrical practice of the fraudulent hypnotist and, on the other, seems to picture Adele in various trances of her own creation.

12   See Roustang (1994), pp. 109–10.

13   I would ask you to think back to the discussion of the role of *La Carte du pays de Tendre* in Malle's *Les Amants*, for the reorganization of Mathilde's apartment can be usefully compared to Jeanne's reorganization of her world according to that map.

14   Compare these statements of Roustang with the following passage from Breton's *First Surrealist Manifesto*:

Why should I not concede to the dream what I sometimes refuse to reality? … Why should I not expect more of the dream sign than I do of a daily increasing degree of consciousness? Could not dreams as well be applied to the solution of life's fundamental problems? … I am obliged to consider the waking state as a phenomenon of interference… [whereas] the mind of the dreaming man is fully satisfied with whatever happens" (Breton (1924), pp. 67–8.).

15 Lest this designation seem arbitrary, I invite you to take another look at the series of scenes between Nico and the openly gay man in the café. Clearly the gay friend is telling Nico that the best way to get in touch with his homosexuality is to undergo hypnosis.

16 This is actually a quote from Leo Spitzer that finds its way into Roustang's book. (R 99).

Chapter 7   Cinema and/as Mourning: Anne Fontaine's *How I Killed My Father*

1 Freud, "Mourning and Melancholia," p. 112.

2 By this time you will have discovered that all of the chapters of this study are connected. If the film begins with a character in a trance, it certainly enjoys a connection to the questions of dreaming and hypnosis that we have already explored.

3 New Yorker Films Publicity Packet: interview, p. 5.

4 Lim, D. (2002), "Shock Waves," *The Village Voice* (August 21). See also Burr, T. (2003), *The Boston Globe* (December 19); Dawson, T. (2002), *The BBC* (June 19); Mitchell, E. (2002), *The New York Times* (August 23); and Ebert, R. (2002), *The Chicago Sun Times* (November 22).

5 Borde's tendency to spy on his family may be the first of a series of references to Hamlet which will be explored in more detail below (pp. 155–6). For a discussion of the prominent role played by spying and deception in Shakespeare's play and the Amleth saga, see Jones, E. (1976[1949]), *Hamlet and Oedipus*. New York: W. W. Norton, pp. 148–9.

6 Robbe-Grillet, A. (1962), "Introduction," *Last Year at Marienbad*, trans. Richard Howard. New York: Grove Press, p. 12.

7 Isaacs, S. (1952), "The Nature and Function of Fantasy." In Klein, M., and Riviere, J. (eds.), *Developments in Psychoanalysis*. London: Hogarth Press, p. 112.

8 Freud, S. (1917), "Mourning and Melancholia." In *S. E.* XIV, pp. 243–5. Hereafter indicated in the body of the essay by "MM" and page numbers.

9 Ernst Jones (1976) was the first to insist on Hamlet's incestuous and parricidal feelings as constituting the barrier to any action. See *Hamlet and Oedipus*, esp. pp. 92–100.

10 Laing, R. D. (1965), *The Divided Self*. Baltimore, MD: Penguin Books, pp. 40–1, 112.

11 Laing (1965), pp. 46–7. Ernst Jones (1976) notes in his study of Hamlet that "psychoneurosis means a state of mind where the person is unduly, and often painfully driven or thwarted by the 'unconscious' part of his mind, that buried

part that was once the infant's mind and still lives on side by side with the adult ... and signifies *internal* mental conflict" (p. 97). I do not need to emphasize how much these terms seem also to apply to Jean-Luc.

12 Miller, J. H. (1990), *Versions of Pygmalion*. Cambridge, MA: Harvard University Press, p. 4. Miller notes that "the story of Pygmalion dramatizes the process by which an anthropomorphism takes place [and thus] makes the story of Pygmalion a prosopopoeia of prosopopoeia" (p. 4).

13 We recall that in the opening sequence of the film, one of Jean-Luc's patients confesses, "I have a two-year-old child. I've calculated that when he's 20, I'll be an old man. I won't have any prestige or authority in his eyes. I can't be affectionate with him. I feel like he's a stranger. Almost a threat." In retrospect this sounds like a projection from Jean-Luc onto his client!

14 Mulvey, L. (1989), "The Oedipus Myth." In *Visual and Other Pleasures*. Bloomington, IN: Indiana University Press, p. 198.

15 I invite you to think about Truffaut's comment that Hitchcock is "the man that we love to be hated by." It is in some way this connection that we will be exploring in moving from a discussion of Fontaine's character to her thoughts about cinema.

16 These are the feelings ascribed by Christopher Bollas (1987) to the abandoned child in his book, *The Shadow of the Object*. New York: Columbia University Press, pp. 3–4.

17 The term is again Bollas's (1987), p. 4.

18 Abraham, N. and Torok, M. (1994), *The Shell and the Kernel: Renewals of Psychoanalysis*, trans. Nicholas T. Rand. Chicago: The University of Chicago, pp. 113–17 passim.

19 Abraham, N. and Torok, M. (1994), p. 127.

20 Ernst Jones (1976) notes that for Hamlet, to kill Claudius is to kill himself and thus his moral fate is bound up with his uncle's (p. 88). Jones further notes the presence of the themes of masks and self-deception in *Hamlet* (pp. 149–50).

21 Abraham, N. and Torok, M. (1994), p. 130.

22 Anne Fontaine, New Yorker Films Publicity Packet: Interview, p. 1.

23 Here again we see a parallel with Ernst Jones's (1976) discussion of Hamlet in which Jones argues that Shakespeare effects a *decomposition* of the father into various attributes, some good, the others bad (pp. 122, 131). We might wonder, ultimately if the entire discourse on Africa in this film isn't an allegory of death that would suggest that Maurice had long ago committed suicide and that the letter of the film's opening and closing scenes represents a level of Jean-Luc that simply refuses to believe his father committed suicide years before and engages in a recuperative fantasy: "Perhaps my father is still alive and has continued all these years to be an important doctor in Africa."

24 In "Reflections on Trauma, Absence and Loss," in Peter Brooks and Alex Woloch (eds.) (2000), *Whose Freud?* New Haven, CT: Yale University Press,

p. 183, Dominick LaCapra notes, "In converting absence to loss, one assumes that there was (or at least could be) some original unity, whose wholeness, security or identity that others have ruined, polluted or contaminated and thus made 'us' lose. To regain it, one must somehow get rid of or eliminate those others – or perhaps the sinful other in oneself."

25 Anne Fontaine, "Interview," pp. 2, 4.

26 Although Freud himself was careful to separate the work of mourning (*Der Trauerarbeit*) from the work of dreams (*Die Traumarbeit*), it is significant I believe that the first word of his essay on mourning is, in fact, the word "Dreams"! (MM, p. 243).

27 Santner, E. L. (1990), *Stranded Objects: Mourning, Memory and Film in Postwar Germany*. Ithaca, NY: Cornell University Press, pp. 68–9.

28 Derrida, J. and Stiegler, B. (1996), *Ecographies de la télévision*. Paris: Editions Galilée, p. 133, trans. mine.

Chapter 8   Cinema and/as Terror: Michael Haneke's *Caché*

1 Camus, A. (1957[1942]), *L'étranger*. Paris: Gallimard, pp. 93–5 passim. Trans. S. Stuart Gilbert (1946), as *The Stranger*. New York: Vintage Books, pp. 93–6 passim.

2 See *La Chanson de Roland* (1924; orig. 11th century), ed. T. Atkinson Jenkins. Boston: D. C. Heath, Stanzas 178 and 179.

3 Girard (1977), pp. 61–3.

4 The term *crusade* is borrowed from numerous articles in the American and French press beginning in 2002. See for example: Carroll, J. (2004), *Crusade: Chronicles of an Unjust War*. New York: Holt, which includes this quote from President Bush, "This crusade … this war on terrorism." See also Cockburn, A. and St Clair, J. (2003), *Imperial Crusades*. Petrolia, CA: Verso Books; Chemillier-Gendreau, M. (2003), "Sous le sceau des croisades," *Le Monde diplomatique* (December); Laurent, E. (2003), *La Guerre des Bush*. Paris: Plon.

5 Haneke, M., Boston University Master Class, October 17, 2008.

Chapter 9   Beautiful Fragments: Discontinuity and the French Cinema

1 De Gramont (1969), p. 318.

2 Ibid., p. 322.

3 Ibid., p. 323.

4 Cited in Burch, N. (1980), *French Impressionist Cinema*. New York: Arno Press, p. 58, trans. mine.

5 De Gramont (1969), pp. 324–5.

6   The Blum-Byrnes Accords of 1946 guaranteed French producers exclusivity in Paris theaters a mere 16 weeks a year. That left 36 weeks open to a steady influx of Hollywood films. Nor did increasing the French share to 20 weeks in 1948 make matters much better.

7   The word "maudit" – "accursed" – was coined by Paul Verlaine to describe poets such as Baudelaire whose popularity was always compromised by the anti-social, provocative, dangerous or even self-destructive tendencies of their life and art, whose writing was generally too difficult for the man in the street and who often died before their poetic worth came to be recognized.

8   In each of these films, *The Bourne Identity* (2002), directed by Doug Liman, and *The Bourne Supremacy* (2004) and *Bourne Ultimatum* (2007), both directed by Paul Greengrass, the jumpiness of style is compensated for by a rigorous continuity of character. Matt Damon's presence provides a sure sense of direction throughout.

9   These are exactly the terms used to describe Bresson's revolutionary approach to *Pickpocket*. See above, p. 68.

10   Ebert, R. (2008), *The Chicago Sun Times*, July 10.

11   Barsanti, C. (2008), *Filmcritic.com*.

12   Gleiberman, O. (2008), *Entertainment Weekly*, July 11.

13   Canet plays the role of a consummate equestrian, a profession he himself exercised before taking up film, a further connector between his directorial and dramatic personae and his "real life" identity.

14   "A mesure que le champ intellectuel gage en automomie, l'artiste affirme de plus en plus fortement sa prétention à l'autonomie, proclamant son indifférence à l'égard du public," Bourdieu, P. (1986), "La reproduction des privilèges culturels, ou comment en démocratie, l'aristocratie prend le visage de la méritocratie." In Accardo, A. and Corcuff, P., *La Sociologie de Bourdieu*, Bordeaux, France: Le Mascaret, p. 37, trans. mine.

15   Bazin, A. (1967), "Ontology of the Photographic Image," *What is Cinema?* Vol. I, p. 12.

16   "Ontology," p. 12.

17   "Ontology," p. 13.

18   "Ontology," p. 14. That this notion is central to all of Bazin's work is confirmed by Eric Rohmer, who notes that Bazin's work is "based on one central idea, an affirmation of the objectivity of the cinema in the same way as all geometry is centered on the properties of the straight line." Cited in Andrew, J. D. (1978), *André Bazin*, New York: Oxford University Press, p. 103.

19   Dudley Andrew, *André Bazin*. French version p. 40, Engl. version, pp. 22, 23, 105–6.

20   Andrew, Engl. version, pp. 121, 123.

21   Bazin, "Cinema and Theology," in *Bazin at Work: Major Essays and Reviews from the Forties and Fifties* (1997), trans. from the French by Alain Piette and Bert Cardullo; edited by Bert Cardullo. New York: Routledge, p. 61.

22 Bazin, A. (1973), *Jean Renoir*, ed. with an intro. by François Truffaut. Trans. from the French by W. W. Halsey II and William H. Simon. New York: Simon and Schuster, p. 88.

23 Bazin, *Jean Renoir*, p. 90.

24 Epstein, Jean (1947), *Le Cinema du diable*, Paris: Editions Jacques Melot. All quotations from this edition will be indicated by CD and page number.

25 Tournier has explained that "diabol" has the meaning opposite to symbol: a throwing apart rather than a linking.

26 Epstein, Jean (1946), *L'Intelligence d'une machine*. Paris: Editions Jacques Melot, p. 6.

27 Henri Bergson (1962[1907]), *L'Evolution créatrice*. Paris: Presses Universitaires Françaises, pp. 2, 3, trans. mine.

28 As I wrote this, the *New York Times* published an article announcing that "The organizers of the Beijing Olympics have set up a sex-determination laboratory to evaluate 'suspect' female athletes." Dr Christine McGinn was quoted as saying, "It's very difficult to define what is a man and what is a woman at this point.... It gets really complicated very quickly." *New York Times*, July 30, 2008, C9.

29 Mehlman, J. (1972) "French Freud." *Yale French Studies* 48: 6. See also Lacan, J. (1949), "Le Stade du miroir comme formateur de la fonction du Je," trans. Alan Sheridan (1977) as "The Mirror Stage as Formative of the Function of the I." In *Ecrits: A Selection*. New York: W. W. Norton.

30 Jean-Paul Sartre (1938), *La Nausée*, Paris: Gallimard, Edition Folio, p. 190.

31 For an excellent discussion of the implications of this position, see Hazel E. Barnes (1992), "Sartre's Ontology: The Revealing and Making of Being," in Christina Howells (ed.), *The Cambridge Companion to Sartre*, Cambridge: Cambridge University Press, pp. 13–38.

32 Jean-Paul Sartre (1970), *L'Existentialisme est un humanisme*. Paris: Nagel, pp. 21–55 passim, trans. mine.

References

Books

Abel, R. (1984), *French Cinema: The First Wave, 1915–1929*. Princeton, NJ: Princeton University Press.

Abel, R. (1988), *French Film Theory and Criticism, 1907–1939*. 2 Vols. Princeton, NJ: Princeton University Press.

Abraham, N. and Torok, M. (1994), *The Shell and the Kernel: Renewals of Psychoanalysis*. Trans. Nicholas T. Rand. Chicago: The University of Chicago Press.

Accardo, A. and Corcuff, P. (1986), *La Sociologie de Bourdieu: Textes choisis et commentés*. Bordeaux: Le Mascaret.

Andrew, J. D. (1976), *The Major Film Theories*. Oxford: Oxford University Press.

Andrew, J. D. (1984), *Film in the Aura of Art*. Princeton, NJ: Princeton University Press.

Anon. (1924[11th century]), *La Chanson de Roland*, ed. T. Atkinson Jenkins. Boston: D. C. Heath.

Bahktin, Mikhail (1973), *Problems of Dostoevsky's Poetics*, trans. R. W. Rotsel. New York: Ardis.

Bazin, A. (1958), *Qu'est-ce que le cinéma?* Paris: Editions de cerf. Trans. H. Gray (1967) as *What Is Cinema?* Berkeley, CA: University of California Press.

Bergson, H. (1939[1896]), *Matière et mémoire*. Paris: Presses Universitaires de France.

Bergson, H. (1962[1907]), *L'Evolution créatrice*. Paris: Presses Universitaires de France.

Bollas, C. (1987), *The Shadow of the Object*. New York: Columbia University Press.

Bordwell, D. (1985), "The Classical Hollywood Style, 1917–60." In Bordwell, D., Staiger J., and Thompson, K. (1985), *The Classical Hollywood Cinema: Film Style and Mode of Production to 1960*. New York: Columbia University Press.

Bordwell, D., Staiger, J., and Thompson, K. (1985), *The Classical Hollywood Cinema: Film Style and Mode of Production to 1960*. New York: Columbia University Press.

Bordwell, D. and Thompson, K. (1990), *Film Art: An Introduction*. New York: McGraw Hill.

Bourdieu, P. and Passeron, J.-C. (1979[1964]), *The Inheritors: French Students and Their Relation to Culture*, trans. Richard Nice. Chicago: The University of Chicago Press.

Bowser, E. (1990), *The Transformation of Cinema, 1907–1918*. Berkeley, CA: University of California Press.

Braudy, L. (1976), *The World in a Frame*. New York: Doubleday.

Braudy, L. and Cohen, M. (2004), *Film Theory and Criticism*. Oxford: Oxford University Press.

Bresson, R. (1975), *Notes sur le cinématographe*. Paris: Gallimard. Trans. J. Griffin as *Notes on Cinematography*, New York: Urizen Books.

Breton, A. (1924), *Manifestes du surréalisme*. Paris: Pauvert.

Burch, N. (1980), *French Impressionist Cinema*. New York: Arno Press.

Burch, N. (1990), *Life to Those Shadows*, trans. B. Brewster. Berkeley, CA: University of California Press.

Camus, A. (1957[1942]), *L'étranger*. Paris: Gallimard. Trans. S. Stuart Gilbert (1946) as *The Stranger*. New York: Vintage Books.

Carroll, J. (2004), *Crusade: Chronicles of an Unjust War*. New York: Holt.

Cavell, S. (1979), *The World Viewed*. Cambridge, MA: Harvard University Press.

Chevreul, P. (1854), *De la baguette divinatoire, du pendule dit explorateur et des tables tournantes, au point de vue de l'histoire, de la critique et de la méthode expérimentale*. Paris: Mallet-Bachelier.

Cobban, A. (1965), *A History of Modern France*. New York: Braziller.

Cockburn, A. and St Clair, J. (2003), *Imperial Crusades*. Petrolia, CA: Verso Books.

Conley, T. (2007), *Cartographic Cinema*. Minneapolis, MN: University of Minnesota Press.

Culler, J. (1975), *Structuralist Poetics*. Ithaca, NY: Cornell University Press.

de Gramont, S. (1969), *The French: Portrait of a People*. New York: Putnam's Sons.

Deleuze, G. (1986), *The Movement Image*. Minneapolis, MN: University of Minnesota Press.

Derrida, J. and Stiegler, B. (1996), *Ecographies de la télévision*. Paris: Editions Galilée.

de Saussure, F. (1966[1898]), *Course in General Linguistics*, trans. Wade Baskin. New York: McGraw Hill.

Descartes, R. (1637), *Discours de la méthode* [*Discourse on Method*]. Paris: Le Livre de Poche, p. 14 (trans. mine).

Dostoevsky, F. (n.d.), *Crime and Punishment*, trans. C. Garnet. New York: Modern Library.

Eisenstein, S. (1949), *The Film Form*. New York: Harcourt, Brace and World.

Epstein, J. (1946), *L'Intelligence d'une machine*. Paris: Editions Jacques Melot.

Epstein, J. (1947), *Le Cinéma du diable*. Paris: Editions Jacques Melot.

Forbes, J. (1992), *The Cinema in France after the New Wave*. London: British Film Institute.

Foucault, M. (1966), *Les mots et les choses*. Paris: Gallimard.

French, P. (ed.) (1993), *Malle on Malle*. London: Faber & Faber.

Freud, S. (1900), *The Interpretation of Dreams: The Standard Edition of the Complete Psychological Works of Sigmund Freud*, Vols. IV, V. London: Hogarth Press.

Freud, S. (1905), *Jokes and Their Relation to the Unconscious. The Standard Edition of the Complete Psychological Works of Sigmund Freud*, Vol. VIII. London: Hogarth Press.

Freud, S. (1910), *Five Lectures on Psychoanalysis. The Standard Edition of the Complete Psychological Works of Sigmund Freud*, Vol. XI. London: Hogarth Press.

Freud, S. (1916), "Dreams." In *Introductory Lectures on Psycho-analysis. The Standard Edition of the Complete Psychological Works of Sigmund Freud*, Vol. XV. London: Hogarth Press.

Freud, S. (1917), *Mourning and Melancholia*. In *The Standard Edition of the Complete Psychological Works of Sigmund Freud*, Vol. XIV. London: Hogarth Press.

Freud, S. (1920), *Beyond the Pleasure Principle*. In *The Standard Edition of the Complete Psychological Works of Sigmund Freud*, Vol. XVIII. London: Hogarth Press.

Freud, S. (1952[1924]), *A General Introduction to Psychoanalysis*. New York: Washington Square Press.

Fromm, E. and Nash, M. (1997), *Psychoanalysis and Hypnosis*. Madison, CT: International Universities Press.

Girard, R. (1977), *Violence and the Sacred*, trans. P. Gregory. Baltimore: The Johns Hopkins Press. Orig. pub. (1972) as *La violence et le sacré*. Grasset: Paris.

Grundman, R. (ed.) (2009), *Michael Haneke's Films*. Oxford: Wiley-Blackwell.

Haneke, M. (1992), "Film als Katharsis." In Francesco Bono (ed.), *Austria (in) felix: zum österreichischem Film der 80er Jahre*. Graz: Blimp.

Hayward, S. (1993), *French National Cinema*. New York: Routledge.

Jones, E. (1976[1949]), *Hamlet and Oedipus*. New York: W. W. Norton.

Klibansky, R., Panofsky, E., and Saxl, F. (1964[1905]), *Saturn and Melancholy: Studies in the History of Natural Philosophy, Religion and Art*. London: Nelson.

Kline, T. Jefferson (1992), *Screening the Text: Intertextuality in New Wave French Cinema*. Baltimore, MD: The Johns Hopkins University Press.

Koszarski, R. (1990), *An Evening's Entertainment: The Age of the Silent Feature Picture, 1915–1928*. Berkeley, CA: University of California Press.

Kristeva, J. (1989), *Black Sun: Depression and Melancholia*, trans. Leon Roudiez. New York: Columbia University Press.

Lagerlöf, S. (1995[1906]), *The Wonderful Adventures of Nils*, trans. V. S. Howard. New York: Dover.

Laing, R. D. (1965), *The Divided Self*. Baltimore: Penguin Books.

Lambert, R. S. (1930), *The Prince of Pickpockets: A Study of George Barrington Who Left His Country for his Country's Good*. London: Faber and Faber.

Lankton, S. and Lankton, C. (1983), *The Answer Within: A Clinical Framework of Eriksonian Hypnotherapy*. New York: Brunner/Mazel.

Laurent, E. (2003), *La Guerre des Bush*. Paris: Plon.

Mallecot, J. and Kant, S. (eds.) (1978), *Louis Malle par Louis Malle*. Paris: Athanor.

Miller, J. H. (1990), *Versions of Pygmalion*. Cambridge, MA: Harvard University Press.

Mulvey, L. (1989), *Visual and Other Pleasures*. Bloomington, IN: Indiana University Press.

Pontalis, J.-B. (1977), *Entre le rêve et la douleur*. Paris: Gallimard.

Powrie, P. and Reader, K. (2002), *French Cinema: A Student's Guide*. London: Arnold Press.

Renoir, J. (1970), *The Rules of the Game*, trans. J. McGrath and M. Teitelbaum. London: Lorrimer.

Renoir, J. (1979), *Entretiens et propos*. Paris: Ramsay.

Ricciardi, A. (2003), *The Ends of Mourning: Psychoanalysis, Literature Film*. Stanford, CA: Stanford University Press.

Robbe-Grillet, A. (1962), *Last Year at Marienbad*, trans. Richard Howard. New York: Grove Press.

Roustang, F. (1994), *Qu'est-ce que l'hypnose?* Paris: Editions de Minuit.

Sadoul, G. (1948), *Histoire générale du cinéma*. Paris: Denoel.

Santner, E. L. (1990), *Stranded Objects: Mourning, Memory and Film in Postwar Germany*. Ithaca, NY: Cornell University Press.

Sartre, J. P. (1936), *L'imagination*. Paris: Presses Universitaires de France.

Sartre, J. P. (1938), *La Nausée*. Paris: Gallimard.

Sartre, J. P. (1943), *Being and Nothingness*. New York: Citadel Press.

Sartre, J. P. (1970), *L'Existentialisme est un humanisme*. Paris: Nagel.

Sessonske, A. (1980), *Jean Renoir: The French Films 1924–1939*. Cambridge, MA: Harvard University Press.

Silverman, K. (1988), *The Acoustic Mirror: The Feminine Voice in Psychoanalysis and Cinema*. Bloomington, IN: Indiana University Press.

Sontag, S. (1973), *On Photography*. New York: Dell.

Spitzer, L. (1963), *Classical and Christian Ideas of World Harmony*. Baltimore, MD: Johns Hopkins University Press, p. 23.

Stok, D. (ed.) (1993), *Kieslowski on Kieslowski*. London: Faber & Faber.

Temple M. and Witt, L. (eds.), *The French Cinema Book*. London: The British Film Institute.

Touratier, J.-M., and Busto, D. (eds.) (1979), *Jean-Luc Godard: télévision/écritures*. Paris: Galilée.

Tournier, M. (1970), *Le Roi des aulnes*. Paris: Gallimard.

Truffaut. F. (1975[1954]), *Les Films de ma vie*. Paris: Flammarion. Trans. Leonard Mayhew (1978) as *The Films of My Life*. New York: Simon & Schuster.

Truffaut, F. (1983), *Hitchcock*. New York: Simon & Schuster.

Truffaut, F. (1988), *Correspondance*. Paris: Hatier.

Turk, E. (1989), *Child of Paradise: Marcel Carné and the Golden Age of French Cinéma*. Cambridge, MA: Harvard University Press.

Vigo, J. (1983), *The Complete Jean Vigo*, ed. Pierre Lherminier. Paris: Lorrimer.

Vincendeau, G., *French Cinema in the 1930s: Social Texts and Contexts*. Unpublished PhD thesis, University of East Anglia.

Williams, A. (1992), *Republic of Images*. Cambridge, MA: Harvard University Press.

Wollen, P. (1972), *Signs and Meaning in the Cinema*. Bloomington, IN: Indiana University Press.

Articles

Altman, G. (1931), "Esprit du film." *La Revue des vivants* 5 (October): 529–38. Reprinted in Abel (1988), Vol. II, p. 82.

Aprà, A., Ponzi, M., and Spila, P. (1999), "Bernardo Bertolucci: *Partner*." In Gerard, F., Kline, T. J., and Sklarew, B., *Bernardo Bertolucci Interviews*. Jackson, MS: University Press of Mississippi.

Barnes, H. E. (1992), "Sartre's Ontology: The Revealing and Making of Being." In Christina Howells (ed.), *The Cambridge Companion to Sartre*. Cambridge: Cambridge University Press.

Baudelaire, C. (1961), "Le Dandy," In *Oeuvres completes*. Text selected and annotated by Y.-G. Le Dantec; completed and introduced by Claude Pichois. Paris: Gallimard, pp. 1177–80.

Baudelaire, C. (1964), "Eloge du Maquillage," in *Le Peintre de la vie moderne: Oeuvres Complètes*, ed. Y.-G. Le Dantec with an introduction by Claude Pichois. Paris: nrf Collection de la Pléiade.

Baudry, J.-L. (1975), "Le Dispositif; approches métapsychologiques de l'impression de réalité," *Psychanalyse et cinéma Communications* 23 (February): 56–72. Trans. as "The Apparatus: Metapsychological Approaches to the Impression of Reality in Cinema." In Braudy, L. and Cohen, M. (2004), pp. 206–23.

Bragin, J. (1966), "A Conversation with Bernardo Bertolucci," *Film Quarterly* 20(1) (Fall): 39–44.

Canudo, R. (1926), "Naissance d'un sixième art." In *L'Usine aux images*. Paris: Chiron, pp. 13–26. Reprinted in Abel (1988), p. 59.

Chemillier-Gendreau, M. (2003), "Sous le sceau des croisades," *Le Monde diplomatique* (December).

Clair, R. (1924), "Les Films du mois." *Coeur fidèle* in *Théâtre et Comoedia illustré* February 1. Reprinted in Abel (1988), Vol. I, p. 305.

Collet, J. (1962) "Entretien avec Jean-Luc Godard." *Cahiers du cinéma* 138 (December): 24.

Collet, J., Delhaye, M., Fieschi, J.-A., Labarthe, A., and Tavernier, B. (1962), "François Truffaut." *Cahiers du cinéma* 138 (December): 55.

Cott, J. (1977), "Fires Within: The Chaste Sensuality of Director Louis Malle." *Rolling Stone* 6 (April): 43–4.

De Jean, J (1989), "The Salons, 'Preciosity,' and the Sphere of Women's Influence." In D. Hollier (ed.), *A New History of French Literature.* Cambridge, MA: Harvard University Press, pp. 297–303.

Delluc, L. (1918), "Notes to Myself." In *La Dixième Symphonie, Le Film* 99 (February 4): 3–4. Cited in Abel R. (1988), *French Film Theory and Criticism: 1907–1939,* Vol. I. Princeton, NJ: Princeton University Press.

Delluc, L. (1920), *Photogénie.* Paris: De Brunhoff, pp. 11–12.

Delluc, L. (1923), "Prologue." In *Drames du cinéma.* Paris: Editions du monde nouveau, pp. i–xiv. Reprinted in Abel (1988), Vol. I, p. 285.

Doniol-Valcroze, J. and Godard, J.-L. (1960), "Entretien avec Robert Bresson." *Cahiers du cinéma* 104 (February): 6–7.

Dulac, D. (1924), "Le Procédés expressifs du cinématographe." *Ciné magazine* 4 (July 4): 15–18. Cited in Abel (1988), Vol. I, p. 308.

Epstein, J. (1921a), "Grossissement." In *Bonjour cinéma.* Paris: Editions de la Sirène, pp. 107–8.

Epstein, J. (1921b), "Le Cinéma et les lettres modernes." In *La Poésie d'aujourd'hui: un nouvel état d'intelligence.* Paris: Editions de la Sirène, pp. 171–7.

Epstein, J. (1923), "L'Elément photogénique." *Cinéa-ciné-pour-tous* 12 (May 1): 7. Cited in Abel (1988), Vol. I, p. 207.

Epstein, J. (1928), "Les Images du ciel." *Cinéa-ciné-pour-tous* 107 (April 15): 11–12. Cited in Abel (1984), p. 464.

Faure, E. (1922), "De la cinéplastique." In *L'Arbre d'Eden.* Paris: G. Crès, pp. 277–304. Reprinted in Abel (1988), p. 263.

Fescourt, H. and Bouquet, J.-L. (1926), *L'Idée et l'écran.* Paris: Haberschill and Sergent.

Filteau, C. (1979), "Le Pays de Tendre: l'enjeu d'une carte." *Littérature* 36 (December): 52, 60 (trans. mine).

Frodon, J. M. (1994), "Trois Couleurs Rouge de Kryzsztof Kieslowski." *Le Monde* (May 18).

Gebaston, P. (1990), "Conversation with Marika Green." In *Pickpocket de Robert Bresson.* Paris: Editions Yellow Now (trans. mine).

Gance, A. (1930), "Images d'hier et voix de demain." *Cinéopse* 125 (January): 26.

Isaacs, S. (1952), "The Nature and Function of Fantasy," In Klein, M., and Riviere, J. (eds.), *Developments in Psychoanalysis.* London: Hogarth Press, pp. 110–15.

Jaubert, M. (1936), "Le Cinéma: La musique," *Esprit* 43 (April): 114–19.

Kline, T. J. (1987), "*Last Tango in Paris.*" in *Bertolucci's Dream Loom: A Psychoanalytic Study of Cinema.* Amherst, MA: University of Massachusetts Press, pp. 106–26.

Kline, T. J. (1992), "The ABC's of Godard's Quatations: *A bout de souffle* with *Pierrot le fou.* In *Screening the Text: Intertextuality in the New Wave French Cinema.* Baltimore, MD: The Johns Hopkins University Press, pp. 184–221.

Kline, T. J. (1996), "Truffaut's Adele in the New World: Autobiography as a Subversion of History." In S. Ungar, and T. Conley, (eds.), *Identity Papers: Contested Nationhood in Twentieth Century France.* Minneapolis, MN: University of Minnesota Press, pp. 195–214.

Kline, T. J. (2000), "Dreaming Up the Cinema." *Projections* 13(1): 18–37.

Kline, T. J. (2004), "The French New Wave." In E. Ezra (ed.), *European Cinema.* Oxford: Oxford University Press, pp. 157–75.

Kline, T. J. (2006), "*Last Year at Marienbad*: High Modern and Postmodern." In T. Perry (ed.), *Masterpieces of Modernist Cinema.* Bloomington, IN: Indiana University Press, pp. 208–35.

Lacan, J. (1949), "Le Stade du miroir comme formateur de la fonction du Je." Trans. Alan Sheridan (1977) as "The Mirror Stage as Formative of the Function of the I." In *Ecrits: A Selection.* New York: W. W. Norton.

LaCapra, D. (2000), "Reflections on Trauma, Absence and Loss." In Brooks, P. and Woloch, A. (eds.), *Whose Freud?* New Haven, CT: Yale University Press, pp. 179–88.

Lagarde, C. (2007), Quoted in *The Boston Globe,* July 22: A14.

L'Herbier, M. (1919), "*Rose-France.*" *Commoedia illustré* (December 5). Cited in Abel (1984), *French Cinema: The First Wave, 1915–1929.* Princeton, NJ: Princeton University Press, p. 302.

Lim, D. (2002), "Shock Waves," *The Village Voice* (August 21).

Mehlman, J. (1972), "French Freud." *Yale French Studies* 48(6): 5–9.

Moussinac, L. (1921), "Cinématographie." *Mercure de France* (November 1): 784–91. Reprinted in Abel (1988), Vol. I, p. 250.

Nogueira, R. (1976/77), "Burel and Bresson." *Sight and Sound* 46(1): 20–1.

Pinel, V. (1962), "Le Paradoxe du non-comédien," *Etudes Cinématographiques* 14–15: 81–2 (trans. mine).

Porte, P. (1926), "Le cinéma pur." *Cinéa-ciné-pour-tous* 52 (January 1):12–13. Reprinted in Abel (1988), Vol. I, p. 385.

Vinneul, F. (1939), "L'Ecran de la semaine: *La règle du jeu,*" *Action Française* (July 7): 4. Reprinted in Abel (1988), Vol. II, p. 273.

Vuillermoz, E. (1920), "Devant l'écran: Esthétique." *Le Temps* 3 (March 27). Reprinted in Abel (1988), Vol. I, pp. 226–7.

Vuillermoz, E. (1938), "Cas de conscience." *La Cinématographie française,* 1032 (August 12): 47–8. Reprinted in Abel (1988), Vol. II, p. 250.

Winnicott, D. W. (1967), "The Role of Mother and Family in Child Development." In P. Lomas (ed.), *The Predicament of the Family.* London: Hogarth Press.

Index